OFFSHORE BANK LICENSE

Seven Jurisdictions

Michael Magnusson

Published By:

OPUS OPERIS LLP
Regency House - Westminster Place
York - YO26 6RW - United Kingdom

Registered in the United Kingdom with Company Number OC381062

OPUS
OPERIS

We plant a new tree for every paper book we sell.
See www.opusoperis.co.uk for further details.

ISBN: 978-0-9575438-0-5

Country facts and map illustrations provided courtesy of the Central Intelligence Agency (CIA)

Cover photo provided by iStockphoto.com

"Always be nice to bankers. Always be nice to pension fund managers. Always be nice to the media. In that order."

John Gotti (1940-2002)

Contents

Legal Notice

Introduction

This book contains a compilation of banking laws from jurisdictions that still welcome applications for international bank licenses. I have omitted jurisdictions that used to do so before the regulatory metamorphosis of the entire offshore banking scene took place in the early years of this millennium. All the traditional tax havens and financial centers have been required to adopt major changes to their financial legislation and policies after being subjected to pressure by the Financial Action Task Force (FATF), the Organization for Economic Co-operation and Development (OECD), the Financial Crimes Enforcement Network (FINCEN), the European Union and by the United States, most notably through its passing of the USA Patriot Act in 2001. This legislation resulted in difficulty for smaller offshore banks to obtain or maintain correspondent banking relationships. The USA Patriot Act is obviously a piece of US legislation but its impact is global, particularly because of the ban on "shell banks". Shell Banks are defined as banks without a physical presence and dedicated staff in any country. A US bank opening correspondent accounts for a shell bank will risk heavy regulatory sanctions. Likewise, any non-US bank providing services to a shell bank will risk severing its own US correspondent relationships, or if it does not have a direct relationship with a US bank, its relationships with banks that do. Since banks worldwide need the ability to clear US Dollar payments and to access the US financial markets, the ban on providing services to shell banks in US legislation became a de facto global ban long before other nations adopted similar restrictions through laws and regulations of their own.

It was not long before the offshore jurisdictions saw themselves forced to change the regulatory frameworks for bank licensing to include the requirement for all licensed banks to maintain a local physical presence.

Any jurisdictions allowing for shell banks with a brass plate presence only were destined to end up on blacklists maintained by the FATF, OECD and other international watchdogs and consequently face economic and political sanctions. The current reality is that no internationally recognized jurisdiction will issue a bank license unless the applicant commits to establish a local brick and mortar presence. In some cases this local presence is required to be substantial with qualified management and day-to-day operation capabilities. In other jurisdictions the local presence can be rather symbolic with a one-employee minimum. Many offshore banks are still in reality managed from jurisdictions other than the one issuing their license, including offshore subsidiaries of rather large and reputable "onshore" banks.

Some jurisdictions have decided to only consider branch license applications from established banks already licensed and regulated in other acceptable jurisdictions and are not interested in new banks being formed "from scratch". The jurisdictions featured in this book do accept new private bank formations and the applicable qualification and capital requirements can be considered quite reasonable.

For the sake of completeness, I wish to clarify that an Offshore Banking License (Licence in commonwealth spelling), sometimes referred to as an International Banking License, is a license to engage in banking activities exclusively with customers whom are non-residents of the jurisdiction in which the license was issued. Restricted Offshore Banking Licenses are typically licenses which allow for banking services to be offered to a predetermined identified group of non-resident customers only.

The Physical Presence

As I have mentioned in the Introduction no internationally recognized jurisdiction will issue a banking license unless the applicant has established or committed to establish a physical presence in the jurisdiction issuing the license. Although the particulars and minimum requirements for such physical presence are not always specified in the Banking laws or regulations, it is a standard requirement that needs to be complied with to ensure that the bank cannot be considered a "shell bank". The USA Patriot Act, the name of which is an abbreviation of "**U**niting and **S**trengthening of **A**merica by **P**roviding **A**ppropriate **T**ools **R**equired to **I**ntercept and **O**bstruct **T**errorism", defines a shell bank as a bank which does not have a physical presence in any country. A physical presence is defined as follows:

- a place of business that is located at a fixed address;
- employs one or more individuals on a full time basis; and
- maintains operating records related to its banking activities and
- is subject to inspection by the banking authority that issued its license

The minimum requirement of at least one employee and a fixed address could hardly be considered a cumbersome requirement to comply with for an international banking operation.

A common misconception in offshore circles these days seems to be that no new offshore banks can be started unless the entire operation and management is also established in the jurisdiction issuing the license. This is not the case and I believe that the legislators and regulators are fully aware of the fact that an international bank cannot typically be managed and operated by one employee. The practice of maintaining a rather symbolic presence in the licensing jurisdiction (although more than a brass plate), with actual management and operational support in other jurisdictions has consequently not in any way been terminated by recent regulatory changes. Although each jurisdiction obviously has the capacity to impose their own requirements in regards to physical presence for the banks they license, the definition in the USA Patriot Act is normally used as a guideline for defining a minimum presence.

Several banking laws in this book leave the definition of the required local place of business to be determined on a case-by-case basis at the discretion of the regulator. For example, Section 24(1) of the Montserrat International Banking Act requires the local place of business to have, "such resources (including staff and facilities) and such books and records as the Commission considers appropriate having regard to the nature and scale of business". Other jurisdictions dictate specific minimum requirements, such as St. Vincent and the Grenadines in Section 8(1) of the International Banks Act (2004):

8. (1) A licensee shall have a physical presence in the State which shall include the following:

a) a physical place of business in the State where all books and records are kept;

b) a minimum of two employees, one of whom shall be of senior management level;

c) a designed registered agent, that the Authority has received notification of and who is not an officer of the licensee.

The hiring of a local manager who has documented experience from the financial services industry and a secretary could in this case satisfy the requirement of local staff.

In Vanuatu the minimum requirements for the local physical presence are stipulated in Section 20 of the International Banking Act (No 4 of 2004):

20. Physical presence of licensees and employees in Vanuatu.

(1) Subject to subsections (2) and (3), a licensee must occupy premises in Vanuatu within 30 days, or such longer period as the Reserve Bank allows, after being issued with a licence under section 7.

(2) A licensee must not occupy premises in Vanuatu unless it has obtained the prior written approval of the Reserve Bank.

(3) The Reserve Bank must not give its approval under subsection (2) to any premises unless it is satisfied that:

a) the premises are located at a fixed address in Vanuatu; and

b) the licensee will carry on international banking business under its licence from those premises; and

c) the licensee will maintain at those premises operating records including financial statements relating to the international banking business conducted under its licence; and

d) the employee or employees of the licensee will operate full time from those premises; and

e) those premises adequately symbolize the physical presence of the licensee in

(4) A licensee must within 30 days, or such longer period as the Reserve Bank allows, after being issued with a licence under section 7, appoint such employees, and have in place such facilities, as the Reserve Bank considers appropriate having

regard to the nature and scale of the international banking business to be carried on by the licensee under its licence.

(5) At least one employee of a licensee must have a day-to-day knowledge of the international banking business conducted by the licensee under its licence and sufficient authority within the licensee to participate in the management of that day-to-day international banking business.

(6) A licensee must not change the address of its premises in Vanuatu unless it has obtained the approval of the Reserve Bank in writing for the change.

(7) If a licensee contravenes subsection (2), (4) or (6), the licensee is guilty of an offence, punishable on conviction by a fine not exceeding $250,000.

Considering the current regulatory requirements in all recognized jurisdictions, one must conclude that shell banks can no longer exist. Nevertheless, any foreign (non US) bank seeking to establish a US correspondent relationship will be required to provide a certification to the US authorities declaring that it does not do business with shell banks in its turn. An offshore bank would have to provide the following:

(1) a declaration that it does not do business with shell banks

(2) the name and address of its agent in the US (for serving legal process)

(3) the identity of the beneficial owner(s)

(4) the fixed address

The requirement of a physical presence can hardly be considered a major obstacle for the establishment of a new privately owned offshore bank. This brings us to the requirement of paid up capital, another major factor when identifying a suitable jurisdiction for new bank startups.

Capital Requirements

Just as in the case of the current physical presence requirements in offshore jurisdictions, I frequently come across misconceptions regarding the applicable capital requirements for offshore banks. It is a known fact that many jurisdictions have simply stopped accepting new applications for international banking licenses. Others only accept applications from applicants that are subsidiaries or branches of financial institutions already licensed and regulated in other acceptable jurisdictions. However, the countries that currently do welcome new bank startups also offer quite reasonable, and in some cases surprisingly low, minimum capital requirements.

Among the jurisdictions featured in this book Belize has one of the highest minimum capital requirements for an international banking license, with a USD 3 million minimum. It should be noted however that although the international bank is required to maintain such amount as a minimum net worth on its books at all times, a mere USD 100,000.00 is required to be kept in an account with the Central Bank of Belize. Cayman Islands, one of the most prominent financial centers in the world and home to 233 banks with USD 1.6 trillion in assets, offers restricted Class B banking licenses with a minimum paid up capital requirement of merely C$ 20,000.00 (1 USD equals 0.82 Cayman Dollars). An unrestricted offshore banking license requires a paid up capital of C$ 400,000.00. Anguilla serves as yet another example of reasonable requirements, where an international bank needs to maintain a net worth of USD 250,000.00.

In general the capital requirements have not changed dramatically despite all the regulatory changes of recent years. The jurisdictions still offering international licenses can however be expected to be more diligent than they were in the past when it comes to verifying that the capital has indeed been paid up and that the assets are acceptable. Since paid up capital is not always required to be kept in the jurisdiction issuing the license (at least not in its entirety), regulators have often depended merely on financial statements prepared by foreign auditors when determining whether an applicant has met the adequate capital requirement. As a result, some offshore banks in the past were capitalized by questionable assets. One remarkable example was First Grenada International Bank which was capitalized with a 10,000 carat ruby. Although the ruby could be located, its owner had never heard about the offshore bank that had used it for its capitalization. It was later discovered that the bank was operating a Ponzi scheme. I should mention that Grenada is no longer a viable jurisdiction for offshore bank licensing and consequently not featured in this book.

Requirements of reserve funds and liquid asset ratios (where applicable) vary from jurisdiction to jurisdiction. Please refer to the Banking Law of each jurisdiction for details.

Qualification Requirements

Each jurisdiction applies its own qualification requirements, but in general, the applicant needs to demonstrate that at least one person, either on staff or on the board of directors, has an appropriate background with some banking experience or experience otherwise suitable for the activities in which the new bank is proposing to engage. Each director, shareholder and other principal will also need to be deemed "fit and proper" and provide documents such as police clearance certificate, bank and commercial references, proof of residential address etc. Please refer to the Application Guidelines chapter of this book for further details and examples of questions that each principal would be required to answer.

Example of a "fit and proper" definition from Section 3 of the Cayman Islands Banks & Trust Companies Law (as revised 2009):

3. In determining for the purposes of this Law whether a person is a fit and proper person, regard shall be had to all circumstances, including that person's;

    a) honesty, integrity and reputation;

    b) competence and capability; and

    c) financial soundness

Section 24 of the Belize International Banking Act (2003) provides for an example of typical disqualification criteria for directors, principals, and in this case also for any employees of a licensee:

24. (1) No person shall apply for, or obtain, or be eligible, or continue to be employed, as a director, officer, manager,

secretary or other worker of any licensee licensed under this Act, without prior approval in writing of the Central Bank if-

a) he has been a director of, or directly or indirectly involved in, the management of a bank which has had its licence revoked in accordance with section 25 and section 27 of this Act or section 7 of the Banks and Financial Institutions Act, or in accordance with the banking laws of another country; or

b) he has been dismissed from the management of a bank for an act or conduct involving dishonesty or fraud; or

c) he has been convicted in Belize or elsewhere for any offence triable on indictment in Belize; or

d) he is or becomes bankrupt, suspends payment to, or compounds with, his creditors; or

e) he is, in the opinion of the Central Bank, not a fit and proper person to work or continue to work for a licensee;

f) he is an approved auditor for the licensee as provided in section 30 of this Act, or is an officer of a company which is an approved auditor.

Anguilla

Background

Colonized by English settlers from Saint Kitts in 1650, Anguilla was administered by Great Britain until the early 19th century, when the island - against the wishes of the inhabitants - was incorporated into a single British dependency along with Saint Kitts and Nevis. Several attempts at separation failed. In 1971, two years after a revolt, Anguilla was finally allowed to secede; this arrangement was formally recognized in 1980 with Anguilla becoming a separate British dependency.

Population

15,423 (July 2012 est.)

Capital

The Valley

Official Language

English

Regulatory Authority

Anguilla Financial Services Commission
P.O. Box 1575 - The Valley – Anguilla
British West Indies
Phone: +1 264 497 5881
Fax: +1 264 497 5872
Email: info@fsc.org.ai
Web: www.fsc.org.ai

License Types

Domestic Banks are regulated by the Banking Act 2005 and Offshore Banks by the Anguilla Trust Companies and Offshore Banking Act 2008. There are no restricted Offshore Banking Licenses and no reference is made in legislation to different classes of Offshore Bank Licenses.

Capital Requirements

A licensee must ensure that its paid-up share capital is maintained in an amount not less than USD 250,000 or the equivalent in another currency. The Governor may order a licensee to increase its fully paid-up capital to such greater amount as he may determine, having regard to the nature of the offshore banking business being, or sought to be, undertaken.

Offshore Bank License Fees

Non-refundable application fee:	USD 500.00
License Issuing Fee if before July 1st	USD 5000.00
License Issuing Fee if after July 1st	USD 10,000.00
Annual License Fee:	USD 20,000.00

Anguilla Trust Companies and Offshore Banking Act 2008

TABLE OF CONTENTS

PART 1

PRELIMINARY PROVISIONS

PART 2

OFFSHORE BANKING BUSINESS

PART 3

TRUST BUSINESS

PART 4

MATTERS APPLICABLE TO TRUST BUSINESS AND OFFSHORE BANKING BUSINESS

15. Interpretation

Revocation, Suspension and Surrender of Licence and Variation of Terms of Licence

16. Revocation or suspension of licence
17. Appointment of administrator by the Court
18. Surrender of licence
19. Variation of terms or conditions of licence

Principal Office and Authorised Agent

20. Principal office and authorised agent
21. Operation outside Anguilla

Restrictions on and Change of Names

22. Restrictions on use of certain terms
23. Change of name

Transfer of Shares and Appointment of Directors

24. Transfer of shares
25. Number and appointment of directors
26. Exemption for domestic bank

Obligations of Licensee

27. Annual fee
28. Books and records
29. Display of licence

Administration

Miscellaneous

PART 1

PRELIMINARY PROVISIONS

1. Interpretation

In this Act;

"attorney-at-law" means an attorney admitted to practice before the Eastern Caribbean Supreme Court in Anguilla;

"auditor" means a person who is in good standing as a member of an association of chartered or public accountants or other similar body approved by the Governor as a reputable auditing association;

"authorised agent" means an authorised agent referred to in section 20;

"bank" means a person carrying on banking business;

"banking business" means;

(a) the business of receiving funds through the acceptance of money deposits payable on demand or after a fixed period or after notice or any similar operation through the frequent sale or placement of bonds, certificates, notes or other securities, and the use of such funds either in whole or in part for loans or investment for the account and the risk of the person doing such business; and

(b) any other activity prescribed by the Governor as constituting customary banking practice that a bank engaged in activities described in paragraph (a) may additionally be authorised to do;

"Commission" means the Anguilla Financial Services Commission established under section 2 of the Financial Services Commission Act; (Act 15/2005, s.1)

"company" means a company incorporated or continued under the Companies Act;

"Court" means the High Court;

"dollar" or "$" means a dollar in the currency of the United States of America;

"domestic bank" means a person holding a licence under the Banking Act;

"foreign company" means a foreign company registered under Division 3 of Part 4 of the Companies Act;

"foreign regulatory authority" means an authority in a jurisdiction outside Anguilla that exercises functions corresponding or similar to the functions exercised by the Commission; (Act 15/2005, s.1)

"Inspector" means the Inspector of Trust Companies and Offshore Banks appointed under section 32;

"international business company" means a company incorporated or continued under the International Business Companies Act;

"offshore banking business" means banking business carried on in or from within Anguilla in a currency other than Eastern Caribbean dollars with a non-resident of Anguilla;

"offshore banking licence" means a licence issued under section 6;

"prescribed" means prescribed by regulations made by the Governor under section 40;

"trust" means trust as defined in the Trusts Act;

"trust business" means carrying on the business of acting as trustee of property;

"trust company licence" means a licence issued under section 12.

(2) Subject to subsection (3), for the purposes of this Act, the following are regarded as nonresidents of Anguilla;

a) an international business company;

b) a company or an LLC formed or continued under the Limited Liability Company Act that, at the relevant time does not engage in any revenue generating activities in Anguilla.

(3) An LLC or a company shall not be regarded as engaging in a revenue-generating activity in Anguilla in respect of;

a) any offshore banking business conducted with it by a person holding an offshore banking licence; or

b) any activity which the Governor may prescribe as exempt from paragraph (2)(b).

(4) For greater certainty;

a. a company;

b. an international business company; or

c. an LLC formed or continued under the Limited Liability Company Act; that carries on banking business or trust business outside Anguilla carries on banking business or trust business, as the case may be, from within Anguilla.

2. Application

(1) This Act does not apply to the Caribbean Development Bank.

(2) For greater certainty;

(a) a person, including a domestic bank, that holds an offshore banking licence;

(i) is exempt from the provisions of the Banking Act in respect of offshore banking business, and

(ii) is subject to the provisions of the Banking Act in respect of banking business other than offshore banking business; and

(b) a person holding an offshore banking licence or a trust company licence, other than a domestic bank, does not require a licence under the Trades, Businesses, Occupations and Professions Licensing Act in respect of its offshore banking or trust business.

PART 2

OFFSHORE BANKING BUSINESS

3. Interpretation

In this Part;

"licence" means an offshore banking licence;

"licensee" means a person holding an offshore banking licence.

4. Licence required

(1) No person, including a domestic bank, shall carry on offshore banking business unless he holds a licence that is not suspended under section 16.

(2) A person who contravenes subsection (1) commits an offence and is liable on summary conviction to a fine of $25,000, to a term of imprisonment of 2 years or to both.

5. Application for licence

(1) A company or a foreign company may apply to the Governor for a licence.

(2) An application under subsection (1) must;

(a) contain the information and be in the form prescribed; and

(b) be accompanied by the documentation prescribed.

6. Issuance of licence

If the Governor is satisfied;

(a) that an applicant is;

(i) a fit and proper person, and

(ii) is qualified to carry on offshore banking business;

(b) that the persons having any share or other interest, whether legal or equitable, in the applicant and its directors and officers are fit and proper persons to have an interest in or be concerned with the management of a licensee, as the case may be;

(c) that the applicant intends, if issued with a licence, to commence offshore banking business;

(d) that the applicant satisfies the requirements of this Act in respect of the application and will, upon issuance of the licence, be in compliance with this Act in respect of licensing; and

(e) that issuing the licence is not against the public interest; he may issue a licence to the applicant subject to such terms and conditions as he thinks fit.

7. Restrictions on business that may be carried on by licensee

A licensee that is not a domestic bank may not;

(a) invest in any asset that represents a claim on any person resident in Anguilla except a claim resulting from;

(i) a transaction with another licensee, or

(ii) the purchase of bonds or other securities issued by the Government, a government agency or a company in which the Government is the sole or majority beneficial owner; or

(b) without the written approval of the Governor, carry on any offshore banking business other than that for which the licence has been issued.

8. Maintenance of capital

(1) A licensee, other than a domestic bank, must ensure that its paid-up share capital is maintained in an amount not less than $250,000, or the equivalent in another currency, or such greater sum as may be ordered under subsection (2).

(2) The Governor may, on the recommendation of the Inspector, order a licensee to increase its fully paid-up capital to such

greater amount as he may determine having regard to the nature of the offshore banking business being, or sought to be, undertaken.

(3) A company that contravenes subsection (1) commits an offence and is liable on summary conviction to a fine of $25,000.

(4) Where an offence under this section is committed by a company, a director or officer of the company who knowingly authorised, permitted or acquiesced in the commission of the offence also commits an offence and is liable on summary conviction to a fine of $25,000, to a term of imprisonment for 6 months or to both.

PART 3

TRUST BUSINESS

9. Interpretation

In this Part;

"licence" means a trust company licence;

"licensee" means a person holding a trust company licence.

10. Licence required

(1) Subject to subsection (2), no person shall carry on trust business in or from within Anguilla unless he holds a licence that is not suspended under section 16.

(2) Subsection (1) does not apply to;

(a) a domestic bank that holds an offshore banking licence that is not suspended; or

(b) an attorney-at-law in so far as he is engaged in trust business solely in the practice of law.

(3) A person who contravenes subsection (1) commits an offence and is liable on summary conviction to a fine of $25,000, to a term of imprisonment of 2 years or to both.

11. Application for licence

(1) A company, a foreign company or, subject to section 13(2), an international business company may apply to the Governor for a licence.

(2) An application under subsection (1) must;

(a) contain the information and be in the form prescribed; and

(b) be accompanied by the documentation prescribed.

12. Issuance of licence

If the Governor is satisfied;

(a) that an applicant is;

(i) a fit and proper person, and

(ii) is qualified to carry on trust business;

(b) that the persons having any share or other interest, whether legal or equitable, in the applicant and its directors and officers are fit and proper persons to have an interest in or be concerned with the management of a licensee, as the case may be;

(c) that the applicant intends, if issued with a licence, to commence carrying on trust business in or from within Anguilla;

(d) that the applicant satisfies the requirements of this Act in respect of the application and will, upon issuance of the licence, be in compliance with this Act in respect of licensing; and

(e) that issuing the licence is not against the public interest; he may issue a licence to the applicant subject to such terms and conditions as he thinks fit.

13. Class and extension of licence

(1) A licence shall be in one of the following classes;

(a) a general trust company licence;

(b) a restricted trust company licence.

(2) A general trust company licence must not be issued to an international business company.

(3) A restricted trust company licence is subject to the restriction that the licensee does not undertake trust business on behalf of persons other than those listed in the undertaking accompanying the application for the licence or any amendment to the list filed with the Inspector.

(4) An applicant for a general trust company licence may apply for the licence to extend to a wholly-owned subsidiary of the applicant.

(5) An application under subsection (4) must be made in writing to the Governor accompanied by;

(a) the name of the subsidiary;

(b) documentary proof sufficient to establish that the subsidiary is wholly owned by the applicant;

(c) a description of the type of trust business being, or to be, carried on by the subsidiary; and

(d) any other information or documentation that the Governor considers necessary.

(6) The Governor may, upon granting a general trust company licence to the applicant, extend the licence to include any subsidiary referred to in subsection (4), subject to such terms and conditions as he thinks fit.

14. Maintenance of capital

(1) A holder of a general trust company licence, other than a domestic bank, must ensure that its paid-up share capital is maintained in an amount not less than $250,000, or the equivalent in another currency, or such greater sum as may be ordered under subsection (3).

(2) A holder of a restricted trust company licence must ensure that its fully paid-up share capital is maintained in an amount not less than the amount prescribed by the Governor as being the minimum capital for a restricted trust company, or such greater sum as may be ordered under subsection (3).

(3) The Governor may, on the recommendation of the Inspector, order a licensee to increase its fully paid-up capital to such greater amount than that required under subsection (1) or (2) as he may determine having regard to the nature of the general or restricted trust business being, or sought to be, undertaken.

(4) A company that contravenes subsection (1) or (2) commits an offence and is liable on conviction to a fine of $25,000.

(5) Where an offence under this section is committed by a company, a director or officer of the company who knowingly authorised, permitted or acquiesced in the commission of the offence also commits an offence and is liable on conviction to a fine of $25,000, to a term of imprisonment for 6 months or to both.

PART 4

MATTERS APPLICABLE TO TRUST BUSINESS AND OFFSHORE BANKING BUSINESS

15. Interpretation

In this Part;

"licence" means an offshore banking licence or a trust company licence;

"licensed business" means the trust business or offshore banking business, as the case may be, that the licensee is licensed to carry on;

"licensee" means a person holding an offshore banking licence or a person holding a trust company licence.

Revocation, Suspension and Surrender of Licence and Variation of Terms of Licence

16. Revocation or suspension of licence

(1) The Governor may at any time revoke or suspend a licence if it appears to him;

(a) that the licensee;

(i) is not a fit and proper person or is not qualified to carry on the licensed business,

(ii) is carrying on the licensed business in a manner detrimental to the public interest or to the interests of any of its creditors or, in the case of a holder of an offshore banking licence, of any depositors or, in the case of a holder of a trust company licence, of any beneficiary of a trust of which it is a trustee,

(iii) is insolvent,

(iv) has contravened or is in contravention of any provision of this Act, the Code of Practice issued under section 41 or of the Anti-Money Laundering Regulations,

(v) has breached or is in breach of any term or condition of its licence,

(vi) has ceased to carry on the licensed business, or

(vii) has furnished the Governor or the Inspector with any false, inaccurate or misleading information whether on making application for a licence or subsequent to the issue of the licence; or

(b) that any person having a share or interest in the licensee, whether equitable or legal, or any director or officer of the licensee is not a fit and proper person to have an interest in or to be concerned with the management of a licensee, as the case may be.

(2) The Governor shall revoke a licence if the licensee fails to pay the prescribed annual fee together with the appropriate late payment penalty in full on or before 30th June in the year in which the annual fee was due.

(3) Subject to subsection (4), the period of suspension of a licence under subsection (1) shall not exceed 90 days.

(4) If it is satisfied that is in the public interest to do so, the Court may, on the application of the Inspector, extend the period of suspension of a licence under this section for one or more further periods not exceeding 90 days each.

17. Appointment of administrator by the Court

(1) If a licence is or is about to be suspended or revoked under section 16, the Inspector may apply to the Court;

(a) for the appointment of an administrator to take over and manage the licensed business then carried on by the licensee or carried on by it immediately prior to the revocation or suspension of its licence, as the case may be; or

(b) for an order that the licensee be wound up by the Court or subject to the supervision of the Court under the Companies Act.

(2) An application made under subsection (1) may be made on an ex parte basis.

(3) On an application made under subsection (1), the Court may make such order as it considers necessary to safeguard;

(a) in the case of a holder of an offshore banking licence, the interests of any depositors; or

(b) in the case of a holder of a trust company licence, the interests of any beneficiary of a trust of which the licensee is a trustee.

(4) Without limiting subsection (3), an order made under that subsection may;

(a) grant an administrator the powers of a licensee under this Act;

(b) require the administrator to provide security;

(c) fix the remuneration of the administrator;

(d) require such persons as it considers necessary to appear before the Court for the purposes of giving information concerning the licensed business; and

(e) make any order that could be made by the Magistrate on an application made under section 33.

18. Surrender of licence

(1) A licensee that ceases to carry on the licensed business may apply to the Governor to surrender its licence.

(2) An application under subsection (1) must;

(a) contain the information and be in the form prescribed; and

(b) be accompanied by the documentation prescribed.

(3) If the Governor is satisfied that;

(a) the licensee has ceased to carry on the licensed business and that;

(i) in the case of a person holding an offshore banking licence, the licensee has repaid all deposits accepted by it, or

(ii) in the case of a person holding a trust company licence, the licensee has properly distributed, transferred or otherwise dealt with all trust assets that were held or administered by it; or

(b) if the licensee is being wound up, that it is solvent and is able on demand;

(i) in the case of a company holding an offshore banking licence, to repay all deposits accepted by it, or

(ii) in the case of a person holding a trust company licence, to properly distribute, transfer or otherwise deal with all trust assets that are or were held or administered by it; the Governor may approve the surrender.

(4) In the case of a surrender of a licence under paragraph (3)(b), the Attorney General or the Inspector may apply to the Court for an order that the licensee be wound up by the Court or subject to the supervision of the Court under the Companies Act.

19. Variation of terms or conditions of licence

The Governor may, upon giving reasonable notice to the licensee;

(a) vary or cancel any terms or conditions imposed on the issue of a licence or under the extension of a licence under section 13(4); or

(b) impose new terms or conditions.

20. Principal office and authorised agent

(1) A licensee must have;

(a) a principal office in Anguilla; and

(b) two authorised agents who comply with subsection (2).

(2) Each authorised agent;

(a) must be an individual resident in Anguilla; and

(b) must, prior to his appointment;

(i) have consented in writing to act as an authorised agent, and

(ii) be approved in writing as an authorised agent by the Inspector.

(3) The licensee must appoint its first authorised agents not later than the day of the issue of its licence and shall forthwith notify the Inspector that the approved appointments have been made.

(4) A licensee may not change the address of its principal office or appoint an authorized agent without the prior written approval of the Inspector.

(5) The Inspector in his discretion may in writing revoke an approval given under this section.

(6) Subject to subsection (7), a licensee that contravenes this section commits an offence and is liable on summary conviction;

(a) in respect of a breach of subsection (1), to a fine of $25,000; and

(b) in respect of a breach of subsection (3) or subsection (4), to a fine of $10,000.

(7) A licensee does not contravene subsection (1) when an authorised agent dies or resigns or has his approval revoked under subsection (5) if;

(a) the licensee forthwith submits to the Inspector for approval the name of a person to replace the authorised representative; and

(b) appoints an authorised agent forthwith after he is approved; so long as the licensee has at least 1 authorised agent.

(8) This section does not apply to a domestic bank.

(9) The authorised agents of a licensee shall in their capacity as representatives of the licensee ensure compliance with any statutory requirements under this Act.

21. Operation outside Anguilla

(1) A licensee must not operate a branch, agency or office outside Anguilla without the prior approval of the Inspector.

(2) A licensee who contravenes subsection (1) commits an offence and is liable on summary conviction to a fine of $25,000.

Restrictions on and Change of Names

22. Restrictions on use of certain terms

(1) No person other than a licensee shall, except with the authority of the Governor or under the authority of any other written law;

(a) use, whether in the name under which he is registered or in the description or title under which he carries on business in or from within Anguilla and whether in English or in any language;

(i) the words "bank", "savings" or "trust" or any derivative, or

(ii) any word that, in the opinion of the Governor, suggests trust business or offshore banking business; or

(b) make any representation in any document or in any other manner that is likely to suggest that he is carrying on trust business or offshore banking business.

(2) The Governor may, by written notice, require a licensee who carries on offshore banking business or trust business under a name that is;

(a) identical to that of any other person, whether within or outside Anguilla, or which so nearly resembles that name as to be likely to deceive;

(b) likely to suggest falsely the patronage of or connection with some person whether within or outside Anguilla; or

(c) likely to suggest falsely that he has special status in relation to or derived from the Government or has the official approval of, or acts on behalf of, the Government or of any of its departments or officials;
forthwith to change the name and in default of compliance may revoke the licence.

(3) A person who contravenes subsection (1) commits an offence and is liable on summary conviction to a fine of $25,000, to a term of imprisonment of 1 year or to both.

(4) A licensee who fails to change his name within 7 days of the date of receipt of a written notice under subsection (2) commits an offence and is liable on summary conviction to a fine of $10,000 and to a daily default fine of $500.

23. Change of name

A licensee shall not change its name without the prior written approval of the Inspector.

Transfer of Shares and Appointment of Directors

24. Transfer of shares

(1) No share or other interest, whether legal or equitable, in a licensee shall be issued, transferred or otherwise disposed of without the prior written approval of the Governor.

(2) The Governor may exempt any company from the provisions of subsection (1), subject to such terms and conditions as he thinks fit.

25. Number and appointment of directors

(1) A licensee shall have not less than 2 directors.

(2) Subject to subsection (3), no appointment of a director or other senior officer of a licensee shall be made without the

prior written approval of the Inspector.

(3) Subsection (2) does not apply to a licensee that is exempted in writing by the Inspector.

(4) An exemption under subsection (3) may be granted subject to such terms and conditions as the Inspector considers fit and may be revoked by the Inspector in writing.

26. Exemption for domestic bank

Sections 24 and 25 do not apply to a domestic bank.

Obligations of Licensee

27. Annual fee

A licensee shall pay the prescribed annual fee on or before 15th January of each year and any penalties for late payment of such fee as may be prescribed by regulation.

28. Books and records

(1) A licensee shall keep within Anguilla;

(a) such books and records as accurately reflect his licensed business; and

(b) such further books and records in respect of its licensed business as the Commission may require.

(2) A licensee that contravenes subsection (1) commits an offence and is liable on summary conviction to a fine of $10,000 or to imprisonment for a term of 6 months or to both.

29. Display of licence

A licensee must prominently display its licence on the premises where its licensed business is carried on.

30. Accounts

(1) Every licensee shall have its accounts audited by an auditor annually or at such other periods as the Governor or the Inspector may require.

(2) The licensee shall forward the audited accounts to the Inspector within 6 months from the end of the financial year of the licensee unless prior written approval for an extension has been granted by the Inspector.

(3) Where a licensee changes its auditor, the licensee shall, when required by the Inspector, authorise the former auditor to disclose the circumstances that gave rise to the change, and when so authorised, the auditor shall disclose such circumstances.

31. Directions for the reporting of information

(1) The Inspector may, by notice published in the Gazette, issue directions to licensees for the making of returns, or the furnishing of documentation, to him for regulatory purposes.

(2) A notice under subsection (1) must specify the period within which returns must be made or documentation filed.

(3) Directions issued under subsection (1) may make different provision in relation to different persons, circumstances or cases.

(4) A licensee that fails, within the period specified, to make a return or furnish documentation to the Inspector in accordance with directions issued under subsection (1) commits an offence and is liable on summary conviction to a fine of $5,000.

Administration

32. Inspector

(1) There is established the office of Inspector of Trust Companies and Offshore Banks as a public office to which appointments are to be made in accordance with section 66 of the Constitution of Anguilla.

(2) Under the general supervision of the Governor, the Inspector is responsible for ensuring the proper administration of this Act.

(3) The functions of the Inspector include;

(a) monitoring trust business and offshore banking business;

(b) advising the Governor on all matters concerning the regulation and supervision of trust business and offshore banking business;

(c) examining and evaluating all applications for;

(i) trust company licences, and

(ii) offshore banking licences, and making recommendations to the Governor concerning such applications;

(d) examining and, if he thinks fit, reporting to the Governor upon returns made and documents filed by licensees under this Act;

(e) where he thinks fit or when required by the Governor, the examination in such manner as he considers necessary, the affairs or business of any licensee for the purpose of satisfying himself that the provisions of this Act, the Code of Conduct issued under section

41 or the Anti-Money Laundering Regulations are being complied with and that the licensee is in a sound financial position and is carrying on its business in a satisfactory manner;

(f) the provision of assistance in the investigation of any offences under the laws governing banking and other commercial activities committed by the licensee, his directors, agents or officers; and

(g) reporting to the Governor regarding the examination of any documents produced to him in the course of the performance of his functions.

(4) For the purposes of performing his functions under subsection (3), the Inspector shall be entitled;

(a) to have access to and take copies of such books, records, vouchers, documents, cash and securities and all other financial instruments of any licensee;

(b) to request such information, matter or thing from any person who, he has reasonable grounds to believe, is carrying on offshore banking business or trust business in contravention of any part of this Act; and

(c) to call upon the authorised agent, or manager, of the licensee for such information or explanation; as the Inspector may reasonably require for the purpose of enabling him to perform his functions under this Act.

(5) Where in the conduct of an examination of the affairs or business of a licensee carried out under paragraph (3)(e) the Inspector, or a person acting under his authority, obtains access to the name and title of a settlor or of an account of a depositor, he must not disclose the information obtained to any other person unless authorised to do so by order of the Court made on the application of the Inspector.

(6) The Court may make an order under subsection (5) if it is satisfied that;

(a) the Inspector has adduced prima facie evidence of illegal activity; and

(b) there are reasonable grounds for believing that the information sought to be disclosed will be of value in the investigation of that illegal activity.

(7) Notice of an application by the Inspector for an order permitting disclosure under subsection (5) must be served on the licensee from whom the Inspector obtained the document or information at least 5 days prior to the hearing or such shorter period as the Court may allow and the licensee shall be entitled to be heard at the hearing of the application.

(8) Where the Inspector is satisfied that there is prima facie evidence of illegal activity carried on by any licensee and for any reason is unable to obtain information he requires from such licensee, the Inspector may apply to the Magistrate for an order of the Magistrate directing the licensee to provide to the Inspector the information that he requires.

(9) Where the Magistrate is satisfied that the Inspector has adduced prima facie evidence of illegal activity carried on by a licensee and that the Inspector is unable to obtain such information as is referred to in subsection (8), the Magistrate shall, on application made by the Inspector, issue an order directing the licensee to provide to the Inspector such information.

(10) Any licensee who contravenes the order of the Magistrate commits an offence and is liable to a fine of $25,000, to a term of imprisonment for 1 year or to both.

(11) With the written approval of the Governor, the Inspector

may authorise in writing any person to assist him in the performance of his functions under this Act.

(12) If the Magistrate is satisfied by information on oath given by the Inspector or by a person authorised by the Governor to assist the Inspector that there is reasonable ground for suspecting that an offence against this Act has been or is being committed by a licensee, the Magistrate shall, on application made by the Inspector, issue an order authorising him to take such action as the Magistrate may consider necessary in the interest of the depositors or of the beneficiaries of any trust or other creditors of the licensee and to preserve any assets of the licensee.

33. Power of search

(1) If the Magistrate is satisfied by information on oath given by the Inspector or by a person authorised by him;

(a) that a licence has been revoked or suspended under section 16;

(b) that there are reasonable grounds for believing that an offence under this Act has been or is being committed and that evidence of the commission of the offence is to be found on any premises or in any vehicle, vessel or aircraft specified in the information; or

(c) that any document that ought to have been produced under section 32(4) and has not been produced is to be found at any premises or in any vehicle, vessel or aircraft specified in the information; he may grant a search warrant authorising the Inspector, together with any other person named in the warrant, to enter the premises or any premises upon which the vehicle, vessel or aircraft may be located at any time within 1 month from the date of the warrant and to search the premises or the vehicle, vessel or aircraft.

(2) The Inspector or any other person authorised by a warrant to search any premises or any vehicle, vessel or aircraft;

(a) may search every person who is found in or whom he has reasonable grounds to believe to have recently left, or to be about to enter, those premises or that vehicle, vessel or aircraft; and

(b) may seize any document found on the premises or in the vehicle, vessel or aircraft that he has reasonable grounds for believing ought to have been produced under section 32(4).

(3) Where under this section a person has any power to enter any premises or a vehicle, vessel or aircraft, he may use such force as is reasonably necessary for the purpose of exercising that power.

34. Attorney General may apply to Court

Where a licensee or a person who has at any time been a licensee is being wound up voluntarily, the Attorney General may, when being requested by the Inspector, apply to the Court for leave to intervene on behalf of any interested party, if he considers that the winding up is not being conducted in the best interests of its depositors, the beneficiaries of any trust, or other creditors and the Court shall make such order as it shall consider appropriate.

Miscellaneous

35. Insurance

(1) The Inspector may by written notice require a licensee to effect a policy of insurance with an approved insurance company and maintain it.

(2) The policy of insurance shall insure against;

(a) losses arising out of claims of negligence or breach of duty by the licensee or by an employee;

(b) the dishonesty of employees or of the licensee;

(c) loss of documents; and

(d) such other risks as the Inspector may stipulate; in such amount and of such nature as the Inspector determines having due regard to the nature and type of business carried on by the licensee.

(3) The licensee shall effect the policy of insurance within the time specified in the notice or any extension of the time given by the Inspector.

(4) The licensee shall without delay give notice to the Inspector in writing if;

(a) he is unable to obtain insurance as required by the Inspector; or

(b) he ceases to maintain the insurance.

(5) A licensee who contravenes this section commits an offence and is liable on summary conviction to a fine of $10,000, to a term of imprisonment of 1 year or to both.

36. Confidentiality

(1) For the purposes of this section, "protected person" means;

(a) a person who has applied for a licence under this Act;

(b) a licensee;

(c) a customer of a licensee;

(d) a settlor or beneficiary of a trust of which the licensee is a trustee; or

(e) a company managed by a licensee.

(2) Subject to subsection (3), the Inspector, a person acting under the Inspector's authority, and a person authorised by the Governor under section 32(12) to assist the Inspector must not disclose to any person information that the Inspector, the person acting under the Inspector's authority, or the person authorised by the Governor under section 32(12) has acquired in the course of his duties concerning the affairs of a protected person or in the exercise of his functions under this Act.

(3) Subsection (2) does not apply to a disclosure;

(a) required or permitted by any court of competent jurisdiction in Anguilla;

(b) to the Governor;

(c) to any person for the purpose of discharging any duty or exercising any power under this Act;

(d) in respect of the affairs of a protected person made with the consent of that person;

(e) if the information disclosed is or has been available to the public from any other source;

(f) where the information disclosed is in a summary or in statistics expressed in a manner that does not enable the identity of a protected person to which the information relates to be determined; or

(g) made by the Inspector to a foreign regulatory authority upon the written request of that authority.

(4) The Inspector may not disclose information concerning the affairs of a protected person to a foreign regulatory authority under paragraph (3)(g) unless he is satisfied;

(a) that the foreign regulatory authority is subject to adequate legal restrictions on further disclosure; and

(b) that the information disclosed is reasonably required by the authority for the purposes of its regulatory functions.

(5) Paragraph (3)(g) does not apply to information to which section 32(5) applies.

(6) The Governor may issue guidelines to the Inspector concerning the discharge of his functions under this section.

(7) Any person who contravenes the provisions of this section commits an offence and is liable on summary conviction to a fine of $10,000.

37. Immunity

No liability attaches to the Governor, the Inspector or any person acting under the authority of the Governor or the Inspector for an act done in good faith in the discharge or purported discharge of his functions under this Act.

38. Gazette notices

(1) The Governor shall cause notice of the issue, revocation or suspension of a licence to be published in the Gazette.

(2) A notice of issue of a licence published in the Gazette must specify the terms and conditions, if any, to which the licence is subject.

39. Appeals

(1) A decision of the Governor under section 7, section 13(6), section 14(2) or section 19 is final and conclusive and shall not be called into question in any court of law.

(2) An appeal lies to the Court from a decision of the Governor to suspend or revoke a licence under section 16.

(3) Unless the Court otherwise orders, an appeal made under subsection (2) does not operate to suspend the decision of the Governor.

40. Regulations

The Governor in Council may make regulations generally for giving effect to the provisions of this Act and specifically;

(a) requiring the payment of fees under this Act and prescribing them, including;

(i) fees for filing an application,

(ii) fees for the issuance of a licence, and

(iii) annual fees;

(b) controlling the form of advertising undertaken by licensees;

(c) prescribing anything required or permitted to be prescribed by this Act; and

(d) exempting any trust company from this Act or any provision of this Act, subject to such conditions, if any, as are imposed in respect of the exemption.

41. Code of Practice

(1) The Inspector may issue a Code of Practice with respect to the procedures to be followed by, and the conduct expected of, a licensee in the operation of its licensed business.

(2) The Code of Practice may include;

(a) due diligence procedures;

(b) record keeping requirements; and

(c) audit requirements.

(3) The Code of Practice may make different provision in relation to different persons, circumstances or cases.

(4) The Inspector must publish the Code of Practice and any amendments thereto in the Gazette.

42. Offences

(1) A person who with intent to deceive, or for any purpose of this Act makes any representation that he knows to be false or does not believe to be true commits an offence and is liable on summary conviction to a fine of $25,000, to imprisonment for a term of 1 year or to both.

(2) A person who;

(a) assaults or obstructs the Inspector or other person in the performance of his functions under this Act;

(b) uses any insulting language to an Inspector or other person in the performance of his functions under this Act;

(c) by the offer of any gratuity, bribe or other inducement prevents or attempts to prevent an Inspector or other person from performing his functions under this Act; or

(d) contravenes any provision of this Act or regulations, for which no penalty is specifically provided; commits an offence and is liable on summary conviction to a fine of $5,000, to imprisonment for a term of 1 year or to both.

(3) A licensee that carries on business contrary to the terms or conditions of its licence or, in the case of the holder of a restricted trust company licence, in contravention of the restriction, commits an offence and is liable on summary conviction to a fine of $25,000.

(4) Where an offence under this Act is committed by a company, a director or officer of that company who knowingly authorised, permitted or acquiesced in the commission of the offence also commits the offence and is liable on summary conviction to;

(a) a fine of the amount specified for the offence;

(b) to a term of imprisonment as specified for the offence, if any; or

(c) to both a fine and imprisonment.

(5) Notwithstanding that the offence is punishable only on summary conviction, the Proceeds of Criminal Conduct Act applies to the following offences;

(a) section 4(2);

(b) section 8(3);

(c) section 8(4);

(d) section 10(3);

(e) section 14(4);

(f) section 14(5);

(g) section 21(2);

(h) section 35(5);

(i) section 42(1); and

(j) section 42(4), where the offence committed by the company is an offence referred to in paragraphs (a) to (f).

43. Citation

This Act may be cited as the Trust Companies and Offshore Banking Act, Revised Statutes of Anguilla, Chapter T60.

Barbados

Background

The island was uninhabited when first settled by the British in 1627. Slaves worked the sugar plantations established on the island until 1834 when slavery was abolished. The economy remained heavily dependent on sugar, rum, and molasses production through most of the 20th century. The gradual introduction of social and political reforms in the 1940s and 1950s led to complete independence from the UK in 1966. In the 1990s, tourism and manufacturing surpassed the sugar industry in economic importance.

Population

287,733 (July 2012 est.)

Capital

Bridgetown

Official Language

English

Regulatory Authority

Central Bank of Barbados
Tom Adams Financial Centre
Spry Street - Bridgetown
PO Box 1016 - Barbados
West Indies BB11126
Phone: +1 246 436 6870
Fax: +1 246 427 9559
Email: supervision@centralbank.org.bb
Web: www.centralbank.org.bb

License Types

Domestic Banks are regulated by the Financial Institutions Act 1996 and Offshore Banks by the International Financial Services Act 2002 which replaced the Offshore Banking Act. There are no restricted Class B Licenses but capital requirements vary depending on whether or not a bank will accept third party funds.

Capital Requirements

A licensee that accepts third party deposits is required to have a stated or assigned capital of at least USD 4,000,000. A licensee that does not accept third party deposits is required to have a stated or assigned capital of at least USD 1,000,000. See the International Financial Services Act for further details about reserve requirements etc.

Offshore Bank License Fees

License Issuing Fee	USD 25,000.00
Annual License Renewal Fee:	USD 25,000.00

International Financial Services Act 2002
Chapter 325

ARRANGEMENT OF SECTIONS

Preliminary

PART I
INTERNATIONAL FINANCIAL SERVICES

Licensing Requirements

Financial Obligations

19. Capital.
20. Reserves.
21. Dividends.
22. Restriction on business activities.

Trust Activities

23. Separation of trust assets.
24. Common trust fund.
25. Declaration of trust.
26. Trust funds awaiting disposition.
27. Contents of declaration.
28. Dealing with trust assets.
29. Interest in common trust fund.
30. Status of licensee as trustee.
31. Application of Mutual Funds Act.

Abandoned Property

32. Abandoned property.
33. Disposal of abandoned property.
34. Sale of abandoned property.
35. Payment into Consolidated Fund.
36. Claims against property.
37. Refusal to pay claims.
38. Offence re: abandoned property.

Part II

ADMINISTRATION OF LICENSEES

Directors and Officers

39. Meaning of "director".
40. Cessation of office by director and senior officer.

Audit and Inspection

Offences

Part III

WINDING UP OF LICENSEES

67. Interruption of winding up.
68. Duty of Central Bank.
69. Powers of High Court.
70. Notice of application.
71. Appointment of custodian.
72. Functions of custodian.
73. Inventory of assets.
74. Effect of seizure.
75. Execution against assets.
76. Reorganisation.
77. Contents of plan.
78. Modification of plan.
79. Compulsory winding up.
80. Termination of employment.
81. Right of lessor.
82. Settlement of trust accounts.
83. Statement of accounts.
84. Contents of boxes.
85. Claims.
86. Objections.
87. Distribution of assets.
88. Priority of claims.
89. Left-over assets.
90. Abandoned funds.
91. Completion of winding up.

PART IV

SPECIAL TAXING PROVISIONS

92. Definitions: "resident of Barbados" and "beneficial interest".

Tax Exemptions

93. Exemption from tax.
94. Transfer of assets: exemption.
95. Withholding tax and report concerning dividends etc.

PART V

MISCELLANEOUS AND TRANSITIONAL

CHAPTER 325
INTERNATIONAL FINANCIAL SERVICES

An Act to repeal the Off-shore Banking Act; to make new provision in relation to international financial services; and to provide for related matters.

Preliminary

1. This Act may be cited as the International Financial Services Act.

2. (1) In this Act,

"advertisement" means any form of advertising, whether notified or Published;

(a) in a newspaper, magazine, journal or other periodical publication;

(b) by the display of posters or notices;

(c) by means of circulars, brochures, pamphlets or handbills;

(d) by an exhibition of photographs or cinematograph films;

(e) by way of sound broadcasting or television; or

(f) by way of any other media;

"approved entity" means any entity approved by the Minister that is organised or formed under an enactment;

"articles" means, in the case of a company, its articles of incorporation and, in the case of a society with restricted liability, its articles of organisation;

"auditor" means an auditor described in section 50 and includes a partnership of auditors;

"business", in relation to a licensee, means the international financial services business of the licensee;

"capital" includes the quota of a society with restricted liability;

"Central Bank" means the Central Bank of Barbados;

"common trust fund" has the meaning given to that expression in section 24;

"Community" means the Caribbean Community established by Article 2 of the Treaty;

"company" includes a society with restricted liability and an approved entity;

"director" means a director within the meaning of section 39;

"eligible company" has the meaning given to that expression in section 5(8);

"foreign bank" means a bank incorporated outside Barbados;

"group" means,

(a) in relation to a company, that company and

(i) any other company which is its holding company or subsidiary;

(ii) any other company which is a subsidiary of its holding company;

(iii) any company which directly or indirectly controls or is controlled by any company referred to in sub-paragraph (i) or (ii);

(iv) any company which is controlled by a person who directly or indirectly controls a company referred to in sub-paragraph (i), (ii) or (iii);

(v) any company in which a group of relatives has a controlling interest;

(b) in relation to a person other than a company,

(i) a group of relatives where each member of the group is substantially dependent upon the same income source;

(ii) a group of persons in which one member has power directly or indirectly to control the other members;

(iii) any other group of persons that may be prescribed by the Central Bank;

"international financial service" has the meaning given to that expression in section 4;

"licensee" means a person licensed under the provisions of this Act, and "licence" shall be construed accordingly;

"Member State" means a Member State of the Community, excluding an Associate Member within the meaning of Article 231 of the Treaty;

"prescribed" means prescribed by regulations;

"prescribed person" means a company or an organisation that is licensed or organised under any of the enactments set out in the Schedule;

"qualified foreign bank" has the meaning given to that expression in section 5(9);

"relative", in respect of any person, means the spouse, parent, brother, sister, child or step-child of that person;

"resident of Barbados" has the meaning given to that expression in section 92;

"senior officer", in relation to a company, means the chief executive officer and the chief finance officer of the company, by whatever name called;

"share" includes the quota of a society with restricted liability, and "shareholder" shall be construed accordingly;

"society with restricted liability" means an organisation that is organised under the Societies With Restricted Liability Act;

"Treaty" means the Revised Treaty of Chaguaramas establishing the Caribbean Community, including the CARICOM Single Market and Economy, that was signed in the Bahamas on 5th July, 2001.

(2) For the purposes of this Act, "associate" means, when used to indicate a relationship with any person,

(a) a company in which that person beneficially owns or controls, directly or indirectly, shares or securities convertible into shares carrying more than 20 per cent of the voting rights under all circumstances or by reason of the occurrence of an event that has occurred and is continuing, or a currently exercisable option or right to purchase those shares or convertible securities;

(b) a partner of that person acting on behalf of the partnership of which they are partners;

(c) a trust or estate in which that person has a substantial beneficial interest or in respect of which he serves as a trustee or in a similar capacity; or

(d) a relative of that person or a relative of the spouse of that person if the relative has the same residence as that person.

(3) For the purposes of this Act,

(a) a company is affiliated with another company if one of them is the subsidiary of the other or both are subsidiaries of the same company or each of them is controlled by the same person;

(b) if two companies are affiliated with a third company at the same time, they are affiliated with each other at that time.

(4) For the purposes of this Act,

(a) a company is the holding company of another if that other company is its subsidiary;

(b) a company is a subsidiary of another company if it is controlled by that other company.

(5) For the purposes of this Act, a licensee is controlled by another company or by an individual, trust or government if at the relevant time it is effectively controlled directly or indirectly by that other company, individual, trust or government

(a) through being an associate of that other company, individual, trust or government;

(b) through being an affiliate of that other company;

(c) through the holding of shares of an incorporated or unincorporated body, but subject to subsection (6);

(d) through the holding of membership in an unincorporated body;

(e) through voting trusts or other agreements relating to the voting of shares;

(f) through the holding by an unincorporated body of a substantial portion of the licensee's borrowings;

(g) through management control of an unincorporated body; or

(h) through any other means.

(6) For the purposes of this Act, a company is controlled by a person if shares of the company that carry voting rights sufficient to elect a majority of the directors of the company are held directly or indirectly, other than by way of security only, by or on behalf of that person.

3. The Minister may by order amend the Schedule.

PART I

INTERNATIONAL FINANCIAL SERVICES

Licensing Requirements

4. (1) For the purposes of this Act, "international financial service" means;

(a) international banking business as described in subsection (2); or

(b) any other financial service, related to or ancillary to an activity described in subsection (2), which the Central Bank may by regulations declare to be an international financial service for the purposes of this Act.

(2) For the purposes of subsection (1), "international banking business" means;

(a) the business of receiving foreign funds through

(i) the acceptance of foreign money deposits payable upon demand or after a fixed period or after notice;

(ii) the sale or placement of foreign bonds, foreign certificates, foreign notes or other foreign debt obligations or other foreign securities; or

(iii) any other similar activity involving foreign money or foreign securities;

(b) the business of using the foreign funds so acquired, either in whole or in part, for

(i) loans, advances and investments;

(ii) the activities of the licensee for the account of or at the risk of the licensee;

(iii) the purchase or placement of foreign bonds, foreign certificates, notes or other foreign debt obligations or other foreign securities; or

(iv) any other similar activity involving foreign money or foreign securities; or

(c) the business of accepting in trust from persons resident outside Barbados or from prescribed persons

(i) amounts of money in foreign currencies or in foreign securities or both;

(ii) foreign personal property or foreign movable property; or

(iii) foreign real property or foreign immovable property.

5. (1) Subject to subsection (5),

(a) no person shall carry on any international financial service in or from within Barbados at any time when that person is not a licensee;

(b) no licence may be issued under this Act to any person other than an eligible company or a qualified foreign bank.

(2) Any person who contravenes subsection (1)(a) is guilty of an offence and is liable on conviction on indictment to a fine of $100,000.

(3) Where there is reasonable cause to believe that any company has contravened subsection (1), the Central Bank may cause an examination to be made of that company; and the provisions of this Act shall apply mutatis mutandis for the purposes of the examination as if the company was a licensee.

(4) A person who holds any funds obtained from carrying on any international financial service from within Barbados during any period in which he did not hold a licence under this Act shall repay those funds in accordance with the direction of the Minister.

(5) This Act does not apply to any international financial service

(a) being carried on immediately before 10th June, 2002 with the approval of the Exchange Control Authority by a bank licensed under the Financial Institutions Act;

(b) carried on after 10th June, 2002, with the approval of the Exchange Control Authority by a bank licensed under the Financial Institutions Act; and any such international financial service may, notwithstanding this Act, be carried on until otherwise directed by the Exchange Control Authority.

(6) Notwithstanding subsection (1), a company is not required to be licensed under this Act where that company receives foreign funds, from affiliates or associates in the manner described in section 4(2)(a), which are used for

(a) the purposes of loans or advances to, or investments in, affiliates or associates of that company; or

(b) the purposes specified in section 4(2)(b).

(7) Where a licence is issued to a company described in subsection (6), section 12 shall apply and the licence shall be subject to such conditions and restrictions as may be specified in the licence by the Minister.

(8) For the purposes of this Act, "eligible company" means a company which is incorporated or registered under the Companies Act, a society with restricted liability or an approved entity;

(a) whose objects or business activities are restricted to the carrying on of any international financial service from within Barbados;

(b) which has at least one director who is a citizen of a Member State and who is resident in Barbados;

(c) whose articles and bye-laws are acceptable to the Central Bank; and

(d) whose stated capital accords with the requirements of section 19.

(8A) For the purposes of this Act, an eligible company that is licensed under this Act to carry on;

(a) international banking business under section 4(1)(a); or

(b) any other financial service related or ancillary to

international banking business under section 4(1)(b) shall be regarded as an international bank and shall be regulated by the Central Bank in accordance with this Act.

(9) For the purposes of this Act, "qualified foreign bank" means

(a) a company that at 10th June, 2002 is a foreign bank that is licensed under the Financial Institutions Act; or

(b) a company that is a foreign bank with the capitalisation and assets specified in section 19 and that is not licensed under the Financial Institutions Act at 10th June, 2002; or

(c) a company approved by the Central Bank that is directly or indirectly a wholly-owned subsidiary of a foreign bank.

6. (1) A licence shall not be granted under this Act unless the company;

(a) has a place of business in Barbados approved by the Central Bank which will be its registered office;

(b) has, if the Central Bank so directs, appointed a person in Barbados who is approved by the Central Bank to be its agent; and

(c) has appointed a person in Barbados who is approved by the Central Bank to be its agent in the absence or inability to act of the person referred to under paragraph (b).

(2) A licensee shall not

(a) cease to have a place of business in Barbados;

(b) change its place of business without the written approval of the Central Bank;

(c) cease to have an authorised agent if required under subsection (1);

(d) change its authorised agent without the written approval of the Central Bank.

(3) For a period of 9 months no action shall be taken against a company to which section 114 applies if the company does not comply with subsection (1) or (2).

7. (1) An applicant for a licence under this Act to carry on an international financial service from within Barbados must

(a) show that it is an eligible company or a qualified foreign bank;

(b) give the names and addresses of its directors;

(c) give particulars of the international financial service it proposes to carry on from within Barbados;

(d) give the names and addresses of the shareholders and the number of shares directly or indirectly held by them; and

(e) provide such other information of a financial or other nature as the Minister may require in any general or particular case.

(2) An application for a licence by an eligible company must be accompanied by;

(a) a copy of the articles and bye-laws of the applicant, certified by the Registrar of Corporate Affairs and Intellectual Property Office; and

(b) such other documents as may be prescribed.

(3) An application for a licence by a qualified foreign bank must be accompanied by the prescribed documents.

(4) An application for a licence shall be signed by not less than 2 directors of the applicant.

8. Where a company has appointed a citizen of a Member State who is a resident of Barbados to its board of directors in order to become an eligible company, that director need not subscribe for nor acquire any shares of the company, either by way of qualification or otherwise, notwithstanding anything to the contrary in the articles of the company.

9. (1) On receipt of an application for a licence, the Minister may cause an investigation to be made of the applicant, its financial circumstances and any associates or affiliates of the applicant, as the Minister considers necessary in the public interest.

(2) In particular, in respect of the applicant, the Minister may require an examination to be made of;

(a) the financial status and history of the applicant and any of its directors, associates or affiliates;

(b) the character and experience of the directors;

(c) the adequacy of its capital for the purpose of the business it intends to carry on;

(d) the needs of the public or persons it intends to serve; and

(e) its earning prospects and its prospects as an employer.

10. (1) Subject to subsection (2), the Minister shall issue or refuse a licence within 3 months of the receipt of the application.

(2) Where additional information is required by the Minister for the purposes of this section, he shall issue or refuse a licence

within 14 days after the expiration of the period mentioned under subsection (1) or within 14 days of the receipt of the information, whichever is the later.

(3) Where the Minister is of the opinion that it is in the public interest to do so, he may issue a licence to the applicant upon payment of the prescribed fee.

11. (1) Where the Minister refuses a licence under this Act, he shall inform the applicant of the grounds for his refusal.

(2) Where the Minister states that the refusal is in the public interest, he need not state any other ground.

12. (1) A licence issued under this Act must show the kind of international financial service to be carried on from within Barbados by the licensee.

(2) A licence is subject to such conditions as the Minister may specify in respect of the kind of international financial service to be carried on by the licensee from within Barbados.

(3) A licence under this Act remains valid until revoked or suspended, but it is a condition of every licence that an annual fee be paid by the licensee in the amount and at the time prescribed.

(4) It is a condition of a licence that the licensee must obtain the written approval of the Central Bank,

(a) before creating a branch, subsidiary company, agency or representative office; or

(b) before opening a place of business outside Barbados.

(5) Subsection (4) does not apply to a licensee that is a qualified foreign bank within the meaning of paragraph (a) or (b) of section 5(9), but the licensee shall not, without notifying the

Central Bank of its intention to do so, create any branch, subsidiary company, agency or representative office.

(6) It is a condition of every licence that the licensee must notify the Central Bank in writing of any change in the directors or senior officers within 14 days of the change.

13. (1) It is a condition of a licence that

(a) any shares of the licensee's capital will be in registered form;

(b) the licensee will not, without the approval of the Minister,

(i) enter into a merger, amalgamation or consolidation;

(ii) transfer, otherwise than in the ordinary course of its business, the whole or any substantial part of its assets or liabilities;

(iii) change its name from that set out in its licence;

(iv) alter its articles;

(v) transfer any of its shares or alter its share structure;

(vi) take any action to reduce or impair in any respect its capital; or

(vii) repurchase its own shares or take any action which may have a similar effect;

(c) the licensee will not knowingly in the course of its business accept any deposit in trust or for the account of a beneficial owner, who is a resident of Barbados, other than a prescribed person; and

(d) the licensee will not, without the written approval of

the Minister, accept or keep a resident of Barbados, other than a prescribed person, as a customer of its international financial services business.

(2) It is a condition of a licence issued to a qualified foreign bank that it will, in the manner and to the extent prescribed, separate its international financial services business from its other business in Barbados and keep separate records of its international financial services business and will permit and assist in an audit of all its undertakings in Barbados by auditors approved by the Central Bank.

(3) Before giving an approval to any matter mentioned in subsection (1)(b), the Minister may carry out such of the investigations specified in section 9 as he thinks fit.

(4) No person or group that is under the control of another person or group shall, without the approval of the Minister and subject to such conditions as he may consider necessary, acquire or hold shares of a value of more than 10 per cent of the stated capital of the licensee.

(5) Subsection (1)(b) and subsection (4) do not apply to a qualified foreign bank within the meaning of paragraph (a) or (b) of section 5(9).

(6) Where approval has been obtained to increase the shareholding in accordance with subsection (4), no person or group that is under the control of another person or group shall hold shares the value of which exceeds the amount approved by the Minister.

(7) Any person who contravenes this section is guilty of an offence and is liable on conviction on indictment to a fine of $25 000.

14. A licensee shall display in a conspicuous place at each place where it does business a copy of its licence under this Act.

15. (1) The Minister may revoke a licence if the licensee

(a) does not within 6 months after the issue of its licence commence business;

(b) fails to comply with a condition of its licence;

(c) is in breach of any duty or obligation imposed upon it by this Act or commits an offence under this Act or under the Money Laundering and Financing of Terrorism (Prevention and Control) Act;

(d) ceases to carry on business under its licence;

(e) in the opinion of the Minister, is carrying on business in a manner that is detrimental to the public interest or to the interest of its depositors;

(f) provides any false or misleading information in respect of its application under this Act or fails to inform the Minister where there is a material change in respect of the information so supplied.

(2) Where the Minister intends to revoke a licence under subsection (1), he shall give the licensee written notice of his intention and a reasonable opportunity to show cause why the licence should not be revoked.

(3) The Minister must give notice in writing to the licensee of the revocation of the licence.

(4) Where it appears to the Minister that there are grounds on which his power to revoke a licence is exercisable but the circumstances are not such as to justify revocation, he may place restrictions on the licensee instead of revoking the licence.

16. (1) Any person who is aggrieved by the revocation of a licence by the Minister under section 15 may, within 30 days of

the giving of the notice under section 15(3), appeal the revocation to a Judge in chambers.

(2) The Minister may, pending an appeal under subsection (1) of any person aggrieved by the revocation of a licence, suspend the revocation of the licence in relation to any existing business of the licensee, pending the determination of the appeal.

(3) Where the Minister revokes a licence and there is no appeal or where there is an appeal and the appeal is disallowed, the notice of revocation must be published in the Official Gazette and in a daily newspaper published and circulated in Barbados.

17. No licensee may be granted a licence under a name that so closely resembles the name of an existing bank, trust company or other company carrying on business in Barbados or elsewhere as would, in the opinion of the Central Bank, mislead or confuse the persons for whom it intends to provide any service.

18. Where documents relating to an action arising out of the operations of a licensee have been served on the licensee, the licensee shall notify the Central Bank of such service within 14 days of the service of the documents.

19. (1) A licence may be issued under this Act to a company

(a) that accepts third party deposits if the stated or assigned capital of the company is at least $4,000,000;

(b) that does not accept third party deposits if the stated or assigned capital of the company is at least $1,000,000.

(2) The Minister may by order alter the sums specified in subsection (1).

(3) No action shall be taken for a period of one year after 10th June, 2002 against a company to which section 114 applies if the company fails to increase its stated or assigned capital in

accordance with subsection (1).

(4) A licensee shall not at any time have a capital adequacy ratio of less than the prescribed percentage.

(5) The capital adequacy ratio shall be calculated in the prescribed manner.

(6) For the purposes of this section, "assigned capital" means such portion of the capital of a company represented by such unencumbered assets as approved by the Central Bank and specifically assigned by the company to its local branch operations.

20. (1) Subject to subsection (2), a licensee shall maintain a reserve fund and shall out of its net profits of each year and before any dividend is paid transfer to the fund

(a) a sum equal to not less than 25 per cent of those profits wherever the amount of the reserve fund is less than the stated capital of the licensee; or

(b) such other sum as is prescribed.

(2) Subsection (1) does not apply to a licensee for which it is shown to the satisfaction of the Central Bank that the stated capital and aggregate reserves of the licensee are adequate in relation to its business.

21. A licensee shall not declare or pay a dividend if there are reasonable grounds for believing that

(a) the licensee is, or would after the payment be, unable to pay its liabilities as they become due; or

(b) the realizable value of the licensee's assets would thereby be less than the aggregate of its liabilities, stated capital and reserve accounts.

22. (1) Subject to this section, a licensee

(a) shall not grant to a person or group that is under the control of another person or group, any advance or credit, or give any financial guarantee or incur any other liability on behalf of such person or group so that

(i) the total value of the advances, credit facilities, financial guarantees or other liabilities at any time exceed 25 per cent of the sum of the stated capital and published reserves of the licensee;

(ii) where a portion of the facilities referred to in sub-paragraph (i) is unsecured, that portion exceeds 10 per cent of the sum of the stated capital and published reserves of the licensee;

(b) shall not grant unsecured advances or unsecured credit of an aggregate amount in excess of $40,000 or of 1 per cent of the sum of stated capital and published reserves of the licensee, whichever is the greater, or give any financial guarantee in excess of such amount without security, or incur any other liability in excess of that amount without security,

(i) to or on behalf of any of its directors whether or not such advances, credit, guarantees or other liabilities are obtained by or on account of the directors jointly or severally;

(ii) to or on behalf of any person in whom it or any of its directors is interested as a director, partner, manager or agent or as guarantor; or

(iii) to its holding company, any subsidiary or affiliate or any director thereof;

(c) shall not grant credit facilities on terms and conditions more favourable than the terms and conditions generally applicable to borrowers to

(i) its holding company or any subsidiary or affiliate;

(ii) any firm in which any director or officer or the relative of such officer or director has an interest or controls 20 per cent or more of the voting shares;

(iii) any person if the credit facilities are guaranteed by an officer, director, or any relative of the officer or director;

(iv) any person who controls more than 20 per cent of the licensee's shares;

(d) shall not grant to its officers or employees unsecured advances or unsecured credit which exceed in aggregate, for any one officer or employee, one year's emoluments of that officer or employee;

(e) shall not, except in so far as may be necessary with respect to the interests or shareholding that a licensee may acquire in satisfaction of debts due to it,

(i) engage, whether on its own account or on a commission basis, in the wholesale or retail trade, including the business of import and export, or otherwise have a direct interest in any commercial, agricultural, industrial or other undertaking; or

(ii) acquire or hold, in an aggregate amount exceeding 25 per cent of the sum of the stated capital and published reserves of the licensee, any part of the share capital of any commercial, agricultural, industrial or other undertaking, but all such interests or shareholding, as the case may be, shall be disposed of within a period not exceeding 5 years unless permission to extend this period has been given by the Central Bank;

(f) shall not without the approval of the Central Bank, invest in the shares of an entity so that the value of the investment at any time exceeds 10 per cent of the sum of the stated capital and published reserves of the licensee.

(2) Subject to this section, a licensee

(a) shall not purchase, acquire or lease real estate unless

(i) such real estate is necessary for the purpose of conducting its business or providing housing or amenities for its staff, having regard to any reasonable requirements for future expansion of its business or staff; and

(ii) the market value of the real estate does not exceed the stated capital of the licensee, except that where the licensee exercises its legal right in respect of any property which is the security for any debt, the licensee may acquire such property, but in that case the property shall not be retained for a period in excess of 5 years without the permission of the Central Bank;

(b) shall not acquire, deal in or underwrite its own shares or the shares of its holding company;

(c) shall not grant any advance against the security of its own shares, or the shares of its holding company or a subsidiary of the licensee.

(3) Subsections (1) and (2) do not apply where the licensee does not accept third party deposits.

(4) Where prior to 10th June, 2002, a licensee has given to any person any advance, credit or financial guarantee or incurred any liability referred to in subsection (1) or (2), no action shall be taken under this Act against the licensee in respect of such advance, credit, guarantee or liability for a period of 2 years after 10th June, 2002.

(5) Subsection (4) does not apply where the licensee has within the period specified in that subsection increased the amount of advance, credit, guarantee or liability or where the licensee fails to comply with the conditions given by the Central Bank.

(6) For the purposes of

(a) this section, "published reserves" means the statutory reserves of the licensee together with the retained earnings as published in the audited financial statements;

(b) this Part, "third party deposits" means deposits from persons other than a licensee's shareholders, its holding company, its subsidiaries, its associates or its affiliates.

23\. (1) A licensee shall, in carrying on its business, keep all assets held in trust separate from its other assets.

(2) Subject to section 24, it is the duty of a licensee in carrying on its business to keep separate from those of its other accounts the assets of each trust account, unless they are properly identified as the property of the trust account.

24\. (1) A licensee may, in the course of its business, establish, maintain and administer one or more common trust funds and, subject to subsection (2), invest assets held in trust accounts in a common trust fund.

(2) The assets of a trust account may only be invested in a common trust fund if the instrument creating the trust expressly permits the investment, and the consent in writing of any co-trustee is obtained to the investment.

(3) For the purposes of this Act, a "common trust fund" is a trust that operates by the process of pooling funds from a number of participants in the trust who share, as beneficiaries under the trust, in the income or other gains derived from the acquisition, holding, management or disposal of assets acquired for the trust.

25. (1) Every common trust fund of a licensee shall be established, administered and maintained in accordance with a written declaration of trust in a form approved by the directors of the licensee.

(2) A certified copy of a declaration of trust and any amendments to it shall be deposited with the Central Bank; and any person interested in the trust fund to which the declaration relates, as beneficiary or otherwise, is entitled upon request to be supplied with a copy of the declaration at the expense of the licensee.

(3) A licensee may sell assets held by it in a trust account to another trust account held by it, if

(a) the transaction is fully disclosed to the parties who have an interest in those accounts and the prior written consent of the parties is obtained in respect of the transaction;

(b) the transaction is fair to both accounts; and

(c) the transaction is not prohibited by the terms of the instruments creating the trusts.

26. (1) Subject to subsection (2), a licensee holding trust funds awaiting investment or distribution shall not hold those

funds uninvested or undistributed any longer than is reasonable for the proper management of the account.

(2) Unless it is contrary to the terms of the instrument establishing the trust, the trust funds described in subsection (1) may be held in the commercial or savings department of the licensee, subject to such conditions as may be prescribed.

27. A declaration of trust establishing a common trust fund must, subject to or in addition to other prescribed provisions, contain provisions relating to

(a) the manner in which the common trust fund is to be administered;

(b) the investment powers of the licensee with respect to the common trust fund, including the nature of investment to be made by the common trust fund;

(c) the allocation and apportionment of income, profits and losses of the common trust fund;

(d) the terms and conditions governing the admission or withdrawal of investments for participation in the common trust fund;

(e) the auditing and settlement of accounts of the licensee with respect to the common trust fund;

(f) the basis and method of valuing assets in the common trust fund;

(g) the basis on which the common trust fund may be liquidated or interests therein may be disposed of;

(h) the expenses to be charged for management of the common trust fund; and

(i) such other matters as are necessary or proper to define the rights of participants in the common trust fund.

28. Subject to the terms of the instrument creating the trust, the assets comprising the funds of the trust may be sold, converted, re-invested, exchanged, transferred or otherwise changed or disposed of at any time by the licensee administering the trust.

29. (1) Each beneficiary of a trust account that participates in a common trust fund has a beneficial interest in so much of the common trust fund as is proportionate to the amount of that participation.

(2) An interest in a common trust fund is not negotiable or assignable, but an interest in the fund may be disposed of in the manner provided by the declaration of trust or as may be prescribed in the absence of any provision relating thereto in the declaration of trust establishing the fund.

30. The licensee in the carrying out of its trust business has all the powers, rights, duties and obligations applicable to trustees but subject to any requirements under this Act.

31. Sections 24 to 30 shall apply subject to the provisions of the Mutual Funds Act.

32. (1) Property of the following kinds held or owing in the course of its business by a licensee in respect of which no activity has been evidenced for a period of 10 years is abandoned property:

(a) any general deposit, that is, a demand, saving or matured time deposit, made with the licensee, together with any interest or dividends but exclusive of legal charges;

(b) funds that were paid towards the purchase of shares or other interests in a licensee;

(c) any sum payable on cheques or other instruments for which the licensee is liable;

(d) intangible personal property or movable property and any income or increment thereon held in trust; and

(e) the contents of a safe deposit box upon which the lease or rental period has expired and in respect of which the licensee has given notice, by registered mail sent to the last known address of the lessee, of its intention to deliver the contents into the custody of the Central Bank.

(2) Activity is evidenced in respect of the property described in subsection (1) if the owner has

(a) within 10 years of the date of deposit increased or decreased the amount of the deposits, or presented a document for the crediting of interest in respect of the deposit;

(b) within 10 years of paying funds for the purchase of shares or other interests mentioned in subsection (1)(b), increased or decreased the amount of the funds or presented a document for the crediting of dividends in respect thereof or acknowledged the receipt of a statement that no dividends were paid, as the case may be;

(c) within 10 years of establishing a trust or within any 10-year period thereafter, increased or decreased the principal, or accepted payment of income in respect of any funds held in a fiduciary capacity; or

(d) within 10 years of making the last deposit, inquiry or communication concerning any item mentioned in subsection (1) corresponded with the licensee concerning the item, or otherwise indicated an interest in the item as evidenced by a memorandum in respect of the item by the licensee.

33. (1) Where there is abandoned property, a licensee shall within 60 days of the end of each financial year,

(a) report to the Central Bank all its holdings of abandoned property within the meaning of this Act;

(b) publish in the Official Gazette and in a daily newspaper which is published and circulated in Barbados, a notice containing

(i) the name of the owner;

(ii) the particulars concerning any abandoned property; and

(iii) a statement requiring the beneficial owner of the property to submit a claim to that licensee within 90 days of the publication of the notice; and

(c) mail a copy of the notice referred to in paragraph (b) to the beneficial owner of the property at his last-known address.

(2) A licensee shall convey to the Central Bank, in the prescribed manner, any abandoned property which remains unclaimed after the expiration of 90 days of the publication of the notice under subsection (1)(b).

(3) The licensee shall be reimbursed by the Central Bank for the cost of the publication and mailing of the notices under subsection (1).

(4) After a licensee has complied with subsections (1) and (2), interest shall cease to accrue on any property which has been abandoned; and the licensee is relieved from any liability to the beneficial owners of the property to the extent of the value of the property deposited or conveyed to the Central Bank.

34. (1) The Central Bank may by public auction sell any property that has been conveyed to it under section 33, after the expiration of 30 days after the date of receipt of the property and at any time before the expiration of the period specified in section 35.

(2) The public auction under subsection (1) may be held after such reasonable advertising of the sale as the Central Bank considers suitable.

35. The Central Bank shall after a period of 6 years pay into the Consolidated Fund all monies received by it as abandoned property and the proceeds of the public auction of any abandoned property less, in each case,

(a) an amount deducted by the Central Bank for reasonable expenses incurred by it in connection with the sale of abandoned property; and

(b) an amount deducted by the Central Bank for payment to the licensee of the cost of the publication and mailing of the notices under section 33(3).

36. (1) A person who claims a beneficial interest in any abandoned property deposited with or conveyed to the Central Bank, may make a claim for the value thereof within 6 years of the publication of the notice under section 33(1) and in the prescribed manner.

(2) Where the Central Bank is satisfied that a claimant is entitled to the abandoned property, the Central Bank shall deliver up the property or make payment for the value thereof, as the case requires.

(3) The Central Bank shall be reimbursed from the Consolidated Fund for any amounts paid in respect of claims made under this section.

37. (1) Where the Central Bank admits or refuses a claim under section 36, it shall forthwith notify the claimant of its decision.

(2) A person aggrieved by a refusal of his claim for abandoned property by the Central Bank may, within 21 days of receiving notice of the refusal, appeal the decision to a Judge in chambers, who may make such order thereon as he considers equitable.

38. A licensee that fails to report to the Central Bank any abandoned property in its possession or that fails to deposit with or convey to the Central Bank any abandoned property as required by this Act is guilty of an offence and is liable on conviction on indictment to a fine of $25,000.

Part II

ADMINISTRATION OF LICENSEES

Directors and Officers

39. For the purposes of this Act,

(a) "director" means an individual occupying that position and performing the functions of a director however his position is designated;

(b) "director" includes the manager of a society with restricted liability;

(c) a reference to "directors" refers to the board of directors or the body directing the affairs of a company or firm.

40. (1) A director or a senior officer of a licensee shall cease to hold that office

(a) if he becomes bankrupt or suspends payment to his creditors;

(b) if he is convicted in Barbados of an offence triable on indictment;

(c) if he is convicted outside Barbados of an offence that would be triable on indictment had it been committed in Barbados;

(d) if he makes an arrangement with his creditors; or

(e) if he becomes the auditor of the licensee.

(2) Where a person ceases to hold office under subsection (1), that person may not be appointed to any other office of the licensee without the consent of the Central Bank.

(3) Where subsection (1) or (2) is contravened, the director or the senior officer, as the case may be, and the licensee are guilty of an offence and are liable on conviction on indictment to a fine of $25,000 or to imprisonment for 12 months, or to both.

41. (1) A person who has been a director or a senior officer of a company whose licence is revoked under this Act shall not be appointed to the office of director, the office of senior officer or to any other office of any licensee without the approval of the Central Bank.

(2) Where subsection (1) is contravened, the director, senior officer or officer, as the case may be, and the licensee are guilty of an offence and are liable on conviction on indictment to a fine of $25,000 or to imprisonment for 12 months, or to both.

42. (1) A director of a licensee who is interested, directly or indirectly, in an advance or loan from the licensee shall,

as soon as possible, declare the nature of his interest to its directors at a meeting thereof.

(2) Subsection (1) does not apply when the interest of a director in an advance or a loan consists only of being a creditor of, or having an interest in, a firm that is interested in an advance or a loan from the licensee if, in either case, the interest of the director is not a substantial interest.

(3) A declaration by a director of a licensee that he is interested in any advance or loan that may, after the date of the declaration, be made by the licensee, is a sufficient declaration of interest in relation to any advance or loan made after the declaration, if

(a) the declaration specified the nature and extent of the interest; and

(b) the interest of the director is not different in nature from or greater than, the nature and extent so specified in the declaration at the time any advance or loan is made.

(4) Notwithstanding sections 88, 89 and 90 of the Companies Act, a director or an officer of a licensee shall not be present at or in any way participate in a meeting of the Board of Directors or a committee of the Board of Directors of that licensee when a loan, an advance or any other credit facility is being considered for

(a) the director, officer or any of his relatives; or

(b) a company in which the director, officer or a relative owns more than 25 per cent of the stated share capital.

43. (1) A director of a licensee who holds any office or has any interest in any property whereby, directly or indirectly, his functions under this Act are likely to be in conflict with his

personal interest shall declare the nature, character and extent of that office or interest to the directors at a meeting thereof.

(2) A declaration required under this section shall be made

(a) at the first meeting of the directors that is held after the acquisition by the declarant of that relevant office or interest; or

(b) if the declarant was not at that time a director, after he becomes a director.

44. A director of a licensee who has declared any interest referred to in section 42 or 43 shall

(a) cause the declaration made by him thereunder to be brought up and read at the next meeting of the directors after it was given; and

(b) cause the declaration to be recorded in the minutes of the meeting at which it was made or read, or both.

45. A director of a licensee who contravenes section 42, 43 or 44 is guilty of an offence and is liable on conviction on indictment to a fine of $25,000 or to imprisonment for 12 months, or to both.

46. (1) A person who has acquired confidential information concerning a licensee

(a) as a director, officer, employee, or auditor of the licensee;

(b) as a custodian of the licensee; or

(c) as an employee of the Central Bank, shall not disclose that information to any person except as permitted under subsection (2), or use that information for any personal benefit not related to the duties through which the information was acquired.

(2) Subsection (1) does not apply to the giving of confidential information

(a) where the information is a general credit rating of a person that is supplied by a director, officer or employee of the licensee following a bona fide business request;

(b) where the information is given with the written authorization of the beneficiary or his legal representative;

(c) where the information is lawfully required to be disclosed by an order of the High Court; or

(d) where the information is lawfully required to be disclosed pursuant to any other enactment.

(3) In this section "confidential information" means information concerning the identity of a depositor, settlor or beneficiary of a trust, or concerning the assets, liabilities, transactions or other information in respect of a depositor, settlor or beneficiary of a trust.

(4) A person who contravenes subsection (1) is guilty of an offence and is liable on conviction on indictment to a fine of $25,000 or to imprisonment for 12 months, or to both.

47. (1) A licensee shall in respect of its business submit to the Central Bank in the prescribed form,

(a) not later than 21 days after the end of each 3-month period, a quarterly statement of its assets and liabilities; and

(b) within such time as the Central Bank may determine, such other returns as the Central Bank requires.

(2) The Central Bank may require a licensee to submit

(a) such further information as it considers necessary for the proper understanding of any statement or return furnished by the licensee pursuant to subsection (1);

(b) any information it considers necessary in respect of any holding company, subsidiary or affiliate of the licensee; and the information shall be submitted within such time and in such manner as the Central Bank requires.

(3) The Central Bank may require the licensee to appoint an auditor to examine and report to the Central Bank, in such manner as the Central Bank may determine, on returns submitted by the licensee.

(4) The Central Bank may cause to be prepared and published in the Official Gazette consolidated statements aggregating all the figures in the quarterly returns of licensees.

(5) A licensee which contravenes subsection (1) is guilty of an offence and is liable on conviction on indictment to a fine of $25,000.

48. (1) Subject to section 47(4) and subsection (2) of this section, no statement, returns or information furnished or submitted by a licensee in respect of its business shall be communicated or disclosed.

(2) The Central Bank may, without the consent of a licensee, disclose information received to

(a) any supervisory or regulatory authority of financial institutions in Barbados; and

(b) the appropriate supervisory or regulatory authority of financial institutions of another country, at the request of that authority, where there is a branch, holding company or affiliate of the licensee operating in that country.

(3) A person who discloses confidential information contrary to subsection (1) is guilty of an offence and is liable

on conviction on indictment to a fine of $25,000 or to imprisonment for a term of 12 months, or to both.

49. (1) Not later than 4 months after the close of its financial year or such longer period as the Central Bank may allow, a licensee shall forward to the Central Bank such number of copies of its balance sheet and profit and loss account as may be prescribed and the full and correct names of the directors of the licensee.

(2) The balance sheet and the profit and loss account must bear the certificate of an auditor on its face.

(3) Where a licensee is a qualified foreign bank, this section applies in respect only of the international financial services carried on by the licensee in Barbados.

(4) A licensee which contravenes this section is guilty of an offence and is liable on conviction on indictment to a fine of $25,000 and, in addition, to a further fine of $25,000 for each month during which the offence continues after a conviction is obtained.

50. For the purposes of this Act, an auditor is a person

(a) who is in good standing as a member of an association of chartered or public accountants or other similar body;

(b) who is authorized to practise in Barbados; and

(c) who is approved by the Central Bank.

51. (1) The annual balance sheets and profit and loss account of a licensee shall be audited at least once in every financial year by an auditor within the meaning of section 50.

(2) It is the duty of the auditor to submit a report to the shareholders and to the directors of the licensee.

(3) The auditor shall note in his report any instances where the operations of the licensee might not in the opinion of the auditor be in compliance with the requirements of this Act, the regulations, the conditions of the licensee's licence or the licensee's articles or bye-laws.

(4) The report of the auditor shall be read with the report of the directors at the annual meeting of the shareholders of the licensee.

(5) A copy of the report of the auditor shall be displayed by the licensee in a conspicuous place at its offices in Barbados and shall be published by the licensee in the Official Gazette.

(6) If the Central Bank has reasonable grounds for being dissatisfied with the annual report of an auditor appointed by a licensee, the Central Bank may appoint another auditor to make an independent report.

(7) A licensee shall give notice in writing to the Central Bank

(a) if it fails to appoint or if it terminates the appointment of an auditor within 90 days of the issue of its licence; or

(b) if it fails to appoint or if it terminates the appointment of an auditor within 90 days of the annual general meeting; and the notice shall state the reasons for its failure to appoint an auditor or the reasons for the termination of the appointment, as the case may be.

(8) Where a licensee fails to appoint an auditor pursuant to this section, the Central Bank may appoint an auditor who

(a) shall have all the powers of an auditor appointed by the licensee to carry out an audit;

(b) shall report to the Central Bank; and

(c) shall comply with the requirements of subsection (3).

(9) The remuneration of an auditor shall be paid by the licensee to which he is appointed, and if the auditor is appointed under subsection (8) his remuneration shall be such amount as the Central Bank determines.

(10) In the case of a licensee that is a qualified foreign bank, this section applies only in respect of the international financial services carried on by the licensee, subject to the conditions of its licence.

(11) An auditor of a licensee shall forthwith give written notice to the Central Bank if he

(a) resigns before the expiration of his term of office; or

(b) does not seek re-appointment.

(12) For the purposes of this section, unless the context otherwise indicates, "auditor" means a person appointed under subsection (1).

52. (1) No person may be appointed an auditor of a licensee

(a) if he has any proprietary interest in the licensee;

(b) if he is a director, or agent of the licensee or of an affiliate of the licensee; or

(c) if he is an officer or employee of the Central Bank.

(2) A former director or a former senior officer shall not be eligible for appointment as an auditor of the licensee within a period of 2 years after the termination of that person's term of office.

53. (1) The Central Bank may, if it considers necessary, cause an examination to be made by any of its officers or any person

authorized by it of the affairs of a licensee, to determine whether the provisions of this Act or the regulations made hereunder are being complied with or whether the licensee is in a sound financial condition.

(2) Where necessary, the Central Bank may in respect of any holding company, parent company or any other company that holds shares in a licensee

(a) inspect the books of the company; or

(b) request any information from the appropriate authorities in any country where the company is located.

54. An auditor, officer or employee of a licensee shall produce for an examiner appointed by the Central Bank under section 53, at such time as the examiner fixes, all books, minutes, cash, securities, vouchers and other documents and records relating to its assets, liabilities and business generally, and shall give the examiner such information concerning its affairs and business as he may request.

55. An auditor, officer or employee of a licensee who is required under this Part to make any disclosure to the Central Bank or to a person authorized by the Central Bank shall not by reason of making that disclosure be regarded as being in breach of his duty to the licensee.

56. If any of the matters referred to in section 54 are not produced, or the information relating thereto is not given to the examiner, the auditor, officer or employee of the licensee is guilty of an offence and is liable on conviction on indictment to a fine of $25,000 and, in addition, to a further fine of $2,500 for each day during which the offence continues.

57. (1) Where the Central Bank is of the opinion that an examination of a licensee indicates that the licensee is carrying on its business in an unlawful manner or is in an

unsound financial condition, the Central Bank, after service of notice in writing,

(a) may require that the licensee immediately take such remedial measures as the Central Bank considers necessary; and

(b) may, with the approval of the Minister,

(i) appoint a person who in the opinion of the Central Bank has had training and experience in the business of the licensee concerned to advise the licensee on the action to be taken to remedy the situation; or

(ii) suspend the licence of the licensee for a period not exceeding 3 months.

(2) A person appointed under subsection (1)(b)(i) shall be paid by the Central Bank such remuneration as the Central Bank may determine, and the remuneration shall be charged to the licensee concerned.

(3) A licensee that is required to take remedial measures or whose licence is suspended under this section may within 21 days of the service of the notice under subsection (1) make representations in writing to the Central Bank as to why the Central Bank should not take the action intended.

(4) Where a licensee is aggrieved by the decision of the Central Bank under subsection (3), the licensee may within 30 days after it is notified of the Central Bank's decision appeal to the Minister.

(5) Where the Central Bank is of the opinion that the operations of a foreign office of a licensee present a threat to the licensee's financial soundness, the Bank may require the licensee to make such changes in the operations of the office

as are considered necessary; or the Bank may require the licensee to close the office.

58. (1) The Minister may by notice in writing revoke a licence granted under this Act where;

(a) the licensee fails to take remedial measures within the period specified; or

(b) the licensee fails within the period of suspension to desist from the behaviour which resulted in the suspension, or fails to take any action required by the Central Bank.

(2) A licensee that is aggrieved by the revocation of its licence under subsection (1) may, within 30 days of the receipt of the notification, apply to the High Court for an order requiring the Minister to revoke the cancellation of its licence; and the Court may make such order as it thinks fit in the circumstances.

59. (1) Upon giving prior notice to the Minister, the Central Bank may seize the management and control of a licensee in any of the following circumstances, namely:

(a) when the realizable value of the licensee's assets is less than the aggregate of its liabilities and capital accounts, or the licensee's financial condition suggests that it will shortly be in that circumstance;

(b) when its business is being conducted in an imprudent manner or is not being conducted in accordance with this Act;

(c) when the licensee refuses to submit to the inspection of its records or operations by an auditor appointed under section 51 or an examiner appointed under section 53; or

(d) when its licence has been revoked or suspended.

(2) A seizure of the management and control of a licensee under this section is effected by placing a notice to that effect on the premises of the licensee and by putting officers of the Central Bank into the offices of the licensee, or by designating officers of the licensee to be officers of the Central Bank, or by both such measures.

(3) A licensee aggrieved by a seizure under this section may institute proceedings in the High Court for recovery of its administration and control; and the High Court may make such order in respect thereto as seems just and consistent with the purposes of this Act.

60. (1) A licensee that engages in advertising practices that are likely to mislead concerning

(a) the relationship of the licensee with the Government of Barbados, the Central Bank or any department or office thereof;

(b) the true interest rate paid on deposits or charged on credit;

(c) the true returns on the management of investments;

(d) the insured or guaranteed status of deposits or of other liabilities or of investments managed by it; or

(e) the financial condition of the designated institution, is guilty of an offence and is liable on conviction on indictment to a fine of $25,000 or imprisonment for 5 years, or to both.

(2) A licensee shall in respect of its business furnish the Central Bank with copies of all its advertisements,

(a) 6 months after the first issue of its licence under this Act, and

(b) thereafter at 6-monthly intervals.

(3) Any licensee which contravenes subsection (2) is guilty of an offence and is liable on conviction on indictment to a fine of $25,000.

61. A director, officer, employee or agent of a licensee, who, with intent to deceive

(a) makes any false or misleading statement or entry in a book, account, record, report or statement of the licensee, or omits a statement or entry that should be made therein; or

(b) obstructs the carrying out by an auditor of his proper function under this Act; or

(c) obstructs the examination of a licensee as required pursuant to this Act, is guilty of an offence and is liable on conviction on indictment to a fine of $25,000 or imprisonment for 5 years, or to both.

PART III

WINDING UP OF LICENSEES

62. (1) Except with the written approval of the Central Bank, no licensee may be wound up voluntarily.

(2) Approval for a voluntary winding up of a licensee may be given by the Central Bank only if it is satisfied that

a) the licensee is solvent and has sufficient assets to repay its depositors and other creditors without delay; and

(b) subject to subsection (3), the winding up has been approved by the holders of at least two-thirds of the outstanding voting shares of the licensee.

(3) Where the Central Bank finds in respect of a licensee that there is imminent danger of its insolvency, and certifies to the Minister the existence of an emergency, the Minister may waive the requirement for shareholder approval of the winding up of the licensee voluntarily, if

(a) the winding up is to be effected in whole or in part through the sale of any of the assets of the licensee to another licensee; and

(b) the deposit liabilities of the licensee to be wound up are to be assumed by that other licensee.

63. Where a licensee receives the approval of the Central Bank to its voluntary winding up, the licensee shall

(a) cease to do business immediately and retain only such staff as is necessary for an orderly winding up;

(b) repay its depositors and other creditors; and

(c) wind up all operations undertaken before the receipt of the approval to wind up.

64. (1) Within 30 days of the receipt of the approval of the Central Bank to the winding up of a licensee, a notice of voluntary winding up shall be sent by the licensee in the prescribed manner or by personal service to the depositors and creditors of the licensee and to other persons having any interest in its funds or other property.

(2) The notice described in subsection (1) shall also be published in the Official Gazette and placed in a conspicuous place on the premises of each office or branch of the licensee to be wound up.

65. (1) The approval of the Central Bank to the voluntary winding up of a licensee does not adversely affect the rights of a

depositor or other creditor of the licensee to settlement in full of his claim or the rights of any person having an interest in the funds or property of the licensee to settlement of that interest.

(2) All claims made by persons described in subsection (1) shall be settled by the licensee concerned within such time as the Central Bank may determine.

66. (1) The assets of a licensee being voluntarily wound up that remain after settlement of the claims described in section 65 are to be distributed among the shareholders of the licensee in proportion to their respective rights.

(2) Notwithstanding subsection (1), no distribution of the remaining assets of a licensee may be made

(a) before all claims of depositors and other creditors have been settled or, in the case of a disputed claim, before the licensee has deposited with the Central Bank sufficient funds to meet any liability that could arise under that claim;

(b) before any funds that are payable to a depositor or other creditor who has not made his claim have been deposited with the Central Bank; or

(c) before any funds or property held by the licensee that could not be returned in accordance with section 65 to the persons who have an interest therein have been deposited with or transferred to the Central Bank, together with the relevant records.

67. (1) If the Central Bank determines that the assets of a licensee that is being voluntarily wound up are not sufficient for the full discharge of the obligations of the licensee, or that the completion of such a winding up is being unduly delayed, the Central Bank may seize the management and control of the licensee after posting a notice to that effect on

the premises of the licensee and by putting officers of the Central Bank into the offices of the licensee.

(2) Where the Central Bank seizes the management and control of a licensee under subsection (1), it shall immediately begin proceedings for the compulsory winding up of the licensee or for its reorganisation in accordance with this Act.

68. The Central Bank shall begin proceedings in the High Court

(a) for the compulsory winding up of the licensee; or

(b) for the reorganisation of the licensee; within 30 days after the Central Bank has seized the administration and control of a licensee under this Act.

69. Proceedings under section 68 in respect of a licensee, may be made by way of application to the High Court and the Court may thereupon order

(a) the compulsory winding up of the licensee;

(b) the reorganisation of the licensee subject to such terms and conditions as the court may determine; or

(c) the return of the management and control of the licensee to its shareholders, directors and officers, subject to such safeguards or conditions, if any, as the court may consider necessary for the purposes of this Act.

70. The Central Bank shall give notice of the application

(a) to the directors and shareholders of the licensee; and

(b) to the depositors and other creditors of the licensee, forthwith after it makes an application to the High Court under section 69 in relation to a licensee.

71. (1) If the High Court orders the compulsory winding up or reorganisation of a licensee pursuant to an application under

section 69, the High Court shall appoint a custodian to be responsible to the Court and to supervise the winding up or reorganisation of the licensee.

(2) The Central Bank or other suitable person may be appointed as the custodian under subsection (1).

(3) If the Central Bank is not appointed custodian, it may contribute to the fees payable to the custodian appointed under this section as remuneration for the custodian's services.

72. (1) The custodian has the exclusive power and duty to manage and control the affairs of the licensee for which he has been appointed.

(2) Without limiting the powers or duties of the custodian under subsection (1), the custodian may, in respect of the licensee for which the custodian has been appointed,

(a) continue or discontinue its operations;

(b) stop or limit the payment of its obligations;

(c) employ staff;

(d) execute any instrument in its name;

(e) initiate, defend and conduct in its name any action or proceeding to which the licensee is or might be a party;

(f) end the seizure of the licensee by restoring it to its directors and shareholders; and

(g) reorganize or wind up the licensee in accordance with this Act.

73. (1) The custodian shall make an inventory of its assets and forward a copy of the inventory to the Registrar of the Supreme Court forthwith after assuming the management and control of a licensee.

(2) The copy of the inventory forwarded to the Registrar under subsection (1) shall be kept available for the inspection of interested persons at all reasonable times.

74. Where the administration and control of a licensee is seized under this Act

(a) any statutory, contractual, or other term or condition on the expiration of which a claim or right of the licensee would expire or be extinguished shall be extended by 6 months from the date of the seizure;

(b) an attachment or lien, other than a lien that was in existence during the 6 months immediately preceding the seizure, shall be vacated and no attachment or lien, other than a lien created by a custodian in the application of this Act, attaches to any of the assets of the licensee during the period the seizure continues; and

(c) a transfer of any assets of the licensee that is made after or in contemplation of its insolvency or seizure, with intent to effect a preference, is void.

75. No execution may be returned against the assets of a licensee whose administration or control has been seized under this Act except such as the High Court may order in respect of an execution effected, pursuant to a judgment that was rendered before the seizure, for an amount not exceeding $5,000.

76. (1) Where the reorganisation of a licensee has been ordered by the High Court, the custodian shall develop a plan of reorganisation and deliver a copy thereof to each of the depositors and other creditors of the licensee who under the plan would not receive full restitution or payment of their claims.

(2) A copy of the reorganisation plan must be accompanied by

a notice requiring that objections to the plan be delivered to the custodian not later than 30 days after the last copy has been delivered under subsection (1).

(3) If within the time limited therefor by subsection (2) the custodian does not receive objections in writing to the reorganization from persons who in the aggregate hold at least one-third of the total amount of deposits and other liabilities of the licensee, the custodian may carry out the reorganisation plan referred to in subsection (1).

(4) Where an objection to the reorganisation plan is received from one-third or more of the persons described in subsection (3),

(a) the custodian shall submit further reorganisation plans in like manner until such time as fewer than one-third of the persons described in subsection (3) object within the time limited therefor; or

(b) he may refer the matter back, at any time, to the High Court for further directions.

(5) The High Court may extend the time limited by subsection (2) and, upon cause shown, may exempt the custodian from delivering the plan to some or all of the persons mentioned in subsection (1).

77. A reorganisation plan developed by the custodian of a licensee must, so far as is practicable,

(a) be equitable to all classes of depositors;

(b) provide for bringing in new funds to establish adequate ratios between

(i) capital and deposits; and

(ii) liquid assets and deposits; and

(c) provide for the removal of any director or any officer or employee responsible for the circumstances that led to the seizure of the licensee.

78. Where, in the course of the reorganisation of a licensee, it appears to the custodian that circumstances render the plan or its execution undesirable, he may apply to the High Court for an order

(a) to modify the plan; or

(b) to wind up the licensee compulsorily.

79. (1) Where the High Court under section 69 or 78 orders the compulsory winding up of a licensee, the custodian appointed therefor by the Court may, subject to subsection (2), perform the functions of the licensee.

(2) The custodian of a licensee described in subsection (1) may not, without an order of the High Court to do so,

(a) sell any assets or transfer any property of the licensee that has a value exceeding $100,000;

(b) create a security interest in any asset or property of the licensee in favour of a creditor who extends new credit to the licensee;

(c) compromise or release any claim, the amount of which exceeds $100,000; or

(d) pay any claim, other than one in respect of an obligation incurred by the custodian in the exercise of his winding up functions, before the schedule referred to in section 85(c) has been approved by the High Court.

80. Subject to any law of Barbados governing conditions of employment, the custodian of a licensee that has been ordered by the High Court to be compulsorily wound up shall terminate,

not later than 9 months after the making of the order of the High Court

(a) any employment contract of the licensee;

(b) any contract for services to which the licensee is a party; and

(c) any obligations of the licensee as a lessee of property.

81. A lessor of any property referred to in section 80

(a) must be given notice of a period not less than 90 days of the intended termination of the obligations of a licensee thereunder;

(b) has no claim for rent thereunder other than rent accrued on the date of the termination of the obligation of the licensee; and

(c) has no right to damages by reason only of any termination of the obligations of the licensee, notwithstanding any term of the lease to the contrary.

82. A custodian of a licensee that has been ordered to be wound up shall take such action as is necessary to terminate all the trust functions of the licensee and to settle its trust accounts.

83. (1) Within 60 days after the granting of an order for the compulsory winding up of a licensee, the custodian shall deliver a statement of account to any depositors and other creditors, any lessees of safe-deposit boxes and any bailors of property held by the licensee.

(2) A notice specifying that any objection to the statement of account is to be made on a date specified in the notice, not being later than 60 days after the delivery of the notice, must accompany the statement of account, and invite the lessees

of safe-deposit boxes and bailors of property to withdraw their property from the licensee in person.

(3) The High Court on application of the custodian for cause shown may exempt the custodian from delivering a statement of account to any person mentioned in subsection (1).

(4) For the purposes of this section, a "statement of account" is a statement of the nature and amount for which a claim of a person described in subsection (1) is shown on the books of the licensee.

84. (1) A safe-deposit box maintained by a licensee that is being compulsorily wound up may be opened in the manner specified by the custodian of the licensee if the contents of the safe-deposit box have not been withdrawn before the expiration of the period specified in a notice under section 83.

(2) The contents of a safe-deposit box opened under subsection (1), and any unclaimed property held by the licensee as trustee, together with any inventories pertaining thereto, shall be turned over to the Central Bank and held by it for 10 years unless sooner claimed by a person entitled thereto.

(3) On the expiration of 10 years from the day any property was turned over to the Central Bank under subsection (2), the property becomes abandoned property.

85. Not later than 90 days after the last day specified in the notice for filing claims against a licensee being compulsorily wound up, the custodian shall

(a) reject any claim of which he doubts the validity;

(b) determine the amount, if any, owing to each known depositor or other creditor, and the priority of his claim under this Act;

(c) prepare for filing with the High Court a schedule of the actions proposed to be given for the purpose of the compulsory winding up of the licensee;

(d) notify each person whose claim is allowed in full; and

(e) publish, once a week for 3 consecutive weeks in the Official Gazette,

(i) a notice of the date and place where the schedule referred to in paragraph (c) will be available for inspection; and

(ii) the date, not being earlier than 30 days from the date of the publication, on which the custodian will file that schedule with the High Court.

86. (1) Within 20 days of the filing of a schedule under section 85(c), a depositor or other creditor, a shareholder of the licensee concerned or any other interested person may file with the High Court any objection he has to any action proposed in that schedule.

(2) After notice is served on the custodian and such interested parties as the High Court may require, the High Court shall hear the objection and make such order as it considers just in the circumstances.

(3) Where the High Court allows an objection, the order must set out the manner in which the schedule referred to in section 85(c) is to be modified.

87. (1) Where a schedule has been filed under section 85(c) in respect of a licensee, the custodian may make a partial distribution to the claimants against the licensee whose claims are undisputed or allowed by the High Court, if the custodian establishes an adequate reserve for the payment of disputed claims against the licensee.

(2) As soon as practicable after all objections against the distribution proposed by the custodian have been heard and determined, final distribution of the assets of the licensee concerned shall be made by the custodian.

88. (1) The following claims have priority against the general assets of a licensee being compulsorily wound up under this Act:

(a) first, the necessary and reasonable expenses incurred by the custodian in carrying out his functions under this Act;

(b) secondly, the wages and salaries of the officers and employees of the licensee that accrued during the 3 months immediately preceding the seizure of the licensee under this Act;

(c) thirdly, any moneys owing to the Government of Barbados;

(d) fourthly, the fees and assessments owing to the Central Bank;

(e) fifthly, the savings and time deposits in amounts not exceeding $5,000 respectively; and

(f) sixthly, deposits other than those mentioned in paragraphs (a) to (e).

(2) After payment with interest at such rate as the High Court determines of all claims against the licensee, all remaining claims against the licensee that were not filed within the time limited therefor under this Act may then be paid.

(3) Where the amount available to pay the claims of any class of claimant specified in this section in respect of priorities is not sufficient to provide payment in full to all claimants in

that class, the amount available shall be distributed by the custodian on a pro rata basis among the claimants in that class.

89. The assets of a licensee being compulsorily wound up that remain after the final distribution to claimants pursuant to section 87 shall be distributed by the custodian among the shareholders of the licensee in proportion to their respective rights.

90. (1) Any funds of a licensee being compulsorily wound up under this Act that remain unclaimed after the final distribution under section 87, and not subject to distribution under any other provision of this Act, shall be deposited with the Central Bank by the custodian of the licensee.

(2) Funds deposited with the Central Bank under subsection (1) must be held by the Bank for 10 years unless earlier claimed by a person entitled thereto.

(3) On the expiration of the 10 years referred to in subsection (2) in respect of any funds, those remaining unclaimed become abandoned property.

91. (1) Where all the assets of a licensee being wound up have been distributed or dealt with as required by this Act, the custodian shall render an audited statement to the High Court.

(2) If the High Court is satisfied with the audited statement rendered by the custodian in respect of a licensee being wound up, it may by order direct the Registrar of Companies to strike the name of the licensee from the register of companies under the Companies Act and publish notice thereof in the Official Gazette.

(3) Where its name is struck off the register of companies, the licensee is thereupon dissolved and its licence under this Act is revoked.

Part IV

SPECIAL TAXING PROVISIONS

92. (1) For the purposes of this Act, the following are residents of Barbados:

(a) an individual ordinarily resident in Barbados;

(b) a citizen of Barbados who is not ordinarily resident in Barbados but owns a dwelling in Barbados;

(c) any incorporated or other body, formed or organised in Barbados, the majority of the shares or other ownership of which is not beneficially held by persons resident outside Barbados;

(d) any incorporated or other body, wherever incorporated, formed or organised, that is controlled by a person described in paragraph (a) or (b) or by the Government of Barbados;

(e) the Crown in right of Barbados and any agency thereof;

(f) a trust

(i) established by a resident as defined in any of paragraphs (a) to (e), other than a trust for the administration of pension or like funds for the benefit of individuals a prescribed majority of whom are persons who are Vresident outside Barbados; or

(ii) in which residents as defined in any of paragraphs (a) to (e) have more than a prescribed percentage of the beneficial interest; or

(g) any incorporated or unincorporated body that is controlled, directly or indirectly, by a trust defined in this section as a resident of Barbados.

(2) A reference in this Part to any beneficial interest or to anything being beneficially owned or held, includes ownership through a trustee, legal representative, agent or other intermediary.

93. (1) Except as provided by this Part, no income tax, capital gains tax or other direct tax or impost shall be levied in Barbados upon the profits or gains of a licensee in respect of the international financial services it carries on from within Barbados.

(2) Except as provided by this Part, no income tax, capital gains tax or other direct tax or impost shall be levied in Barbados in respect of any dividends or earnings attributable to the shares or securities of a licensee that are beneficially owned by another licensee or by a person who is not a resident of Barbados.

(3) Except as provided by this Part, no tax, duty or impost shall be levied upon the increment in value of the property or other assets in Barbados of a licensee, other than upon such of them as are distributed to residents of Barbados.

94. (1) Except as provided by this Part, no tax, duty or other impost shall be levied upon a licensee, its shareholder or transferees in respect of the transfer of all or any part of its securities or other assets to another licensee or to a person who is not a resident of Barbados.

(2) Where a person who is not a resident of Barbados or a licensee transfers shares of a licensee that are held by that person or licensee to another person who is not a resident of Barbados or to another licensee, the transfer is exempt from the payment of any tax, duty or impost thereon.

(3) Except as provided by this Part,

(a) no income tax or capital gains tax; and

(b) no other direct tax or impost, shall be levied or collected in Barbados in respect of any dividends, interests or other returns from any shares, securities, deposits or other borrowings of a licensee or any assets managed by a licensee, if the dividends, interest or other returns are in respect of shares, securities, deposits or other borrowings or assets beneficially owned by a person who is not a resident of Barbados; but the onus of establishing ownership lies upon the licensee.

95. (1) Notwithstanding any provision of the Income Tax Act, but subject to subsection (2), no licensee need withhold any portion of

(a) any dividend, interest or other returns payable to any person in respect of any borrowings of the licensee or in respect of that person holding shares or securities of the licensee; or

(b) any fee payable to any person.

(2) All dividends, interests or other returns attributable to the shares or securities of, or the management of assets by, a licensee and all fees that are payable to a resident of Barbados and known as such by the licensee, shall be reported to the Commissioner of Inland Revenue.

96. Where a trust is established by a settlor who is not a resident of Barbados in favour of another person who is not a resident of Barbados, the trust is exempt from any tax, duty or impost in Barbados if the funds of the trust consist solely of foreign currency or foreign securities and the trust is under the management of a licensee.

97. (1) By way of income tax but in lieu of income tax at the rates specified in the Income Tax Act there shall be levied and paid to the Commissioner of Inland Revenue, upon the

profits and gains of a licensee in respect of the international financial services carried on by it from within Barbados, tax at the following rates:

(a) 21/2 per cent on all profits and gains up to $10,000,000;

(b) 2 per cent on all profits and gains in amounts exceeding $10,000,000 but not exceeding $20,000,000;

(c) 11/2 per cent on all profits and gains in amounts exceeding $20,000,000 but not exceeding $30,000,000; and

(d) 1 per cent on all profits and gains exceeding $30,000,000.

(2) A licensee may elect to take a credit in respect of taxes paid to a country other than Barbados where such an election does not reduce the tax payable in Barbados to a rate of less than 1 per cent of the profits and gains of the licensee in any income year.

(3) Except in so far as this Act operates to exempt a licensee from liability to income tax under the Income Tax Act, the provisions of that Act shall apply mutatis mutandis to a licensee.

98. (1) Where in the opinion of the Minister it is in the public interest to do so, the Minister may by agreement give such assurance or guarantee regarding the future taxing of a licensee as it may require before commencing to carry on international financial services from within Barbados.

(2) An assurance or guarantee referred to in subsection (1) is subject to affirmative resolution of the House of Assembly.

99. (1) Where a tax levied in Barbados is in the nature of a service charge or utility charge for a service provided by the

Government of Barbados, a licensee is not exempt from that charge under this Part.

(2) A service or utility charge includes a charge or fee levied or imposed for the issue of any incorporation, registration or licence required in Barbados.

100. The Minister may by order exempt a licensee, in respect of its business, from all or so much of any duty payable under the Customs Act as the Minister deems expedient in respect of any goods imported by the licensee, if the licensee satisfies the Minister that the goods concerned

(a) are not being made or manufactured in Barbados;

(b) are essential as equipment or fixtures for doing business from within Barbados; and

(c) are not merely goods that will be used up or expended in the ordinary course of business.

101. (1) Where the Minister is satisfied that a licensee must use the services of specially qualified persons in order to do its business effectively from within Barbados and that

(a) it is unable to acquire those services within the Caribbean Community; and

(b) it is unable to retain or hire those services from outside the Caribbean Community without special tax benefits being made available, the Minister may authorize an international financial service benefit for the employment of those specially qualified persons who are not residents of the Caribbean Community.

(2) For the purposes of this section,

(a) "Caribbean Community" means the Caribbean Community within the meaning of the Caribbean Community Act;

(b) an "international financial service benefit" is a benefit whereby, notwithstanding any provision of the Income Tax Act or the Exchange Control Act, a prescribed percentage of an employee's or contractor's salary, fees and any other emoluments from a licensee

(i) is exempt from income tax or other tax in Barbados;

(ii) may be paid in a foreign currency in a trust account without being liable to income tax or other tax in Barbados as to the amount paid or any earnings thereon; or

(iii) may be paid in some other prescribed manner in another currency or otherwise without being liable to income tax or other tax in Barbados.

102. (1) The dividends, royalties, interest, foreign securities, funds, gains and assets generated or managed by a licensee in the course of its business are exempt from the provisions of the Exchange Control Act.

(2) Section 11(2) of the Exchange Control Act does not apply to a person who proposes to incorporate an eligible company.

(3) Except section 11(2), Part IV of the Exchange Control Act, does not apply to a licensee in respect of its international financial services business.

PART V

MISCELLANEOUS AND TRANSITIONAL

103. Upon the written request of a licensee, the Central Bank may extend the time within which any document or information required from the licensee must be sent to the Central Bank.

104. (1) Subject to subsection (2), the Central Bank may publish any information furnished to it under this Act.

(2) No information concerning the business of a licensee shall be published by the Central Bank that might disclose the individual affairs of the directors or staff of a licensee or its customers without the prior written consent of all persons whose interests might be disclosed by the publication.

105. (1) Subject to subsection (2), no person other than a licensee may, without the approval of the Central Bank, use the word

(a) "bank" or any of its derivatives in any language; or

(b) any other word indicating the carrying on of international banking business from within Barbados, in the name, description or title under which that person carries on business or intends to carry on business in Barbados, or make any representation to that effect in any bill-head, letter paper, notice or advertisement.

(2) Subsection (1) does not apply

(a) to a bank licensed under the Financial Institutions Act; or

(b) to such person as the Central Bank may exempt from the provisions of subsection (1).

(3) A person who contravenes subsection (1) is guilty of an offence and is liable on conviction on indictment to a fine of $25,000.

106. Neither the Governor of the Central Bank nor any officer of the Bank shall be liable in damages for anything done or omitted in the discharge or purported discharge of his respective functions under this Act, unless it is shown that the act or omission was in bad faith.

107. The Minister may delegate to the Central Bank any of his functions under this Act other than the function of issuing or revoking a licence.

108. Where an international bank that is licensed in another jurisdiction intends to establish a representative office in Barbados, it must seek the approval of the Minister before doing so; and where the Minister gives his approval, he may specify such conditions as he deems fit.

109. (1) The Central Bank may make regulations

(a) respecting the operation of common trust funds;

(b) respecting the information to be recorded in relation to trust accounts of a licensee;

(c) approving the manner of using, investing or managing any property or funds outside or within Barbados by a licensee;

(d) in respect of loans and other assets;

(e) in respect of the treatment of interest;

(f) in respect of loan concentrations;

(g) in respect of major acquisitions or investments by licensees;

(h) in respect of related party transactions;

(i) in respect of matters relating to self-dealing;

(j) in respect of foreign exchange risks and market risks;

(k) regarding the issue of advertisements by licensees;

(l) in respect of such matters as may affect the safety and soundness of licensees;

(m) in respect of such acts, matters or things as are required by this Act to be prescribed;

(n) generally for giving effect to this Act.

(2) All regulations made under this Act

(a) shall be made with the approval of the Minister; and

(b) are subject to negative resolution.

110. (1) Part IV of the Companies Act relating to the winding up of a company does not apply to a licensee.

(2) Division B of Part V of the Companies Act does not apply to a licensee.

111. The Bankruptcy and Insolvency Act, does not apply to a licensee.

112. The Financial Institutions Act does not apply to a licensee in respect of its international financial services business.

113. All regulations, orders and notices made under the Off-shore Banking Act shall, except in so far as they are inconsistent with this Act, continue to have effect as though made or issued under this Act.

114. A company licensed at 10th June, 2002 under the Off-shore Banking Act shall, from that date, be deemed to be licensed under this Act and the provisions of this Act shall apply accordingly.

115. The Off-shore Banking Act is repealed.

Belize

Background

Belize was the site of several Mayan city states until their decline at the end of the first millennium A.D. The British and Spanish disputed the region in the 17th and 18th centuries; it formally became the colony of British Honduras in 1854. Territorial disputes between the UK and Guatemala delayed the independence of Belize until 1981. Guatemala refused to recognize the new nation until 1992 and the two countries are involved in an ongoing border dispute. Guatemala and Belize plan to hold a simultaneous referendum to determine if this dispute will go before the International Court of Justice at The Hague, though they have not yet set a date. Tourism has become the mainstay of the economy.

Population

327,719 (July 2012 est.)

Capital

Belmopan

Official Language

English

Regulatory Authority

Central Bank of Belize
Gabourel Lane
Belize City - Belize
Phone: +501 223 6194
Email: info@centralbank.org.bz
Web: www.centralbank.org.bz

License Types

Domestic Banks are regulated by the Banks & Financial Institutions Act and Offshore Banks by the International Banking Act 2003 which replaced the Offshore Banking Act 1996. Belize offers unrestricted offshore Class A as well as restricted Class B licenses.

Capital Requirements

Class A licensees are required to maintain a paid up capital of at least USD 3,000,000 and Class B licensees are required to maintain USD 1,000,000. See the International Banking Act for further details about reserve requirements etc. A minimum of USD 100,000 is required to be kept in an account at the Central Bank of Belize.

Offshore Bank License Fees

Non Refundable Application Fee:	USD 2,500.00
License Issuing Fee Class A	USD 20,000.00
License Issuing Fee Class B	USD 15,000.00
Annual Renewal Fee Class B	USD 20,000.00

Annual Renewal Fee Class A:

Banks with assets up to USD 30M:	USD 20,000.00
Banks with assets up to USD 100M:	USD 25,000.00
Banks with assets above USD 100M:	USD 40,000.00

International Banking Act 2003
Chapter 267

ARRANGEMENT OF SECTIONS

PART I

Preliminary

PART II

Licensing Requirements

PART III

Types and Requirements of International Banking Licences

15. Types of licences.
16. Unrestricted "A" Class International banking licence.
17. Restricted "B" Class International banking licence.
18. Additional capital requirements.
19. Change of "B" Class Licence to "A" Class Licence.
20. Carrying on of International banking business by domestic and foreign banks.
21. Penalty for infringing capital requirements.

21:01 Deposit and Liquid Asset Requirement.
21:02 Single borrower limits of banks.
21:03 Extension of credit to insiders.

PART IV

Prohibited Activities and Disqualification of Directors, Management and Workers

22. Prohibited transactions.
23. Prohibition on the use of the words "bank", etc.
24. Disqualification of directors, management and workers.

PART V

Revocation of Licences

25. Grounds for revocation of licence and voluntary surrender.
26. Consequences of revocation of licence.
27. Preventive actions by Central Bank in the interest of depositors, etc.
28. Appeal against revocation.

PART VI

Accounting Records, Inspections and Audits

PART VII

Secrecy and Disclosure

PART VIII

Exemptions from Taxes, Duties and Exchange Control

PART IX

Winding up, Dissolution and Abandoned Property

PART X

Miscellaneous

Part I

Preliminary

1. This Act may be cited as the International Banking Act.

2. In this Act, unless the context otherwise requires,

"advertisement" means any form of advertising whether notified, published, mailed or electronically transmitted by any means or device,

(a) in a newspaper, magazine, journal or other publication;

(b) by the display of cinematographic notices;

(c) by means of circulars, brochures, pamphlets or handbills;

(d) by an exhibition of photographs or cinematographic films;

(e) by way of sound broadcasting or television;

(f) by way of computer networks, satellite and telephone; or

(g) by way of solicitation in any form.

"affiliate" in relation to another person means any person which controls, is controlled by or is under common control with, the first person, and includes any or all of the following;

(a) a holding company, parent company or subsidiary company of that person;

(b) a subsidiary of a holding company, or parent company of that person; or

(c) a controlling shareholder of that person (if a company) which, either alone or in association with any person or persons, is entitled to exercise or control the exercise of ten percentum or more of the voting power at a general or special meeting of that person;

"capital" means the net worth of a person, determined in accordance with generally accepted accounting principles as the excess of assets over liabilities;

"Central Bank" means the Central Bank of Belize, established by the Central Bank of Belize Act;

"control" means the power, directly or indirectly, to appoint or remove a majority of the Board of Directors or trustees of a company or to exercise ten percentum or more of the voting power at a general or special meeting of such company;

"demand deposit" means any deposit payable to a depositor upon the demand of such person, or with a maturity or withdrawable by the depositor upon advance notice of less than seven days; by cheque, draft or other similar means;

"deposit" means:-

(a) the unpaid balance of money received or held by a company in the usual course of business and for which it has given or is obligated to give credit to a demand, passbook savings or time account or which is evidenced by its certificate of deposit, certificate of indebtedness or other similar obligation;

(b) money received or held by a company or the credit given for money or its equivalent received or held by a company, in the usual course of business for a special or specific purpose regardless of the legal relationship thereby established, including but not limited to escrow funds, funds held as security for an obligation due to the company or others, funds deposited by a debtor to meet maturing obligations, funds held to meet its acceptance of letters of credit but does not include funds which are received by the company for immediate application to the satisfaction or reduction of indebtedness to the receiving company; or

(c) an outstanding draft (including advice or authorization to charge the company's balance at another company), cashier's cheque, money order, or other officer's cheque received by a company and which has been issued by another company in the usual course of business for any purpose, including but not limited to those issued in payment for services, dividends or purchases;

"deposit liabilities" means those liabilities of a bank represented by deposits held by that bank;

"director" means an individual occupying the position of director or alternate director of a company by whatever name he may be called and includes a member of a local board of a company whose head office is situated outside Belize or which is incorporated outside Belize;

"dollar" means a unit of currency of the United States of America;

"domestic bank" means a bank holding a valid banking licence under the Banks and Financial Institutions Act;

"foreign bank" means a foreign company holding a valid banking licence under the laws of a country other than Belize;

"foreign company" means a company incorporated in a country other than Belize;

"foreign licensee" means a foreign bank holding a valid licence to carry on International banking business from within Belize, issued under this Act;

"foreign money" means a currency other than the Belize dollar;

"holding company" means any company which has control over any bank that is or becomes a licensee by virtue of this Act. A company has control over a bank if:-

(a) the company directly or indirectly or acting through one or more other persons owns, controls, or has power to vote ten percentum or more of any class of voting shares of the bank; or

(b) the company controls in any manner the election of a majority of the directors of the bank;

"international bank" means a company licensed under this Act to carry on the business of international banking;

"international banking" or "international banking business" shall have the meaning assigned to it in section 3;

"licence" means a licence granted under this Act, and "licensed" shall be construed accordingly;

"licensee" means a company holding a valid licence under the provisions of this Act to carry on international banking business from within Belize;

"local company" means a company incorporated in Belize under the Companies Act, or the International Business Companies Act;

"local licensee" means a local company holding a valid licence granted under this Act to carry on international banking business from within Belize;

"Minister" means the Minister for the time being responsible for banks and banking who has been assigned such responsibility under section 41 of the Belize Constitution;

"non-resident" means a person who is not a resident of Belize within the meaning of "resident" as hereinafter defined;

"officer" means the chairman or deputy chairman of the board of directors, president, vice president, managing director, manager, financial controller, secretary or treasurer of a company, or any other individual who holds the title or performs any function similar to that of the holder of those offices;

"person" means an individual, sole proprietor, partnership, company, incorporated or unincorporated association, trust, estate, joint venture or any similar entity, organisation, company or other body of persons including a political sub-division of Government such as a City Council or a Town Board.

"resident" means-

(a) a person ordinarily resident in Belize, irrespective of nationality, or a person who engages in a trade or business in Belize: Provided that an Export Processing Zone Developer or an Export Processing Zone Business established under the Export Processing Zone Act, or a Commercial Free Zone Developer or a Commercial Free Zone Business established under the Commercial Free Zone Act, may conduct banking business with a licensee so, however, that a licensee shall not provide loans or advances to any of the said entities above the amount of one million dollars for a single borrower or a group of related borrowers without the prior written approval of the Central Bank; or

(b) any incorporated or other body, wherever incorporated, formed or organized, that is controlled by a person described in (a) above; or

(c) any company incorporated under the International Business Companies Act (other than a Public

Investment Company) that holds or owns shares, debt obligations or other securities in a company incorporated under the Companies Act, or has any of its shares, debt obligations or other securities beneficially owned or held by any person or company resident in Belize.

"subsidiary" in relation to another company, means a company in which that other company is entitled to exercise or control the exercise of more than fifty percentum of the voting power at a general or special meeting;

"unsecured loans, advances and extensions of credit" means loans, advances and extensions of credit made without tangible security or realisable collateral or in respect of any advances and extensions of credit made with tangible security or realisable collateral, any part of which exceeds the fair or market value, as determined in a manner acceptable to the Central Bank, of the assets comprising the security given;

3. "International banking" or "International banking business" means:-

   (a) receiving, borrowing or taking up foreign money exclusively from non-residents at interest or otherwise on current account, savings account, term deposit or other similar account and which according and subject to arrangement is repayable on the cheque, draft, order, authority or similar instrument of the customer, and investing the foreign money so received by lending, giving credit or otherwise exclusively to non-residents; or

   (b) carrying on exclusively with non-residents such other activities as are customarily related or ancillary to international banking.

Part II

Licensing Requirements

4. (1) No person shall carry on offshore banking business from within Belize unless he holds a valid licence granted under this Act.

(2) A person who not being duly licensed under this Act-

(a) acts as an offshore bank, whether on his own account, in partnership or otherwise;

(b) holds himself out as being licensed as an offshore bank; or

(c) takes or uses any name, title, addition, or description implying or likely to lead another person to believe that he is licensed as an offshore bank, commits an offence and is liable on summary conviction to a fine not exceeding one hundred thousand dollars or to a term of imprisonment not exceeding five years, or to both such fine and term of imprisonment.

5. (1) No licence may be issued under this Act to any person other than an eligible company.

(2) A body corporate or proposed to be incorporated is an eligible company if-

(a) it is incorporated or registered under the Companies Act or the International Business Companies Act as a company limited by shares, or it is a foreign bank;

(b) its shares are in registered form and not in bearer form;

(c) its memorandum and articles of association are acceptable to the Central Bank; and

(d) its authorized and paid up capital accords with the requirements of sections 16 or 17, as the case may be, and section 18 of this Act.

(3) Notwithstanding anything contained in the Companies Act, or the International Business Companies Act, no company may be incorporated or registered under those Acts, whose objects include the carrying on of offshore banking business from within Belize unless its incorporation or registration has been consented to by the Central Bank.

6. (1) An eligible company desirous of carrying on offshore banking business from within Belize shall make an application to the Central Bank for the grant of a licence in the prescribed form.

(2) An application under subsection (1) shall show that the applicant is an eligible company. The Central Bank may also require that such application-

(a) give particulars of, but not limited to:-

(i) the names and addresses of its directors and principal shareholders;

(ii) the ultimate beneficial ownership of the company or proposed company where the shareholders of record are, or are to be, corporations, trusts or other legal entities or organizations, or where the shareholders of record are acting as nominees for or under the direction of any other person notwithstanding anything to the contrary contained in any other law;

(iii) the shareholding structure and management of the company;

(iv) the financial standing of the company, if applicable;

(b) contain a detailed business and financial plan of the company;

(c) provide particulars of referees, guarantors and other third parties;

(d) provide details of any subsidiary or affiliated company;

(e) provide details of any overseas office which the company has or proposes to open;

(f) provide the names and addresses of the external auditors of the company or proposed company, including the experience of the auditors in auditing banks;

(g) provide such other information of a financial or other nature as the Central Bank may require in any general or particular case; and

(h) be accompanied by a non-refundable fee as may from time to time be prescribed by the Central Bank.

(3) In addition to the requirements of subsection (2), a foreign bank shall further supply to the Central Bank when making its application, a written statement from the banking supervisory authority in its country of incorporation, and the banking supervisory authority in the country where its principal office is located if different, confirming that the authority has no objection to the application.

(4) An application for a licence and all documents submitted pursuant to this Act in support of the application shall be signed by the directors of the eligible company or proposed company making the application.

(5) Documents submitted to the Central Bank under subsection (4) may be produced in evidence in any court of law or before the Appeal Board established under the Banks and Financial Institutions Act.

7. (1) On receipt of an application from an eligible company for a licence under this Act, the Central Bank may cause such investigation to be made of the applicant company or proposed company, its financial standing, and of any associates or affiliates of the applicant company or proposed company, as the Central Bank considers necessary to satisfy itself that the applicant meets the criteria of licensing and that it will conduct its business in a sound and prudent manner.

(2) Without prejudice to the generality of subsection (1), the Central Bank may require an examination or investigation to be made of any or all of the following:

(a) the financial status and history of the applicant company and any of its directors, associates, principal shareholders or affiliates;

(b) the character and experience of the directors and managers thereof;

(c) the adequacy of its capital for the purpose of the business it intends to carry;

(d) the earning prospects and viability of the proposed offshore bank;

(e) the source of funds for capitalization;

(f) any other matter relating to the fitness and propriety of the applicant company, its directors, beneficial owners or management;

(g) the adequacy of the applicant company's liquidity;

(h) the adequacy of the applicant company's provision for non-performing and doubtful assets; and

(i) the adequacy of the applicant company's accounting methods and records.

(3) For the purposes of this section, "associate" when used to indicate a relationship with any person, means:

(a) a company of which the person so referred to beneficially owns or controls, directly or indirectly, shares, or securities convertible into shares, carrying more than twenty five per centum of the voting rights;

(b) a partner of the person so referred to, acting on behalf of the partnership;

(c) a trust or estate in which the person so referred to has a substantial beneficial interest or in respect of which he serves as a trustee or in a similar capacity.

(4) For the purposes of this section:

(a) one company is affiliated with another company if that company is the subsidiary of the other or both are subsidiaries of the same holding company or each of them is controlled by the same person;

(b) if two companies are affiliated with the same company at the same time, they are affiliated with each other at that time;

(c) a company is the holding company of another if that other company is a subsidiary of the first-mentioned company;

(d) a company is a subsidiary of another company if it is controlled by that other company.

(5) [Repealed by Act 34 of 2002]

8. (1) The Central Bank may grant a licence under this Act upon the payment of the prescribed fee and subject to such terms and conditions as it may specify; or it may refuse to grant a licence.

(2) Where a licence is granted subject to the condition that the terms and conditions thereof may be varied subsequent to its issue, the Central Bank may at any time revoke any of the original terms and conditions or impose additional terms and conditions.

9. (1) Where the Central Bank refuses to grant a licence under this Act, it shall inform the applicant of the grounds for such refusal.

(2) Where the Central Bank states that the refusal to grant a licence was in the public interest, he need not give details of that refusal, or state any other ground.

10. (1) A licence granted under this Act remains valid until revoked pursuant to this Act, but it is a condition of every licence that an annual fee be paid not later than the second day of January of each succeeding year by every class of licensee as prescribed by the Central Bank from time to time.

(2) Every licensee who defaults in paying the prescribed annual licence fee in respect of a licence granted under this Act by the due date and who continues to transact offshore banking business shall be liable to pay, upon being called upon by the Central Bank to do so, an amount equal to three times the amount of the unpaid fee.

11. (1) It is a condition of every licence granted under this Act that:-

(a) a local licensee shall not change his name without the prior approval of the Central Bank;

(b) a licensee shall not knowingly in the course of his business accept any deposit for the account of a beneficial owner who is a resident of Belize;

(c) a local licensee shall not open outside of Belize a subsidiary, branch, agency or representative office without the prior written approval of the Central Bank;

(d) the prior written approval of the Central Bank is required for the appointment of directors of a local licensee;

(e) the Central Bank is notified as soon as a person ceases to be a director of a local licensee.

(f) a licensee shall not amend its memorandum or articles of association without the prior approval of the Central Bank;

(g) a licensee shall not merge or consolidate with any other licensee under this Act or the Banks and Financial Institutions Act, or either directly or indirectly acquire any material portion of the assets of, or assume any material portion of the liabilities of, another licensee under this Act or the Banks and Financial Institutions Act or any other institution without the prior consent of the Central Bank.

(2) No person, either alone or with any associate or associates, shall, without the prior written consent of the Central Bank, acquire control over any voting shares of a local licensee where such acquisition would result in that person exercising control equivalent to, or in excess of ten percent, twenty percent, fifty percent or seventy-five percent of the total voting shares issued.

(3) Before giving an approval to any matter mentioned in subsection (2) of this section, the Central Bank may carry out such investigations and examinations as it deems necessary or proper.

(4) Where the Central Bank is of the opinion that the interests of a group of two or more persons are so interrelated that they should be considered as a single unit, the total holdings of that group shall be combined and deemed to be the holdings of a single person for the purposes of this section.

(5) In every case where the provisions of subsection (2) have been violated, the Central Bank may issue an order requiring

divestment of so much of the offending interest as is necessary to secure compliance with the provisions of subsection (2).

(6) The Central Bank may by notice in writing require any licensee to submit within such period and in such form as may be specified by the Central Bank, a list of all shareholders on its register. The Central Bank may also require the licensee to provide the names of the ultimate beneficial owners of such shares.

(7) Every licensee or other person who acts in contravention of this section commits an offence and is liable on summary conviction to a fine not exceeding one thousand dollars for each day during which the offence continues.

12. A licensee shall display in a conspicuous place where he conducts business a copy of his current licence granted under this Act.

13. Every licensee shall use as part of his description or title the word "bank" or one or more of its derivatives in any language.

14. (1) It shall be a condition of every licence granted under this Act that the Central Bank shall be notified forthwith of any change of address of a licensee's business office in Belize.

(2) Every person who fails to comply with the provisions of subsection (1) of this section shall pay, on being called upon by the Central Bank to do so, two thousand dollars for each day that it failed to notify the Central Bank of the change of address.

PART III

Types and Requirements of Offshore Banking Licences

15. The following kinds of licenses may be granted under this Act, namely:-

(a) Unrestricted "A" Class Offshore Banking Licence; and

(b) Restricted "B" Class Offshore Banking Licence.

16. (1) No company shall apply for, or obtain, or be eligible to hold, an "A" Class international banking licence under this Act unless it has at all times capital equivalent to not less than three million dollars or, in the case of a foreign bank, not less than twenty five million dollars. The capital shall be expressed in dollars or in any other foreign currency as the Central Bank may approve in writing.

(2) The holder of an "A" Class international banking licence shall:-

(a) establish, maintain and operate a business office in Belize;

(b) transact international banking business through its business office in Belize without restriction on that business.

(3) For the purposes of this section and section 17, a "business office" shall be a local physical presence in which the bank's business is carried on.

17. (1) No company shall apply for, or obtain, or be eligible to hold, a "B" Class international banking licence under this Act unless it maintains at all times capital equivalent to not less than one million dollars or, in the case of a foreign bank, not less than fifteen million dollars. The capital shall be expressed in dollars or in any other foreign currency as the Central Bank may approve in writing.

(2) The holder of a "B" Class international banking licence shall:-

(a) establish, maintain and operate a business office in Belize; and

(b) transact only such international banking business as may be specified in the licence.

(3) In addition, the holder of a "B" Class international banking licence is prohibited from:-

(a) soliciting or accepting any deposits of money or any other valuable property from the general public; and

(b) issuing to any depositor a cheque book or providing any current deposit or chequing account facilities for the transaction of his international banking business.

18. (1) In addition to the capital requirements of sections 16 and 17, the Central Bank may also require every local licensee to maintain capital in amounts not less than such percentage of that licensee's total assets and off-balance sheet contingencies, commitments, transactions and exposures, calculated in such a manner and using such methods as the Central Bank may prescribe. The Central Bank may also at any time direct a particular licensee to maintain a higher percentage of capital in excess of the minimum specified above if it considers such higher percentage appropriate having regard to the financial condition of such licensee.

(2) For purposes of this section, fully paid-up and unimpaired capital and reserves, mean:-

(a) allotted, called up and fully paid and outstanding share capital, including any amounts which may be paid in excess of the par or stated value of the shares;

(b) perpetual, irredeemable non-cumulative preferred shares, including shares convertible at the issuing licensee's option into common shares;

(c) any other disclosed reserves created or increased by appropriations or retained earnings;

(d) current retained earnings;

(e) subordinated term debt subject to such terms, limits

and restrictions as the Central Bank may from time to time specify; Less:

(f) goodwill and any other intangible assets, except such intangible assets which are readily marketable and have identifiable and consistent streams of cash flows which, in the determination of the Central Bank, may be included in capital under such terms and conditions as the Central Bank may specify; and

(g) current year's losses as reported to the Central Bank irrespective of whether they have been published, and any accumulated losses not previously published.

(3) Whether any reserves or portion of any reserves have been created against identified assets, groups of assets or losses or, in respect of a deterioration in the value of particular assets of the licensee, such reserves or portion of reserves will be considered as being impaired and shall not be included in the capital base of the licensee for purposes of computing the minimum requirements provided in this section.

(4) Any bank which on and from the 5th October, 2002 does not comply with the requirements of this section shall, within six months of the said date, or such longer period as may be approved in writing by the Central Bank, maintain fully paid up and unimpaired capital and reserves, as specified in this section.

(5) The Central Bank may require any or every licensee to comply with such minimum standards of prudent conduct of business as it may by Order prescribe, including, but not limited to, standards relating to liquidity, concentration of risk and provisions against non-performing and doubtful assets.

19. (1) The holder of a "B" Class international banking licence granted under section 17 may, at any time during the term of

the licence, apply to the Central Bank for a change in licence to an "A" Class international banking licence.

(2) In reviewing an application under subsection (1) of this section, the Central Bank shall require such information as it deems necessary and shall have regard to the public interest and such other considerations as it thinks fit to take into account.

(3) The Central Bank may approve an application submitted pursuant to subsection (1) of this section subject to such terms and conditions as it thinks fit; including, but not limited to, an increase in capital to comply with the requirements of an "A" Class international banking licence.

20. (1) A domestic bank licensed under the Banks and Financial Institutions Act may carry on international banking business from within Belize only through a separately capitalized subsidiary company which has been granted an international banking licence under this Act.

(2) A foreign bank may carry on international banking business from within Belize either through a locally incorporated subsidiary which has been granted an international banking licence under this Act or through a branch which is established and administered separately and independently from any branch or subsidiary which may be carrying on banking business licensed under the Banks and Financial Institutions Act.

21. The capital requirements prescribed in sections 16, 17 and 18 shall continue during the subsistence of a licence and a licensee who fails or neglects to maintain such requirements shall pay, on being called upon by the Central Bank to do so, three thousand dollars for each day that it failed to comply with the provisions of the said sections.

21:01(1) Every bank shall maintain an account in its name with the Central Bank a minimum deposit of one hundred thousand dollars on terms and conditions specified by the Central Bank, or such other sum as may from time to time be specified by the Central Bank by thirty days' prior notice in writing.

(2) Every bank shall maintain a minimum aggregate holding of approved liquid assets, which shall be at least twenty four percentum of its total deposit liabilities, or as prescribed by the Central Bank.

(3) For the purpose of this section "approved liquid assets" means assets that are freely and readily convertible into cash without significant loss, free from any charge, lien or encumbrance whatsoever and includes all or any of the following:-

(a) notes and coins which are legal tender in Belize and in the United States of America and such other foreign notes and coins as the Central Bank may specify in writing;

(b) net balances and deposits held with other banks in Belize not exceeding one year to maturity but where such balances are negative they will be subtracted from the approval liquid assets;

(c) cheques and other sight drafts drawn on banks and in the course of collection;

(d) balances and deposits at call and at short notice not exceeding one year to maturity held with banks and financial institutions abroad and denominated in currencies freely convertible into dollars net of any or all of the following balances due within one year:

(i) balances due to banks and financial institutions abroad;

(ii) balances due to head office and other branches abroad;

(iii) balances due to holding company or parent company or any company that owns the majority of the shares of a bank or financial institution;

(e) inland bills of exchange which are financial commercial transactions, which bear the acceptance or confirmation of acceptance of another bank and which are payable in not more than one year from the date on which they were drawn or accepted;

(f) treasury bills and other securities issued or guaranteed by the Government of Belize and maturing in not more than one year; and

(g) treasury bills and other securities which have been issued or guaranteed by governments abroad, which are marketable in money and capital markets abroad, which mature in not more than one year and which are denominated in currencies freely convertible into dollars.

(4) The Central Bank may, by thirty days' prior notice in writing to a licensee, require any licensee to maintain a minimum aggregate holding of liquid assets, which shall be equivalent to such value as the Central Bank may determine.

(5) Any bank which fails to maintain a deposit with the Central Bank as required by subsection (1) of this section shall be liable to pay, on being called upon by the Central Bank to do so, a sum of one thousand dollars for each day that it fails to maintain such deposit.

(6) Any bank which during any quarter fails to maintain a minimum aggregate holding of liquid assets in accordance with this section shall be liable to pay, on being called upon in writing to do so by the Central Bank, a sum equivalent to ten percentum of the amount by which its actual aggregate holding of liquid assets has fallen short of its required

aggregate holdings, and such charge shall be payable to the Central Bank on such day as may be fixed by the Central Bank.

(7) The Central Bank may vary, by thirty days' prior notice in writing to a licensee, the method to be used in computing the liquid assets requirement specified in subsection (2).

21:02(1) The aggregate of unsecured loans, advances and extensions of credit granted by a bank to a person and not secured by collateral having a marketable value as determined by reliable and current valuations at least equal to the total amount of the loan, advances and extensions of credit shall not exceed fifteen percentum of the fully paid up and unimpaired reserves of a licensee.

(2) Except with the prior written approval of the Central Bank, total loans, advances and extensions of credit by a bank to a person shall not exceed twenty five percentum of the fully paid-up and unimpaired capital and reserves of a licensee. These limitations shall be separate from and in addition to the limitations contained in subsection (1).

(3) For the purposes of subsection (1) and (2) above-

(a) the term "loan, advances and extensions of credit" shall include all loans, advances, overdrafts, holdings of papers and all direct and indirect obligations of the borrower as well as off-balance sheet commitments, such as acceptances and guarantees on behalf of the borrower, underwriting facilities, endorsements, placements, documentary credits issued, performance bonds and other contingent liabilities on behalf of such person or any other facility or instrument that the Central Bank may specify in writing; and

(b) the term "person" shall include any group of persons which is under the control of one and the same person.

(4) The limitations contained in subsection (1) or (2) shall not apply to-

(a) loans, advances and extensions of credit to the Government of Belize;

(b) loans, advances and extensions of credit fully secured by bonds, debentures, notes and treasury bills of the Government of Belize or by other such obligations fully guaranteed as to principal and interest by the Government of Belize;

(c) loans, advances and extensions of credit fully secured by the Government of Belize; or

(d) loans, advances and extensions of credit fully secured by a segregated and pledged deposit account in the lending bank.

(5) A licensee shall not grant any loans, advances or extensions of credit against the security of its own shares.

21:03(1) A bank shall not grant or permit to be outstanding unsecured loans, advances and extensions of credit of an aggregate amount in excess of two percentum of the aggregate of its fully paid-up unimpaired capital and reserves or give any financial guarantees in excess of such amount without security, or incur any other liability in excess of such amount without security-

(a) to or on behalf of any one of its directors, officers or principal shareholders, whether such loans, advances and extensions of credit are obtained by or on account of such director, officer or principal shareholder jointly or severally; or

(b) to or on behalf of any partnership, company or any similar entity or organization in which the bank or

any one or more of its directors, officers or principal shareholders as described in subsection (2) is interested whether as a partner, director, officer or guarantor.

(2) For purposes of this section, "principal shareholder" means a person who directly or indirectly or acting through or in concert with one or more persons, owns, controls or has the power to vote more than ten percentum of the voting power at any general or special meeting of a bank. Shares owned or controlled by a spouse, son, daughter, mother or father of a person are considered to be held by that person.

(3) The aggregate of all loans, advances and extensions of credit described in this section shall not exceed fifty percentum of the fully paid-up and unimpaired capital and reserves of a licensee.

21:04(1) Any bank to which sections 21:02 and 21:03 are applicable and which, prior to 5th October, 2002 entered into any transaction which does not comply with the said sections shall, within six months after such the said date, submit a statement thereof to the Central Bank and shall liquidate all such transactions within such reasonable time as shall be determined by the Central Bank but in no case later than one year from the commencement of the said Act.

(2) Any person who fails to comply with the provisions of section 21:02 or 21:03 shall, upon being called in writing to do so by the Central Bank, pay a penalty of five thousand dollars for each day of such failure to comply.

(3) Nothing in section 21:02 or 21:03 shall be deemed to prevent a bank from enforcing any transaction referred to therein against any person who is a party thereto or against whom it could have been otherwise enforced.

PART IV

Prohibited Activities and Disqualification of Directors, Management And Workers

22. (1) A licensee shall not:-

(a) transact any international banking business with any person or entity who is a resident of Belize unless such person or entity-

(i) is a bank licensed under the Banks and Financial Institutions Act or this Act which is transacting business customarily carried on with foreign banks outside of Belize; or

(ii) is transacting such business in the capacity of agent, nominee, legal representative or other similar capacity exclusively for and in respect of non-residents where such persons or entity is not the beneficiary of such business transactions;

(iii) is the Government of Belize or a public statutory corporation wholly owned by the Government of Belize;

(b) transact any business otherwise than in accordance with the terms and conditions of the licence and the provisions of this Act or any regulations made thereunder.

(2) For the purpose of subsection (1) (a) (ii) above, the onus of establishing residency and beneficial interest in such transactions to the satisfaction of the Central Bank shall be on the licensee.

(3) Every person or licensee who acts in contravention of this section commits an offence and is liable on summary conviction to a fine equal to two thousand dollars for each

day during which the offence continues or to imprisonment for a term not exceeding five years, or to both such fine and term of imprisonment.

23. (1) Except with the prior written approval of the Central Bank, no person other than the holder of a valid licence granted under this Act or under the Banks and Financial Institutions Act shall:-

(a) use the word "bank", "savings", "savings and loan" or any of their derivatives in any language, or any other word indicating the carrying on of banking business, or international banking business, in or from within Belize, in the description or title under which such person is incorporated or carrying on business in or from within Belize; or

(b) make, or continue to make, any representation in any billhead, printed form, letter, paper, notice, advertisement, solicitation, computer network, satellite or telephone transmission, or in any other manner whatsoever, that such person is carrying on banking business or international banking business in or from within Belize.

(2) A licensee shall not:-

(a) in the conduct of his international banking business, use or operate under a name other than the name under which he is licensed under this Act;

(b) use, or operate under, a name which so closely resembles or is identical to the name of any company, firm, business house, or other financial entity or institution whether within or outside Belize as is likely to mislead or deceive; or

(c) use, or operate under, a name which is calculated to suggest falsely that such licensee has a special status in relation to, or derived from, the Government of Belize, or has the official backing of or acts on behalf of, the said Government or of any department or official thereof or is recognized in Belize as a national or Central Bank.

(3) No licensee shall engage in advertising practices that are likely to mislead or deceive concerning:-

(a) the relationship of the licensee with the Government of Belize, the Central Bank or any department or office thereof;

(b) the true interest rate paid on deposits or charged on credit;

(c) the true returns on the management of investments;

(d) the insured or guaranteed status of deposits or other liabilities or of investments managed by it; or

(e) the financial condition of the institution.

(4) Every person who contravenes this section commits an offence and is liable on summary conviction to a fine not exceeding twenty five thousand dollars or to imprisonment for a term not exceeding five years, or to both such fine and term of imprisonment.

(5) In this section, the term "printed form" includes a form of which copies are produced by photocopying or by any duplicating or reproduction process, including but not limited to letterpress, photographic, lithographic or stenciling, or any other similar process.

24. (1) No person shall apply for, or obtain, or be eligible, or continue to be employed, as a director, officer, manager, secretary or other worker of any licensee licensed under this Act, without prior approval in writing of the Central Bank if-

(a) he has been a director of, or directly or indirectly involved in, the management of a bank which has had its licence revoked in accordance with section 25 and section 27 of this Act or section 7 of the Banks and Financial Institutions Act, or in accordance with the banking laws of another country; or

(b) he has been dismissed from the management of a bank for an act or conduct involving dishonesty or fraud; or

(c) he has been convicted in Belize or elsewhere for any offence triable on indictment in Belize; or

(d) he is or becomes bankrupt, suspends payment to, or compounds with, his creditors; or

(e) he is, in the opinion of the Central Bank, not a fit and proper person to work or continue to work for a licensee;

(f) he is an approved auditor for the licensee as provided in section 30 of this Act, or is an officer of a company which is an approved auditor.

(2) Every person who contravenes the provisions of subsection (1) above commits an offence and shall be liable on summary conviction to a fine not exceeding ten thousand dollars or to imprisonment for a term not exceeding two years, or to both such fine and term of imprisonment.

(3) Every director and officer of a licensee, in exercising the powers and discharging the duties of that person's office, shall:

(a) act honestly and in good faith with a view to securing the best interests of the licensee; and

(b) exercise the care, diligence and skill that a reasonably prudent person would exercise in comparable circumstances.

(4) A director or officer of a licensee who:

(a) is a party to a material loan, contract or transaction, or a proposed material loan, contract or transaction with the licensee; or

(b) is a director or officer of, or has a material interest in or a material relation to, any person who is a party to a material loan, contract or transaction, or a proposed material loan, contract or transaction with the licensee, shall disclose in writing to the licensee the nature and extent of the material interest or relation.

(5) The disclosure required by subsection (4) above shall be made the director or officer when the matter or proposed contract comes or ought reasonably to have come to the attention of the director or officer.

(6) A general notice in writing to the board of directors by a director or officer, disclosing at the time such person assumes or is appointed to his office and from time to time (but in no event less than annually) every material commercial, financial, agricultural, industrial or other business or family interest that such person has at the time, and stating that the person is to be regarded as interested in any material contract between the licensee and any person named in the disclosure, shall be a sufficient declaration of material interest in relation to any such contract.

(7) A director or officer who has a material interest or a material relation within the scope of subsections (4) to (6) above shall leave any meeting at which the matter is discussed, and shall refrain from voting on any matter related thereto which becomes the subject of action by the board of directors of the licensee, provided that such an interest, if so disclosed, shall not disqualify the interested person for purposes of constituting a quorum.

(8) For the purposes of subsections (4) and (6) above, a director or officer shall be deemed to have a material interest in, or material relation to, another person, if that director or officer, or the spouse, parent, sibling or child of such director or officer.

(a) in the case of another person who is a company, partnership or similar entity, is or during the last fiscal year has been an officer, director or partner of such company, partnership or entity, or owns or has the power to vote, or during the last fiscal year has owned or held the power to vote, ten percentum or more of any class of shares or other equity interest of such company, partnership or entity;

(b) owes money to or otherwise is indebted to, or is a guarantor of any obligation of such other person in an amount exceeding two percentum of the fully paid up and unimpaired capital and reserves of the licensee;

(c) engages or during the last fiscal year has engaged in any transaction with such other person in an amount which exceeds ten percentum of the director's or officer's net worth; or

(d) is the spouse, parent, sibling or child of any person described in paragraphs (b) or (c) above.

(9) Where a director or officer fails to disclose a material conflict of interest in accordance with this section, the Central Bank may request the licensee to suspend the director or officer from office for any period not exceeding one year.

(10) A director or officer who contravenes subsection (4) or (6) of this section commits an offence and shall be liable on summary conviction to a fine not exceeding twenty-five thousand dollars or to imprisonment for a term not exceeding six months, or to both such fine and imprisonment.

(11) Any officer of a licensee who with intent to deceive:

(i) makes any false or misleading statement or entry or omits any statement or entry that should be made in any book, account, report or statement of the licensee; or

(ii) obstructs or attempts to obstruct the proper performance by an auditor of his duties in accordance with the provisions of this Act, or a lawful examination of the licensee by a duly authorised examiner appointed by the Central Bank under section 32 or 33 of this Act, commits an offence and shall be liable on summary conviction to a fine not exceeding fifty thousand dollars, or to imprisonment for a term not exceeding twelve months, or to both such fine and imprisonment.

PART V

Revocation of Licences

25. (1) The Minister may, on recommendation from the Central Bank, revoke a licence if the licensee so requests or if:

(a) the licensee does not within six months after the grant of the licence, or such longer period as the Central Bank may approve in writing, commence international banking business; or

(b) the licensee fails to comply with any term or condition of his licence; or

(c) the licensee is in breach of any duty or obligation imposed upon him by this Act or commits an offence under this Act or any regulations made thereunder; or

(d) the licensee fails to comply with any provision of this Act, or any directive or Order issued by the Minister or the Central Bank under this Act; or

(e) the licensee ceases to carry on international banking business; or

(f) the licensee goes into liquidation or is wound-up or otherwise dissolved; or

(g) the licensee fails to pay the prescribed annual licence fee as provided for under section 10 of this Act; or

(h) the circumstances specified in section 27 (1) exist.

(2) A licensee shall not be allowed to surrender his licence voluntarily and request subsequent revocation unless he produces evidence satisfactory to the Central Bank that he has repaid all of the deposits and other liabilities and has transferred all his assets held or administered by him and that he has ceased carrying on all other forms of international banking business from within Belize.

26. (1) Where a licence is revoked under section 25, the licensee shall forthwith surrender the licence and every copy thereof in his possession to the Central Bank and the Central Bank may appoint any person it deems suitably qualified to properly carry out the functions of an administrator or liquidator with respect to the affairs of the licensee.

Every such person so appointed shall have full power and authority to perform the functions of the administrator or liquidator for that licensee without further action on the part of the Central Bank and with such legal rights and duties under the laws of Belize as may be held by the Central Bank acting in such capacity.

(2) The Central Bank shall promptly give notice of the revocation of the licence and of the appointment of the administrator or liquidator (if any) to the licensee as well as to the creditors, depositors, directors, shareholders, customers, and employees of the licensee and to the relevant authorities in Belize and abroad.

27. (1) If in the opinion of the Central Bank, a licensee is carrying on his business in a manner detrimental to the public interest or to the interest of depositors, creditors and other customers, or has insufficient assets to cover his liabilities, or is contravening any of the provisions of this Act, or regulations made thereunder, the Minister may, on the recommendation of the Central Bank, take one or more of the following measures from time to time as may seem to him necessary:-

(a) revoke the licence pursuant to section 25 of this Act;

(b) impose new conditions upon the licence or amend or revoke existing conditions;

(c) require the removal or substitution of any director or officer of the licensee;

(d) at the expense of the licensee, appoint a person, who, in his opinion, has adequate training and experience, to advise the licensee on the proper conduct of his affairs and to report to him thereon within such time as may be specified; or

(e) require the licensee forthwith to take such measures as he may consider necessary in relation to his business.

(2) If a licensee refuses or fails to take any measure required under paragraph (e) of subsection (1) of this section, he commits an offence and is liable on summary conviction to a fine not exceeding one thousand dollars in respect of every day during which the offence continues.

28. (1) Any licensee who is aggrieved by the revocation of his licence under this Act may within twenty-one days of the communication of the decision to him appeal to the Appeal Board established under Part X of the Banks and Financial Institutions Act and thereafter the provisions of that Part of that Act shall mutatis mutandis apply to appeals under this Act.

(2) Any party aggrieved by a decision of the Appeal Board may appeal to the Court of Appeal on the ground that the decision was erroneous on a point of law and the Court may affirm or set aside the decision appealed against, and may remit the matter to the Appeal Board for rehearing and determination by it.

Part VI

Accounting Records, Inspections and Audits

29. A licensee shall keep his international banking business records in such a manner as will enable his accounts and records to be conveniently and properly audited and examined pursuant to the provisions of this Part of this Act.

30. (1) Every local licensee shall appoint annually an approved auditor whose duties shall be to make a report upon the annual balance sheet, profit and loss accounts and statement of cash flows in respect of his international banking business, and in every such report the auditor shall state whether, in his opinion, proper books and records of account have been kept, whether the balance sheet and other accounts and financial statements are in agreement with the licensee's books and records, and whether the balance sheet, profit and loss accounts and statement of cash flows are complete and fair and properly drawn up and whether it exhibits a true and correct statement of the financial condition and affairs of the licensee, and in any case in which the auditor has called for explanation or information from the officers or agents of the licensee, whether the same was found to be satisfactory.

(2) The report of an approved auditor under subsection (1), along with copies of the balance sheet, profit and loss accounts, statement of cash flows, supplementary notes and management letter, shall be sent by the licensee to

the Central Bank within four months after the close of the licensee's financial year, or such longer period as the Central Bank may in writing approve.

(3) In the case of a foreign licensee, the consolidated audit report and financial statements of the foreign bank as stipulated in subsection (2) of this section shall be sent to the Central Bank within the time stipulated therein.

(4) Every licensee who fails to comply with the requirements of subsection (2) or (3) of this section shall be liable, upon being called upon in writing by the Central Bank to do so, to pay a penalty of five thousand dollars for each day of such failure to comply except where an extension to the period has been granted in writing by the Central bank.

(5) A copy of the report of the auditor shall bear on its face the certificate of the auditor and shall be displayed by every licensee in a conspicuous place in his business office in Belize.

(6) No person having an interest in any local licensee other than as a depositor, and no director, officer or agent of the licensee or of an affiliate of the licensee shall be eligible for appointment as an approved auditor for that licensee; and any person appointed as such auditor to any licensee who subsequently acquires such interest or becomes a director, officer or agent of that licensee shall cease to be auditor.

(7) If the Central Bank, on reasonable grounds, is not satisfied with the annual report of an auditor appointed by a local licensee, it may appoint another auditor to make an independent audit report, and in every such case the Central Bank shall fix the remuneration to be paid by the licensee to such auditor appointed under this subsection.

(8) If a licensee fails to appoint an approved auditor under this section, the Central Bank may appoint an auditor who shall

have all the powers and duties of an auditor appointed by the licensee to carry out an audit. The Central Bank shall fix the remuneration to be paid by that licensee to such auditor appointed under this subsection.

(9) If the auditor appointed under this section becomes aware, during course of his examination of the licensee or at any other time, that the licensee is conducting his affairs in an unsafe and unsound manner, is insolvent or may soon become insolvent, is in contravention of this Act or any terms and conditions that may be attached to his licence, is involved in or is aiding or abetting fraudulent or criminal activity, he shall forthwith report such findings to the Central Bank. Any auditor making such report shall not be legally liable for such disclosure if he acts in good faith.

(10) Any auditor who fails to report his findings to the Central Bank as required under subsection (9) above commits an offence and shall be liable on summary conviction to a fine not exceeding ten thousand dollars.

(11) For the purpose of this section, an approved auditor is an auditor who is a member of one of the professional bodies for the time being declared by the Central Bank by notice in the Gazette to be approved for such purposes.

(12) A licensee shall forthwith give notice to Central Bank if the licensee:

(a) proposes to give special notice to its shareholders of an ordinary resolution removing an auditor before the expiration of his engagement; or

(b) gives notice to its shareholders of an ordinary resolution replacing an auditor at the expiration of his engagement with a different auditor, or if a person ceases to be an auditor of the institution otherwise than in consequence of such a resolution.

(13) An auditor or a licensee appointed under this section shall forthwith give written notice to Central Bank if he:

(a) resigns before the expiration of his engagement;

(b) does not seek to be re-appointed, or

(c) decides to include in his report on the licensee's accounts any qualification that indicates that that the licensee may be carrying on its business in a manner dritrimental to the interests of its depositors or of its creditors, or may have insufficient assets to satisfy its liabilities as they mature or become due, or may be contravening any of the provisions of this Act.

(14) A licensee or auditor who fails to comply with this section commits an offence and shall be liable on summary conviction to a fine not exceeding fifty thousand dollars or to imprisonment for a term not exceeding twelve months, or to both such fine and imprisonment.

(15) No duty to which an auditor may be subject shall be regarded as contravened by reasons of his communicating in good faith to Central Bank, whether or not in response to a request made by it, any information about a licensee or opinion pursuant to an obligation of the auditor under this Act.

(16) This section applies to any matter of which an auditor becomes aware in his capacity as auditor and which relates to the business or affairs of the licensee or any affiliate of the licensee.

31. (1) Every licensee shall, in respect of his operations from within Belize, submit to the Central Bank such returns and information as the Central Bank may prescribe within such time as may be required.

(2) The Central Bank may from time to time request any information which it may require for the purposes of this Act

from any licensee with respect to its operations, the affairs of a particular person and those of its holding company and its affiliates in Belize or abroad, where in relation to its holding company and its affiliates in Belize or abroad, such information pertains directly to the business and financial relationship between the licensee and such holding company or its affiliates in Belize or abroad. The licensee shall supply such information within such period and in such manner as the Central Bank may require.

(3) Any licensee or other person who has reasonable cause to believe that any officer or other person participating in the affairs of the licensee may have committed or aided in the commission of an offence punishable under the Criminal Code or other laws of Belize shall submit a report thereof to the Central Bank within such time and in such manner, and containing such information, as the Central Bank may specify.

(4) Every licensee who fails to comply with the provisions of subsections (1) (2) or (3) above commits an offence and shall on summary conviction forfeit to the Central Bank a penalty of one thousand dollars for every day the offence continues.

(5) Every director, officer or employee of a licensee who knowingly or willfully supplies false or misleading returns or information to the Central Bank under this section commits an offence and shall be liable on summary conviction to a fine not exceeding ten thousand dollars or to imprisonment for a term not exceeding two years, or to both such fine and term of imprisonment.

32. (1) The Central Bank shall have the power to examine every licensee as often as the Central Bank deems necessary. The Central Bank also shall have that power to conduct an examination of any holding company or affiliate of the licensee but only in so far as shall be necessary to examine the business, managerial and financial relationships between each

licensee and its affiliates and the effect of such relationships on the financial condition and operations of the licensee.

(2) The Central Bank shall also have the authority to obtain particulars of the names and addresses of the ultimate beneficial owners of a licensee in cases where the shareholders of record are corporations, trusts or other legal entities or organizations, or where the Central Bank has reason to believe that the shareholders of record are acting as nominees for or under the direction of any other person, notwithstanding anything to the contrary contained in any other law.

(3) The Central Bank may appoint examiners to carry out the performance of its functions under this section. An examiner making the examination of a licensee under subsection (1) above shall have the power to require the production of any books, records, accounts, writings and documents of any kind, as well as any data or information held, stored or transmitted by electronic means.

(4) The Central Bank may assess any licensee it examines under this section such fees and costs as may be necessary to defray the cost of examination; provided that, such fees and costs are determined on a fair and equitable basis taking into account the amount of assets and deposits, and the activities of the licensee being examined, and do not unreasonably discriminate between licensees of a similar character or among classes of similar licensees.

(5) Every licensee, holding company or affiliate of a licensee and every officer or agent of a licensee, its holding company or affiliate shall produce for the examination of any examiner appointed by the Central Bank such books, records, accounts, writings and documents of any kind, and supply the examiner with such other oral information as may be required by such examiner in the performance of the functions specified in subsection (1) and (3).

(6) Any licensee, holding company or affiliate of a licensee or any employee of such licensee, who contravenes the requirements of subsection (5), or who obstructs or impedes the performance by any examiner or officer appointed by Central Bank of the duties specified in subsection (1) and (3), shall be guilty of an offence and shall be liable on summary conviction thereof to a fine not exceeding fifty thousand dollars or to imprisonment for a term not exceeding one year, or to both such fine and imprisonment.

33. (1) The Central Bank may at any time and without notice appoint one or more of its examiners or other qualified persons to carry out a special examination under conditions of secrecy of the books and affairs of any licensee whether in Belize or elsewhere-

(a) where it has reason to believe that such licensee may be carrying on his business in a manner detrimental to the interests of his depositors, creditors or other customers, or is not operating in a sound financial condition or may have insufficient assets to cover his liabilities to the public or may be, either in Belize or elsewhere, contravening any of the provisions of this Act or regulations made thereunder; or

(b) if the licensee suspends payment to depositors or creditors or informs the Central Bank of his intention to do so; or

(c) if the Central Bank has reasonable grounds to believe that the licensee is involved in fraudulent or criminal activity, or is aiding or abetting others in committing fraudulent or criminal activity or is otherwise conducting his business in a manner detrimental to the public interest.

(2) Subject to subsection (3) of section 32, every licensee of whom an examination has been ordered under subsection (1) of this section shall produce to the examiners, or other

persons appointed under this section, at such times and in such places as the examiners or persons may specify, all records, books, accounts, minutes, cash, securities, vouchers and other documents and assets in whatever form in the possession or custody of the licensee or of which he is entitled to possession or custody relating to his assets, liabilities and business generally, and shall give, within such time as the examiners or persons may specify, such oral information concerning his business as may be required.

(3) As soon as may be practicable after the conclusion of an examination under this section, the examiners or persons appointed to carry out the examination shall submit a full report on such examination to the Central Bank.

(4) The Central Bank may order that all expenses of, and incidental to, a special examination under subsection (1) of this section shall be paid by the licensee examined.

(5) Every person who:-

(a) refuses or fails or neglects to produce or obstructs or willfully delays the production of any record, book, document, asset or information required under this section shall pay to the Central Bank, upon being called upon to do so, a penalty of two thousand dollars for each day of the failure to comply; or

(b) knowingly produces any record, book, document or information required under this section which is false or misleading in any material particular commits an offence and is liable on summary conviction to a fine not exceeding two thousand dollars or to imprisonment for a term not exceeding six months, or to both such fine and term of imprisonment.

(6) Any director, officer or employee of a licensee who knowingly or willfully supplies false or misleading information to the

persons authorized to carry out an examination in terms of this section commits an offence and is liable on summary conviction to a fine not exceeding ten thousand dollars or to imprisonment for a term not exceeding two years, or to both such fine and term of imprisonment.

PART VII

Secrecy and Disclosure

34. (1) No person shall disclose any information relating to the affairs of a licensee or any customer of a licensee which he has acquired in the performance of his duties or the exercise of his functions under this Act except where such information:-

(a) is lawfully required or permitted by any law or court of competent jurisdiction in Belize; or

(b) is in respect of the affairs of the licensee or a customer of the licensee with the authority of the licensee or the customer of the licensee which has been voluntarily given, as the case may be; or

(c) is disclosed by the Central Bank to a banking regulatory or supervisory authority outside of Belize where such information is considered necessary for that authority to exercise functions similar to those of the Central Bank pursuant to this Act including any information which will assist that foreign authority in its consolidated supervision of a banking group which controls or is affiliated with the licensee.

(2) [Repealed by Act 34 of 2002]

(3) Every person who contravenes subsection (1) of this section commits an offence and is liable on summary conviction to

a fine not exceeding five thousand dollars or to a term of imprisonment not exceeding six months, or to both such fine and term of imprisonment.

PART VIII

Exemption from Taxes, Duties and Exchange Control

35. (1) Notwithstanding anything contained in any other law-

(a) no income tax or any other direct or indirect tax or impost, shall be levied in Belize upon the profits or gains of a licensee, or upon any interest or dividends earned by a licensee in respect of the international banking business he carries on from within Belize;

(b) no income tax or any other direct or indirect tax or impost shall be levied or collected in Belize in respect of any dividends, interest or other returns from any shares, securities, deposits or other borrowings of a licensee or any assets or property managed by the licensee if the dividends, interest or other returns are in respect of shares, securities, deposits or borrowings or assets or property beneficially owned by a person who is not a resident of Belize.

(2) For the purpose of paragraph (b) of subsection (1) above, the onus of establishing ownership to the satisfaction of the Central Bank shall be on the licensee.

36. Bills of exchange and promissory notes payable on demand and any other document, instrument or certificate executed by or in connection with an international banking business whether within or outside of Belize shall be exempt from stamp duty.

37. The licensee and any international banking business conducted by and in accordance with a licence granted under this Act shall

be exempt from any currency and exchange control restrictions or regulations under the Exchange Control Regulations, 1976.

Part IX

Winding-up, Dissolution and Abandoned Property

38. (1) The provisions of Part VIII of the Banks and Financial Institutions Act shall apply mutatis mutandis to the winding-up and dissolution of licensees under this Act.

(2) The courts of Belize shall have jurisdiction in every such winding up and dissolution.

39. The provisions of Part IX of the Banks and Financial Institutions Act, regarding abandoned property, shall apply mutatis mutandis to the disposition of abandoned property by licensees under this Act.

Part X

Miscellaneous

40. Every person who commits an offence against this Act or any regulations made thereunder for which no penalty is specifically provided is liable on summary conviction to a fine not exceeding ten thousand dollars or to imprisonment for a term not exceeding two years or to both such fine and imprisonment, and, if the offence is a continuing offence, to a further fine not exceeding one thousand dollars for every day during which the offence continues.

41. (1) All fines, forfeitures and penalties recovered or incurred under this Act or regulations made thereunder shall be placed to the credit of the Central Bank.

(2) Where the Central Bank is empowered under this Act to impose a fine or other penalty for failure to comply with any

provisions of this Act or any regulations made thereunder, the Central Bank may, without prejudice to any other remedies available to it under the law, recover such fine or other penalty from the deposit maintained by the licensee with the Central Bank under section 21:01 of this Act.

42. No prosecution in respect of any offence committed under this Act or regulations made thereunder shall be instituted except by, or with the consent in writing of, the Central Bank or the Director of Public Prosecutions.

43. All prosecutions, actions, suits, or other proceedings brought for any offence, or for the recovery of any fines, penalties or forfeitures, under this Act or regulations made thereunder, shall be brought within five years next after the date of the offence committed or the cause of action accrued.

44. Nothing in this Act shall affect any civil remedy that any person may have against a licensee in respect of any matter.

45. (1) The Central Bank may, from time to time, with the approval of the Minister, issue such orders, directives, circulars or make such regulations prescribing all matters and things required or authorized by this Act to be prescribed or provided for, or which are necessary or convenient for the carrying out of, or the giving full effect to the provisions of, this Act.

(2) All regulations made under this Act shall be laid before the National Assembly as soon as may be after the making thereof and shall be subject to negative resolution.

46. Neither the Central Bank, nor any examiner or person responsible for the administration of this Act, shall be liable in damages for anything done or omitted to be done in the discharge or purported discharge of their respective functions under this Act or any regulations made thereunder, unless it is shown that the act or omission was in bad faith.

47. In the event that any act or step is required or permitted to be done under this Act, and no form is prescribed or procedure laid down in this Act or regulations made pursuant to this Act for doing the same, the Central Bank, after consultation with the Minister, may in response to application made to it, or on its own motion, give directions as to the manner in which the same may be done, and any act or step done or taken in accordance with its directions shall be a valid performance of such act or step.

48. (1) Every document filed with the Registrar of Companies or the Central Bank, and all records and accounts required to be kept under this Act shall be in the English language.

(2) Where a document is not in the English language it shall be accompanied by an authentic English translation and in the event of any conflict in meaning between the foreign language and the English version, the English version shall prevail.

49. This Act shall come into operation on such day as the Minister may, by Order published in the Gazette, appoint.

Cayman Islands

Background

The Cayman Islands were colonized from Jamaica by the British during the 18th and 19th centuries and were administered by Jamaica after 1863. In 1959, the islands became a territory within the Federation of the West Indies. When the Federation dissolved in 1962, the Cayman Islands chose to remain a British dependency.

Population

52,560 (July 2012 est.)

Capital

Georgetown

Official Language

English

Regulatory Authority

Cayman Islands Monetary Authority
PO Box 10052
80e Shedden Road
Elizabethan Square
Grand Cayman KY1-1001
Cayman Islands
Phone: +1 345 244 1606
Fax: +1 345 945 6132
Email: ContactBanking@cimoney.com.ky
Web: www.cimoney.com.ky

License Types

Both Domestic and Offshore Banks are regulated by the Banks and Trust Companies Law (2009 revision). Banks authorized to offer banking services locally are required to obtain a Class A licenses while offshore licenses are referred to as Class B. Restricted Class B licenses allow for banking services to be offered to a limited number of pre-identified customers only (suitable for "in-house" or "captive" banks").

Capital Requirements

The minimum capital requirements in Cayman Islands are surprisingly reasonable and license fees relatively high. Class A and Class B licensees are required to maintain a minimum paid up capital of C$ 400,000.00 and restricted Class B licensees a mere C$ 20,000.00. One US Dollar equals 0.82 Cayman Dollars.

Offshore Bank License Fees

Class B Application Fee	C$ 2,000.00
Class B License Issuing	C$ 70,000.00
Class B License Renewal Fee	C$ 60,000.00
Class B Restricted Application Fee	C$ 2,000.00
Class B Restricted License Issuing	C$ 45,000.00
Class B Restricted License Renewal	C$ 40,000.00

BANKS AND TRUST COMPANIES LAW (2009 Revision)

ARRANGEMENT OF SECTIONS

1. This Law may be cited as the Banks and Trust Companies Law (2009 Revision).

2. In this Law;

"authorised agent" means a person so designated by a bank or trust company under paragraph (b) of section 6(2);

"Authority" means the Cayman Islands Monetary Authority established under section 3(1) of the Monetary Authority Law (2004 Revision) and includes any employee of the Authority acting under the Authority's authorisation;

"bank" means a person carrying on banking business;

"banking business" means the business of receiving (other than from a bank or trust company) and holding on current, savings, deposit or other similar account money which is repayable by cheque or order and may be invested by way of advances to customers or otherwise;

"company" means a company incorporated under the laws of the Islands or under the laws of any other country or place;

"controlled subsidiary" means a trust company-

(a) that is incorporated in the Islands;

(b) that is a wholly owned subsidiary of a licensee under section 6(5)(c); and

(c) whose directors and senior officers are directors and senior officers of the licensee or are otherwise persons approved by the Authority as fit and proper persons to be directors and senior officers of licensees holding licences for trust business under section 6(5).

"Court" means the Grand Court;

"debt" has the meaning assigned to that expression in section 2 of the Mutual Funds Law (2009 Revision);

"Governor" means the Governor in Cabinet;

"licence" means a licence granted under section 6;

"licensee" means a person holding a licence under this Law;

"net worth" means excess assets over liabilities as presented under applicable generally accepted accounting principles subject to adjustment for non-admitted assets as determined by the Authority;

"trust business" means the business of acting as trustee, executor or administrator; and

"trust company" means a company carrying on trust business.

3. In determining for the purposes of this Law whether a person is a fit and proper person, regard shall be had to all circumstances, including that person's -

(a) honesty, integrity and reputation;

(b) competence and capability; and

(c) financial soundness.

4. (1) This Law has effect in addition to and not in derogation of any other provisions having the force of law in the Islands.

(2) This Law does not apply to the Cayman Islands Civil Service Association Co-operative Credit Union Limited.

5. (1) No banking business may be transacted from within the Islands, whether or not such business is carried on in the Islands, except by a person who is in possession of a valid licence granted by the Authority authorising him to carry on such business.

(2) Subject to subsection (3) and to such other exemptions and conditions as may be prescribed by regulations made by the Governor under this subsection, no trust company may

carry on trust business from within the Islands, whether or not such business is carried on in the Islands, unless it is in possession of a valid licence granted by the Authority authorising it to carry on such business.

(3) A trust company that is a controlled subsidiary does not require a licence to carry on the business of issuing debt instruments or to carry on other trust business that is-

(a) connected with the trust business of the licensee by which the controlled subsidiary is owned; and

(b) within the scope of that licensee's Trust licence.

(4) Notwithstanding subsection (3), a controlled subsidiary to which that subsection refers shall register with the Authority; and, in order to be registered, such controlled subsidiary shall-

(a) at that time of registration and on or before the 31st day of January every year thereafter during the continuation of the registration, file with the Authority an annual declaration, in such form as the Authority may approve, declaring-

(i) the name of the controlled subsidiary;

(ii) the name of the licensee of which the controlled subsidiary is a subsidiary;

(iii) the names of the directors and senior officers of the controlled subsidiary; and

(iv) that the controlled subsidiary is a controlled subsidiary to which subsection (3) applies; and

(b) at the time of registration and on or before the 31st day of January every year thereafter during the continuation of the registration, pay to the Government the prescribed fee.

(5) A controlled subsidiary that is registered under subsection (4) may, on payment of the prescribed fee, act as a trustee of a trust that is registered as a mutual fund under the Mutual Funds Law (2009 Revision) without being licensed as a mutual fund administrator under that Law, if the licensee by which the controlled subsidiary is owned is itself licensed under that Law to administer such trust.

(6) Whoever contravenes this section or any regulations made under subsection (2) is guilty of an offence and liable on summary conviction to a fine of ten thousand dollars and to imprisonment for one year, and in the case of a continuing offence to a fine of one thousand dollars for each day during which the offence continues.

6. (1) Any person desirous of carrying on banking business and any company desirous of carrying on trust business from within the Islands shall make application to the Authority for the grant of a licence. Every such application shall be in writing and shall be sent to the Authority accompanied by such information and particulars and details as may be prescribed together with the prescribed application fee (which the Authority shall forward to the Financial Secretary for the benefit of the revenue and which shall be refunded if the licence is granted), and the Authority may, if satisfied that the carrying on of such business will not be against the public interest, grant a licence to such person or company subject to such terms and conditions, if any, as the Authority may deem necessary.

(2) A licence shall not be granted to a bank or trust company unless it has-

(a) a place of business in the Islands, approved by the Authority, which will be its principal office in the Islands; and

(b) two individuals or a body corporate, approved by the Authority, resident or incorporated in the Islands to be its agent in the Islands.

(3) Where, in accordance with paragraph (b) of subsection (2), a licensee has appointed two individuals in the Islands to act as its agent in the Islands, the licensee may appoint them to act either separately or jointly.

(4) A licensee shall not-

(a) cease to have a principal office in the Islands;

(b) change its principal office in the Islands without the prior approval of the Authority;

(c) cease to have an authorised agent under paragraph (b) of subsection (2), or

(d) change its agent (or, where the licensee has appointed two individuals to be its agent, either of them) without the prior approval of the Authority.

(5) Licences granted under subsection (1) shall be granted either for carrying on of-

(a) banking business within and outside the Islands but subject to such conditions as may be imposed by the Authority, known as "A" licences;

(b) banking business with the restrictions on that business mentioned in subsection (6), known as "B" licences;

(c) trust business within and outside of the Islands but subject to such conditions as may be imposed by the Authority, known as Trust licences;

(d) banking business with the restrictions on that business mentioned in subsection (6), and incorporating a further restriction that the licensee shall not receive or solicit funds by way of trade or business from persons other than those listed in any undertaking accompanying the application for the licence, known as Restricted "B" licences;

(e) trust business with the restriction that the licensee shall not undertake trust business for persons other than those listed in any undertaking accompanying the application for the licence, known as Restricted Trust licences; or

(f) trust business under a Trust licence to a licensee which is a wholly-owned subsidiary of another licensee and where the sole purpose of that subsidiary is to act as its nominee, known as Nominee (Trust) licences. Any conditions imposed pursuant to this subsection may, at any time, be varied or revoked by the Authority.

(6) The holder of a "B" licence shall not-

(a) take deposits from any person resident in the Islands, other than another licensee, or an exempted or an ordinary non-resident company which is not carrying on business in the Islands;

(b) invest in any asset which represents a claim on any person resident in the Islands, except a claim resulting from-

(i) a loan to an exempted or an ordinary non-resident company not carrying on business in the Islands;

(ii) a loan by way of mortgage to a member of its staff or to a person possessing or being deemed to possess Caymanian status under the Immigration Law (2009 Revision) for the purchase or construction of a residence in the Islands to be owner-occupied;

(iii) a transaction with another licensee; or

(iv) the purchase of bonds or other securities issued by the Government, a body incorporated by statute, or a company in which the Government is the sole or majority beneficial owner; or

(c) without the written approval of the Authority, carry on any business in the Islands other than one for which the "B" licence has been obtained, and, without prejudice to the foregoing restrictions, a holder of a "B" licence which is not a subsidiary or branch of a bank licensed in a country or territory outside the Islands, shall not after the 26th April, 2003 carry on business in the Islands unless it has such resources (including staff and facilities) and such books and records as the Authority considers appropriate having regard to the nature and scale of the business.

(7) Every person to whom a licence is first granted shall, at the date of such grant, pay the prescribed fee to the Financial Secretary for the benefit of the revenue.

(8) Every holder of a licence shall, on or before every 15th day of January after the first grant of the licence, pay the prescribed annual fee to the Financial Secretary for the benefit of the revenue: Provided that, unless the Authority waives the same, there shall be payable to the Financial Secretary for the benefit of the revenue by a licensee who fails to pay the prescribed annual fee by that date a surcharge not exceeding one-twelfth of that fee for every month or part of a month that the fee is not paid.

(9) Without prejudice to the foregoing provisions of this section, if the annual fee referred to in subsection (8) is not paid on or before every 15th day of January after the first grant of the licence, the unpaid annual fee may be sued for by the Crown by action as a civil debt and the Crown may require, and the

court may order, the payment of any penalties accrued in respect of the late payment of the fee.

(10) Whenever it is considered to be in the public interest, the Authority may refuse to grant a licence.

(11) The Authority shall refuse to grant a licence if the Authority is of the opinion that the business to which the application relates would not be carried on by persons who are fit and proper persons to be directors or, as the case may be, managers or officers.

(12) For the purposes of subsection (2)(a)-

"place of business", with reference to any bank applying for the grant of a "B" licence (other than a subsidiary or branch of a bank licensed in a country or territory outside the Islands), means having such resources (including staff and facilities) and such books and records as the Authority considers appropriate having regard to the nature and scale of the business.

(13) In subsection (9)-

"court" means the Grand Court or a court of summary jurisdiction, as the case may be.

7. (1) No shares in a company which is a licensee under this Law shall be issued, and no issued shares shall be transferred or disposed of in any manner, without the prior approval of the Authority.

(2) The Authority may exempt from the provisions of subsection (1) a licensee whose shares are publicly traded on a stock exchange recognised by the Authority, and any such exemption-

(a) shall be subject to a condition that the licensee shall, as soon as reasonably practicable, notify the Authority of-

(i) any change in control of the licensee;

(ii) the acquisition by any person or group of persons of shares representing more than ten per cent of the licensee's issued share capital or total voting rights; or

(iii) the acquisition by any person or group of persons of shares representing more than ten per cent of the issued share capital or total voting rights of the licensee's parent company.

(b) shall be subject to a condition that the licensee shall, as soon as reasonably practicable, provide such information to the Authority, and within such period of time, as the Authority may require for the purpose of enabling an assessment as to whether persons acquiring control or ownership of the licensee in the circumstances set out in paragraph (a) are fit and proper persons to have such control or ownership; and

(c) shall be subject to such terms and other conditions as the Authority may deem necessary.

(3) In subsection (1) the reference to shares being transferred or disposed of includes not only the transfer or disposal of the legal interest in the shares but also the transfer or disposal of any beneficial interest in the shares.

8. (1) Except in the case of a Restricted "B" licence, or a Restricted Trust licence, or a Nominee (Trust) licence, a licence shall not be granted to a bank or trust company unless it has a net worth of not less than four hundred thousand dollars or its equivalent in other currencies, or such greater sum as may be determined by the Authority.

(2) A Restricted "B" licence or a Restricted Trust licence shall not be granted to a bank or trust company unless it has a net worth of not less than twenty thousand dollars or its equivalent in other currencies, or such greater sum as may be determined by the Authority.

(3) A Nominee (Trust) licence shall not be granted to a trust company unless such trust company furnishes a guarantee from the licensee of which it is a wholly-owned subsidiary for liabilities of up to two hundred thousand dollars or its equivalent in other currencies, or such greater sum as may be determined by the Authority.

(4) When the Authority has reasonable cause to believe that there are grounds for doing so, the Authority may require a licensee to increase its net worth by increasing its paid-up capital to such greater sum as the Authority may determine for the nature of the banking business or trust business, current or proposed.

(5) A licensee shall at all times maintain the net worth required by this section unless exempted by the Authority.

9. (1) The Authority may, by notice in writing, require a licensee to maintain such portion of its issued capital, in cash or cash equivalent instruments, in such amounts and in such manner, as the Authority considers appropriate, having regard to the risks arising from the activities of the licensee and such other factors as the Authority considers relevant.

(2) In this section-

"cash equivalent instruments" means a highly liquid security with a known market value and a maturity, when acquired, of less than three months.

10. (1) A licensee holding a licence for the carrying on of banking business and incorporated under the Companies Law (2007 Revision) shall not, at any time, have a capital adequacy ratio of less than ten per cent (or such other percentage as may be determined by the Authority from time to time) as calculated in accordance with such form, content and manner as may be prescribed.

(2) The Authority may, if it considers it to be appropriate in the particular circumstances of a licensee incorporated under the Companies Law (2007 Revision) having regard to the risks arising from the activities of the licensee and such other factors as the Authority considers relevant, vary the capital adequacy ratio applicable to that licensee.

(3) A licensee which fails to comply with the requirements of this section may, for the purposes of section 18, be treated by the Authority as carrying on business in a manner detrimental to the public interest, the interest of its depositors or other creditors.

11. (1) Except with the approval of the Authority, no person, other than a licensee, shall-

(a) use or continue to use the words "bank", "trust", "trust company", "trust corporation", "savings" or "savings and loan" or any of their derivatives, either in English or in any other language, in the description or title under which such person is carrying on business from within the Islands, whether or not such business is carried on in the Islands;

(b) make or continue to make any representation in any billhead, letter, letterhead, circular, paper, notice, advertisement or in any other manner whatsoever that such person is carrying on banking business or trust business; or

(c) in any manner whatsoever solicit or receive deposits from the public.

(2) Except with the approval of the Authority, no company shall be registered, or continue to be registered, by a name which contains the words "bank", "trust", "trust company", trust corporation", "savings" or "savings and loan" or any of their derivatives, either in English or in any other language, in the

description or title under which such company is carrying on business from within the Islands, whether or not such business is carried on in the Islands.

(3) Before giving its approval under subsection (1) or (2), the Authority may require of any person such references and such information and particulars as may be prescribed.

(4) Whenever the Authority considers it to be in the public interest, the Authority may withdraw any approval given under subsection (1).

(5) The Authority may refuse to grant a licence to a bank or trust company or, if such bank or trust company is already in possession of a licence, the Authority may revoke such licence if, in the Authority's opinion, such bank or trust company is carrying on or intending to carry on banking or trust business, as the case may be, under a name which-

(a) is identical with that of any company, firm or business house, whether within the Islands or not, or which so nearly resembles that name as to be calculated to deceive;

(b) is calculated to suggest, falsely, the patronage of or connection with some person or authority, whether within the Islands or not; or

(c) is calculated to suggest, falsely, that such bank or trust company has a special status in relation to or derived from the Government, has the official backing of or acts on behalf of the Government, of any department, branch, agency or organ of Government, or of any officer thereof, or is recognised in the Islands as a national or central bank or trust company.

(6) Whoever contravenes this section is guilty of an offence and liable on summary conviction to a fine of ten thousand

dollars and to imprisonment for one year and, in the case of a continuing offence, to a fine of one thousand dollars for each day during which the offence continues.

12. (1) Every licensee incorporated under the Companies Law (2007 Revision) shall have its accounts audited annually or at such other times as the Authority may require by an auditor, who shall be a chartered accountant, certified public accountant or some other professionally qualified accountant, approved by the Authority.

(2) The audited accounts shall be forwarded to the Authority within three months of the end of the financial year of the licensee, unless prior written approval for an extension has been granted by the Authority.

(3) Every licensee not incorporated under the Companies Law (2007 Revision) shall provide a copy of the audited annual accounts of its head office to the Authority within three months of the end of the financial year of such parent company, unless prior approval for an extension has been granted by the Authority.

(4) When a licensee incorporated under the Companies Law (2007 Revision) changes its auditor, the Authority may require the former auditor to explain the circumstances responsible for such change.

13. (1) If an auditor, in the course of carrying out an audit of the accounts of a licensee, obtains information or suspects that the licensee is-

(a) unable or likely to become unable to meet its obligations as they fall due;

(b) carrying on or attempting to carry on business or is winding up its business voluntarily in a manner that is prejudicial to its investors or creditors;

(c) carrying on or attempting to carry on business without keeping any or sufficient accounting records to allow its accounts to be properly audited;

(d) carrying on or attempting to carry on business in a fraudulent or criminal manner; or

(e) carrying on or attempting to carry on business without compliance with-

(i) this Law or any regulations made hereunder;

(ii) the Monetary Authority Law (2008 Revision);

(iii) the Money Laundering Regulations (2009 Revision); or

(iv) a condition of the licence, the auditor shall immediately give the Authority written notice of his information or suspicion and, in the case of suspicion, his reason for that suspicion.

(2) Without prejudice to subsection (8), if it appears to the Authority that an auditor has failed to comply with subsection (1), the Authority may disqualify him from being an auditor of a licensee; but the Authority may remove any disqualification imposed under this subsection if satisfied that the person in question will in future comply with subsection (1).

(3) A licensee shall not appoint as an auditor a person disqualified under subsection (2).

(4) Where the Authority has granted approval of an auditor under this Law, the approval may be revoked by the Authority if the Authority is of the opinion that the auditor is not sufficiently competent to carry out an audit of the accounts of a licensee or that, in all the circumstances, the auditor is incapable of carrying out the audit objectively.

(5) No person carrying out or charged with the carrying out of any duty, obligation or function under this section shall incur civil liability to any other person for anything done or omitted to be done in respect of the discharge or purported discharge of that duty or function unless it is shown that the act or omission was in bad faith.

(6) A reference in this section to an auditor carrying out an audit of the accounts of a licensee includes an auditor who was engaged to carry out such an audit or who was in the course of carrying out such an audit but resigned before carrying out or completing the audit or whose contract to carry out or complete the audit was otherwise terminated.

(7) Nothing in subsection (1) shall impose on an auditor carrying out an audit of the accounts of a licensee an obligation to do anything that he would not otherwise be required to do in accordance with generally accepted auditing standards, other than the obligation to provide notice and reasons to the Authority.

(8) Whoever contravenes subsection (1) is guilty of an offence and liable on summary conviction to a fine of twenty thousand dollars.

14. (1) A licensee incorporated under the Companies Law (2007 Revision) holding a licence for the carrying on of banking business shall not acquire or hold a beneficial interest in an entity, whether directly or indirectly, so that the value of the interest at any time exceeds twenty per cent of the net worth of the licensee-

(a) except with the prior written approval of the Authority; or

(b) except insofar as may be necessary with respect to any interest acquired by the licensee in satisfaction of debts due to it.

(2) A licensee incorporated under the Companies Law (2007 Revision) holding a licence for the carrying on of banking business shall not acquire or hold a beneficial interest in an entity, whether directly or indirectly, so that the value of the interest at any time exceeds twenty per cent of the net worth of the licensee-

(a) except with the prior written approval of the Authority; or

(b) except insofar as may be necessary with respect to any interest acquired by the licensee in satisfaction of debts due to it, but any such interest acquired in satisfaction of debts shall be disposed of within a period not exceeding five years unless permission to extend such period has been given by the Authority.

(3) Subject to subsections (4) and (5), a licensee holding a licence for the carrying on of banking business shall not purchase, acquire or lease real estate unless the Authority has given prior written approval or-

(a) such real estate is necessary for the purpose of conducting its business or providing housing or amenities for its staff, having regard to any reasonable requirements for future expansion of its business or staff; and;

(b) the market value of the real estate does not exceed twenty per cent of the net worth of the licensee, or such other sum as to the Authority may seem appropriate to a maximum of fifty per cent of the net worth of the licensee.

(4) Where the licensee exercises its legal right in respect of any property which is the security for any debt, the licensee may acquire such property, but in that case the property shall not be retained for a period in excess of five years without the permission of the Authority.

(5) Nothing in this section shall require a licensee-

(a) which holds a licence for the carrying on of banking business; and

(b) which immediately before the 14th November, 2006 owns or leases real estate the market value of which exceeds fifty per cent of the net worth of the licensee, to comply with subsection (3)(b) before the expiry of a period of five years commencing with that date.

(6) A contract, transaction, obligation or instrument entered into by any person shall not be rendered unenforceable merely because it is entered into in connection with banking business carried on by that person in contravention of this section.

15. (1) A licensee holding a Trust Licence shall obtain and maintain adequate professional indemnity insurance, or have in place other appropriate arrangements to cover risks, in respect of its trust business, and such insurance or arrangements shall be subject to review by the Authority.

(2) In conducting reviews under subsection (1), the Authority shall have regard to relevant factors including the nature and scope of the trust business, the financial position and reputation of the licensee and its parent company, and the existence of any group coverage or financial commitment made by the parent company or other appropriate body to cover risks in respect of the licensee's trust business.

16. (1) A licensee shall at no time have less than two directors.

(2) Unless exempted from such a requirement by the Authority, a licensee shall, before the appointment of a director or other senior officer, apply to the Authority for its written approval of such appointment.

(3) The Authority shall refuse to grant approval under subsection (2) if the Authority is of the opinion that the director or other senior officer to whom the application relates is not a fit and proper person to be such director or, as the case may be, senior officer.

(4) Approval granted under subsection (2)-

(a) ipso facto lapses if the director or senior officer becomes bankrupt or is convicted of an offence involving dishonesty; and

(b) may be revoked by the Authority.

(5) Approval granted under paragraph (b) of section 6(2) may be revoked by the Authority.

17. (1) It is the duty of the Authority-

(a) to maintain a general review of banking practice in the Islands;

(b) whenever it thinks fit, to examine, by way of the receipt of regular returns or in such other manner as it thinks necessary, the affairs or business of any licensee carrying on business in or from within the Islands for the purpose of satisfying itself that this Law is being complied with and that the licensee is in a sound financial position and, whenever it thinks fit, to report to the Governor the results of every such examination;

(c) to assist in the investigation of any offence against the laws of the Islands which it has reasonable grounds to believe has or may have been committed by a licensee or by any of its directors or officers in their capacity as such; and

(d) to examine accounts and audited annual accounts forwarded to it under section 10 and to report on them to the Governor whenever it thinks fit.

(2) The Authority may-

(a) examine and make decisions with respect to applications for licences;

(b) examine all proposals and make decisions in respect of the exercise of its powers under sections 18, 19 and 20; and

(c) take all necessary action, including originating applications to the Grand Court, to ensure the proper and just implementation of every provision of this Law.

(3) In the performance of its functions under this Law, the Authority is entitled at all reasonable times-

(a) to have access to such books, records, vouchers, documents,cash and securities of any licensee; and

(b) to request any information, matter or thing from any person who it has reasonable grounds to believe is carrying on banking or trust business in the Islands in contravention of section 5(1) or (2), as the Authority may reasonably require for the purpose of enabling it to perform its functions under this Law.

(4) The Authority may, in writing, authorise any other person to assist the Authority in the performance of its functions under this Law, and the Authority may make provision for the payment of such person's remuneration and expenses whether or not the performance of the function has been completed.

(5) If it appears to it that there is reasonable ground for suspecting that an offence against this Law has been or is being committed by any person, the Authority may, with the approval of the Court, take such action as it considers necessary, in the interests of the depositors or of the

beneficiaries of any trust, or other creditors of that person, to preserve any assets held by that person.

18. (1) Whenever the Authority is of the opinion that-

(a) a licensee is or appears likely to become unable to meet its obligations as they fall due;

(b) a licensee is carrying on business in a manner detrimental to the public interest, the interest of its depositors or of the beneficiaries of any trust, or other creditors;

(c) a licensee has contravened this Law;

(d) a licensee has failed to comply with a condition of its licence;

(e) the direction and management of a licensee's business has not been conducted in a fit and proper manner;

(f) a person holding a position as a director, manager or officer of a licensee's business is not a fit and proper person to hold the respective position; or

(g) a person acquiring control or ownership of a licensee in the circumstances set out in paragraph (a) of section 7(2) is not a fit and proper person to have such control or ownership, the Authority may forthwith do any of the following-

(i) revoke the licence;

(ii) impose conditions, or further conditions, as the case may be, upon the licence and may amend or revoke any such condition;

(iii) require the substitution of any director or officer of the licensee;

(iv) at the expense of the licensee, appoint a person to advise the licensee on the proper conduct of its affairs and to report to the Authority thereon within three months of the date of his appointment;

(v) at the expense of the licensee, appoint a person to assume control of the licensee's affairs who shall, mutatis mutandi, have all the powers of a person appointed as a receiver or manager of a business appointed under section 18 of the Bankruptcy Law (1997 Revision); and Banks And Trust Companies Law (2009 Revision)

(vi) require such action to be taken by the licensee as the Authority considers necessary.

(2) Notwithstanding section 25(1), a licensee may, within seven days of the decision, apply to the Authority for a reconsideration of its decision to revoke a licence under paragraph (i) of subsection (1).

(3) A person appointed under subparagraph (iv) or (v) of subsection (1) or whose appointment has been extended under paragraph (b) of subsection (4) shall from time to time at his discretion and in any case within three months of the date of his appointment or of the extension of his appointment (as the case may be), prepare and furnish a report to the Authority of the affairs of the licensee and of his recommendations thereon.

(4) On receipt of a report under subsection (3), the Authority may-

(a) revoke the appointment of the person appointed under subparagraph (iv) or (v) of subsection (1);

(b) extend the period of his appointment;

(c) subject to such conditions as the Authority may impose, allow the licensee to reorganise its affairs in a manner approved by the Authority; or

(d) revoke the licence and apply to the Court for an order that the licensee be forthwith wound up by that Court in which case the provisions of the Companies Law (2007 Revision) relating to the winding up of a company by that Court shall, mutatis mutandis, apply.

(5) Notwithstanding any provisions herein, the Authority may revoke a licence if the licensee-

(a) has ceased to carry on banking business or trust business; or

(b) goes into liquidation or is wound up or otherwise dissolved.

(6) Whenever the Authority revokes a licence under sub-paragraph (i) of subsection (1), paragraph (d) of subsection (4) or subsection (5) the Authority shall cause notice of such revocation to be gazetted, and may also cause such notice to be published (whether within the Islands or elsewhere) in such newspaper or other publication as the Authority may consider necessary in the circumstances.

19. (1) The Authority may, in any case in which a licensee, or a person who has at any time been a licensee, is being wound up voluntarily, apply to the Court if the Authority considers that the winding up is not being conducted in the best interests of its depositors, the beneficiaries of any trust, or other creditors, and the Court shall make such order as it shall consider appropriate.

(2) Where a petition for the winding up of a licensee, or a person who has at any time been a licensee, is presented by a person other than the Authority, the Authority shall be

served with a copy of the petition by the petitioner and may appear at the hearing of the petition, and the provisions of subsections (3) and (4) shall apply.

(3) A document which relates to a petition for winding up and which is required to be sent to a licensee or former licensee or any of their respective depositors, beneficiaries, or other creditors, shall, in addition, be sent to the Authority.

(4) A person appointed for the purpose by the Authority may-

(a) attend a meeting of creditors of a licensee or former licensee;

(b) attend a meeting of a committee established to discuss a compromise or arrangement; and

(c) make representations as to any matter for decision at any such meeting.

20. (1) A licensee which has ceased to carry on the business in respect of which the licence was granted may apply to the Authority to surrender its licence if it-

(a) has ceased to carry on such business, and produces evidence that it has repaid all deposits held by it and has transferred all trust assets held or administered by it: or

(b) is being wound up voluntarily and produces evidence that it is solvent and able forthwith to repay all deposits held by it and all its other creditors and has transferred all trust assets held or administered by it, and the Authority may thereupon approve the surrender.

(2) In the case of an application under paragraph (b) of subsection (1) the Authority may apply to the Court for the licensee to be wound up either by that Court or subject to its supervision, and on the making of such an order the

provisions of the Companies Law (2007 Revision) relating to the winding up of a company by or subject to the supervision of that Court shall, mutatis mutandis, apply.

21. The Chief Justice may make rules governing the procedure in relation to applications to the Court under section 17(5), paragraph (d) of section 18(4), section 19 and section 20(2).

22. (1) If a Justice of the Peace is satisfied by information on oath given by the Authority or by a person authorised under section 17(4) to assist him either that-

(a) there is reasonable ground for suspecting that an offence against this Law has been or is being committed and that evidence of the commission of the offence is to be found at any premises specified in the information, or in any vehicle, vessel or aircraft so specified; or

(b) any books, records, vouchers, documents, cash or securities which ought to have been produced under section 17(3) and have not been produced are to be found at any such premises or in any such vehicle, vessel or aircraft, he may grant a search warrant authorising the Authority or such person authorised under section 17(4) or any constable of the rank of Inspector or above, together with any other person named in the warrant and any other constables to enter the premises specified in the information or, as the case may be, any premises upon which the vehicle, vessel or aircraft so specified may be, at any time within one month from the date of the warrant, and to search such premises or, as the case may be, such vehicle, vessel or aircraft.

(2) The person authorised by any such warrant to search any premises or any vehicle, vessel or aircraft may search every person who is found in or whom he has reasonable grounds

to believe to have recently left or to be about to enter those premises or that vehicle, vessel or aircraft, as the case may be, and may seize any books, records, vouchers, documents, cash or securities found in the possession of any such person or in such premises or in such vehicle, vessel or aircraft which he has reasonable grounds for believing ought to have been produced under section 17(3): Provided that no female shall, in pursuance of any warrant issued under this subsection, be searched except by a female.

(3) Where under this section a person has any power to enter any premises he may use such force as is reasonably necessary for the purpose of exercising that power.

(4) Whoever obstructs the Authority or any other person in the exercise of any powers conferred on it or him under this section is guilty of an offence and liable on summary conviction to a fine of ten thousand dollars and to imprisonment for one year.

23. Any licensee or any director or officer of a licensee who knowingly or wilfully supplies false or misleading information to the Authority is guilty of an offence and liable on summary conviction to a fine of ten thousand dollars and to imprisonment for one year.

24. Whoever contravenes any provision or requirement of this Law for which no offence is specifically created is guilty of an offence and liable on summary conviction to a fine of ten thousand dollars and to imprisonment for one year.

25. (1) An appeal lies to the Court from any decision of the Authority-

(a) revoking a licence under section 11(5), paragraph (i) of section 18(1), or section 18(4) or (5);

(b) withdrawing any approval under section 11(4); or

(c) requiring a licensee to take certain steps which the Authority may specify under section 18.

(2) An appeal against the decision of the Authority shall be on motion. The appellant within twenty-one days after the day on which the Authority has given its decision shall serve a notice in writing signed by the appellant or his attorney-at-law on the Authority of his intention to appeal and of the general ground of his appeal: Provided that any person aggrieved by a decision of the Authority may, upon notice to the Authority, apply to the Court for leave to extend the time within which the notice of appeal prescribed by this section may be served and the Court upon hearing of such application may extend the time prescribed by this section as it deems fit.

(3) The Authority shall, upon receiving the notice of appeal, transmit to the Clerk of the Court without delay a copy of the decision and all papers relating to the appeal: Provided that the Authority is not compelled to disclose any information if it is considered that the public interest would suffer by such disclosure.

(4) The Clerk of the Court shall set the appeal down for argument on such day, and shall cause notice of the same to be published in such manner, as the Court may direct.

(5) At the hearing of the appeal the appellant shall, before going into the case, state all the grounds of appeal on which he intends to rely and shall not, unless by leave of the Court, go into any matters not raised by such statements.

(6) The Court may adjourn the hearing of an appeal and may, upon the hearing thereof confirm, reverse, vary or modify the decision of the Authority or remit the matter with the opinion of the Court thereon to the Authority.

(7) An appeal against a decision of the Authority shall not have the effect of suspending the execution of such decision.

26. The Authority shall not be liable in damages for anything done or omitted in the discharge or purported discharge of their respective functions under this Law unless it is shown that the act or omission was in bad faith.

27. The Governor may make regulations-

    (a) to prescribe the information, particulars and references which may be prescribed under section 6(1) or 11(3);

    (b) to control the form of advertising by licensees;

    (c) to prescribe fees payable under this Law; and

    (d) generally for carrying this Law into effect.

Montserrat

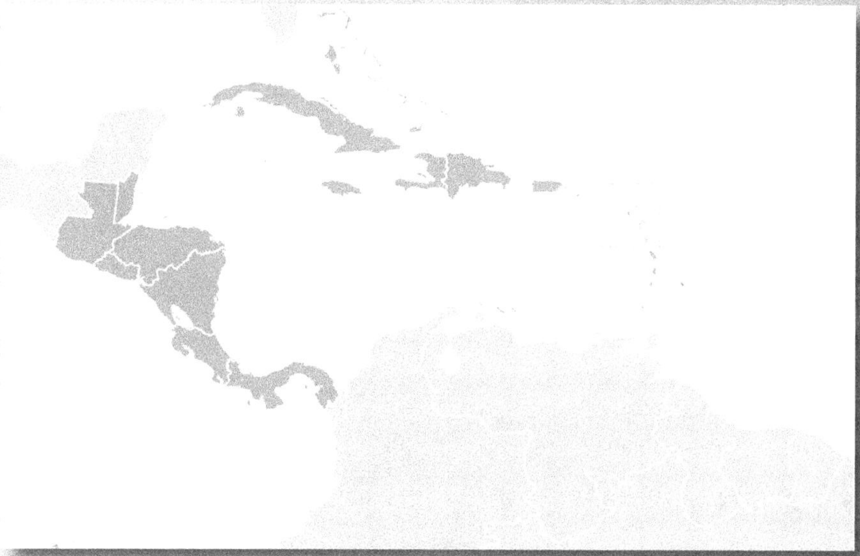

Background

English and Irish colonists from St. Kitts first settled on Montserrat in 1632; the first African slaves arrived three decades later. The British and French fought for possession of the island for most of the 18th century, but it finally was confirmed as a British possession in 1783. The island's sugar plantation economy was converted to small farm landholdings in the mid-19th century. Much of this island was devastated and two-thirds of the population fled abroad because of the eruption of the Soufriere Hills Volcano that began on 18 July 1995.

Population

5,164 (July 2012 est.)

Capital

Plymoth (official), Brades (de facto)

Official Language

English

Regulatory Authority

Financial Services Commission
Phoenix House
P.O. Box 188
Brades - Montserrat
Tel: +1 664 491 6887/8
Fax: +1 664 491 9888
Email: fscmrat@candw.ms
Web: www.fscmontserrat.org

License Types

Domestic Banks are regulated by the Banking Act (as revised 2008) and Offshore Banks by the International Banking and Trust Companies Act 2008. No reference is made to different classes of International Licenses.

Capital Requirements

The minimum paid up capital requirement for an International Banking License is USD 1,000,000.00.

Offshore Bank License Fees

Non-refundable Application Fee	USD 3,000.00
Annual License Fee	USD 19,000.00

CHAPTER 11.04
INTERNATIONAL BANKING AND TRUST COMPANIES

ARRANGEMENT OF SECTIONS

PART 1
PRELIMINARY PROVISIONS

PART 2
INTERNATIONAL BANKING BUSINESS

PART 3
TRUST BUSINESS

15. Application for licence
16. Issuance of licence
17. Class and extension of licence
18. Maintenance of capital
19. Interpretation

Revocation, Suspension and Surrender of Licence and Variation of Terms of Licence

20. Revocation or suspension of licence
21. Appointment of administrator by the Court
22. Surrender of licence
23. Variation of terms or conditions of licence

Principal Office and Authorised Agent

24. Principal office and authorised agent
25. Operation outside Montserrat

Restrictions on and Change of Names

26. Restrictions on use of certain terms
27. Change of name

Transfer of Shares and Appointment of Directors

28. Transfer of shares
29. Number and appointment of directors
30. Exemption for domestic bank

Obligations Of Licensee

31. Annual fee
32. Display of licence
33. Returns and accounts

PART 1

PRELIMINARY PROVISIONS

Short Title

1. This Act may be cited as the International Banking and Trust Companies Act.

Interpretation

2. (1) In this Act;

"attorney-at-law" means an attorney admitted before the Eastern Caribbean Supreme Court to practice in Montserrat;

"auditor" means a person is in good standing as a member of an association of chartered or public accountants or other similar body approved by the Commission as a reputable auditing association;

"authorised agent" means a person licenced under the Company Management Act (Cap. 11.26) or holding a general trust licence under this Act.

"bank" means a person carrying on banking business;

"banking business" means;

(a) the business of receiving funds through the acceptance of money deposits payable on demand or after a fixed period or after notice or any similar operation; through the frequent sale or placement of bonds, certificates, notes or other securities; and the use of such funds either in whole or in part for loans or investment for the account and the risk of the person doing such business; and

(b) any other activity prescribed by the Commission as constituting customary banking practice that a bank engaged in activities described in paragraph (a) may additionally be authorised to do;

"board" means a board of directors or other body responsible for the management of a licensee;

"company" means a company incorporated or continued under the Companies Act (Cap.11.12);

"Commission" means the Financial Services Commission as appointed under the Financial Services Commission Act (Cap. 11.02);

"Commissioner" means the person appointed under section 8 of the Financial Services Commission Act (Cap. 11.02);

"Court" means the High Court;

"dollar" or "$" means a dollar in the currency of the United States of America;

"domestic bank" means a person holding a licence under the Banking Act (Cap. 11.03) or any succeeding legislation;

"financial institution" means a person licensed to undertake banking business;

"foreign company" means a person from outside Montserrat that is registered under Division D of Part III of the Companies Act (Cap.11.02);

"foreign regulatory authority" means an authority in a jurisdiction outside Montserrat which exercises functions corresponding or similar to those exercised by;

(a) the Commission appointed under the Financial Services Commission Act. (Cap.11.02);

(b) the Commission under this Act;

(c) the Commission under the Company Management Act, (Cap.11.26); or

(d) the Commission under the Insurance Act;

"international banking business" means banking business carried on in or from within Montserrat in a currency other than Eastern Caribbean dollars with a non-resident of Montserrat;

"international banking licence" means a licence issued under section 7;

"international business company" means a company incorporated or continued under the International Business Companies Act (Cap. 11.13);

"prescribed" means prescribed by regulations made by the Governor in Council under section 50;

"trust" means the legal relationship created when assets have been placed under the control of a person (a trustee) to be held for the benefit of another (the beneficiary) or for a specified purpose;

"trust business" means carrying on the business of acting as trustee of property;

"trust company licence" means a licence issued under section 16;

"unimpaired capital" means total equity capital in the most recent report plus any subordinated notes and debentures approved by the Commission as an addition to capital structure plus any valuation reserves created by charges to income reported on the most recent report.

(2) Subject to subsection (3), for the purposes of this Act, the following are regarded as non-residents of Montserrat;

(a) an international business company;

(b) a company or an LLC formed or continued under the Limited Liability Company Act (Cap. 11.04) that, at the relevant time does not engage in any revenue generating activities in Montserrat.

(3) An LLC or a company shall not be regarded as engaging in a revenue generating activity in Montserrat in respect of;

(a) any international banking business conducted with it by a person holding an international banking licence; or

(b) any activity which the Commission may prescribe as not being a revenue generating activity in Montserrat.

(4) A company, an international business company; or an LLC formed or continued under the Limited Liability Company Act, (Cap.11.04); that carries on banking business or trust business outside Montserrat carries on banking business or trust business, as the case may be, from within Montserrat.

3. (1) This Act applies, in respect to their international banking business, to a person, including a domestic bank, that conducts international banking business.

(2) A person, including a domestic bank, that holds an international banking licence;

(i) is exempt from the provisions of the Banking Act (Cap. 11.03) in respect of international banking business and 10 CAP. 11.04 International Banking and Trust Companies

(ii) is subject to the provisions of the Banking Act (Cap.11.03) in respect of banking business other than international banking business.

(3) This Act does not apply to the Caribbean Development Bank.

(4) A person holding an international banking licence or trust company licence, other than a domestic bank, does not require a licence under the Trades Licences Act (Cap.15.02), in respect of its international banking or trust business.

PART 2

INTERNATIONAL BANKING BUSINESS

Interpretation

4. In this Part;

"licence" means an international banking licence;

"licensee" means a person holding an international banking licence.

Licence required

5. (1) No person, including a domestic bank, shall carry on

international banking business unless they hold a licence that is not suspended under section 20.

(2) A person who contravenes subsection (1) commits an offence and is liable on summary conviction to a fine of $25,000, or to a term of imprisonment of 2 years or to both for each day that they contravene the subsection.

Application for licence

6. (1) A company or a foreign company may apply to the Commission for a licence.

(2) An application under subsection (1) must;

(a) contain the information and be in the form prescribed in the regulations to this Act; and

(b) be accompanied by the documentation and the fee prescribed in the regulations to this Act, and such other information and documentation that the Commission may deem necessary.

(3) In considering an application for a licence, the Commission may review and investigate the information provided for in regulation 2, but is not limited to the information contained in that regulation.

Issuance of licence

7. (1) If the Commission is satisfied;

(a) that an applicant is;

(i) fit and proper, in accordance with the criteria set out in regulation 3 of the regulations; and

(ii) qualified to carry on international banking business;

(b) that the persons having any share or other interest, whether legal or equitable, in the applicant and its directors and officers are fit and proper to have an interest in or be concerned with the management of a licensee, as the case may be;

(c) that the applicant intends, if issued with a licence, to commence international banking business within 12 months of receiving the banking licence;

(d) that the applicant satisfies the requirements of this Act in respect of the application and will, upon issuance of the licence, be in compliance with this Act in respect of licensing; and

(e) that issuing the licence is not against the public interest; it may issue a licence to the applicant upon payment of the prescribed fee and subject to such terms and conditions as it thinks fit.

(2) If the Commission is of the opinion that it would be undesirable in the public interest to grant the licence, it may refuse to grant the same and need not give any reason for so refusing, but shall still inform the applicant that it has refused to grant the licence.

(3) There is no appeal from the decision of the Commission in subsection (2).

Restrictions on business that may be carried on by licensee

8. (1) A licensee that is not a domestic bank may not;

(a) invest in any asset that represents a claim on any person resident in Montserrat except a claim resulting from;

(i) a transaction with another licensee, or a domestic bank;

(ii) the purchase of bonds or other securities issued by the Government, a statutory corporation or a company in which the Government is the sole or majority beneficial owner; and

(iii) the renting of property, maintenance of books and records and dealing with any other matter or person necessary to carrying out or done in relation to the carrying out of its business; or

(b) without the written approval of the Commission, carry on any international banking business other than that for which the licence has been issued.

(2) A licensee shall not directly or indirectly, without the written approval of the Commission, carry on business as set out in Schedule 3 of the regulations.

(3) A licensee that contravenes subsection (1) or (2) commits an offence and is liable on summary conviction to a fine of $25,000.

Maintenance of capital

9. (1) A licensee, other than a domestic bank, or a branch of a foreign bank, must ensure that its paid up share capital is maintained in an amount not less than $1,000,000, or the equivalent in another currency, or such greater sum as may be ordered under subsection (2).

(2) The Commission may order a licensee to increase its fully paid-up capital to such greater amount as it may determine having regard to the nature of the international banking business being, or sought to be, undertaken and to a capital adequacy ratio, as the Commissioner may from time to time determine.

(3) A company that contravenes subsection (1) commits an offence and is liable on summary conviction to a fine of $25,000 for each week that it contravenes the said subsection.

(4) Where an offence under this section is committed by a company, a director or officer of the company who knowingly authorised, permitted or acquiesced in the commission of the offence also commits an offence and is liable on summary conviction to a fine of $25,000, or to a term of imprisonment for 6 months or to both.

Maintenance of Reserve Fund

10. Every licensee shall maintain a reserve fund and shall out of its net profits of each year transfer to that fund a sum equal to not less than 20% of such profits whenever the amount of the reserve fund is less than 100% of the paid-up capital of the licensee.

Restrictions on distribution of dividends

11. No licensee shall declare, credit or pay any dividend or make any other transfer from profits whenever such declaration, credit, payment or transfer would result in an impairment of the shareholders equity of the licensee or the capital required under section 10.

Maintenance of liquidity

12. Every licensee shall maintain adequate liquidity by way of cash or marketable securities or call or time deposits of less than 12 months with a prime or other acceptable international bank amounting to at least 12% of the total assets or such other percentage as may from time to time be determined by the Commissioner.

PART 3

TRUST BUSINESS

Interpretation

13. In this Part;

"licence" means a trust company licence;

"licensee" means a person holding a trust company licence.

Licence required

14. (1) Subject to subsection (2), no person shall carry on trust business in or from within Montserrat unless he holds a licence that is not suspended under section 20.

(2) Subsection (1) does not apply to an attorney-at-law in so far as he is engaged in trust business that relates solely to the practice of law.

(3) A person who contravenes subsection (1) commits an offence and is liable on summary conviction to a fine of $25,000 or to a term of imprisonment of 2 years or to both for each day that he contravenes the said subsection.

Application for licence

15. (1) A company, a foreign company or, subject to section 17(2), an international business company may apply to the Commission for a licence.

(2) An application under subsection (1) must;

(a) contain the information and be in the form prescribed in the regulations to this Act; and

(b) be accompanied by the documentation and the nonrefundable fee prescribed in the regulations to this Act.

(3) In considering an application for a licence, the Commission may review and investigate the information provided for in regulation 2 of the regulations but is not limited to information contained in that regulation.

Issuance of licence

16. (1) If the Commission is satisfied;

(a) that an applicant is;

(i) a fit and proper person, in accordance with the criteria set out in regulation 3 of the regulations; and

(ii) is qualified to carry on trust business;

(b) that the persons having any share or other interest, whether legal or equitable, in the applicant and its directors and officers are fit and proper persons to have an interest in or be concerned with the management of a licensee, as the case may be;

(c) that the applicant intends, if issued with a licence, to commence carrying on trust business in or from within Montserrat within 12 months of receiving the licence;

(d) that the applicant satisfies the requirements of this Act in respect of the application and will, upon issuance of the licence, be in compliance with this Act in respect of licensing; and

(e) that issuing the licence is not against the public interest; it may issue a licence to the applicant subject to such terms and conditions as it thinks fit.

(2) If the Commission is of the opinion that it would be undesirable in the public interest to grant the licence, it may refuse to grant the same and need not give any reason for so refusing but shall inform the applicant that it has refused to grant the licence.

(3) There is no appeal from the decision of the Commission in subsection (2).

Class and extension of licence

17. (1) A licence shall be in one of the following classes;

(a) a general trust company licence;

(b) a restricted trust company licence.

(2) A general trust company licence shall not be issued to an international business company.

(3) A restricted trust company licence is subject to the restriction that the licensee does not undertake trust business on behalf of persons other than those persons or classes of persons listed in the undertaking accompanying the application for the licence or any amendment to the list approved by the Commission.

(4) An applicant for a general trust company licence may apply for the licence to extend to a wholly owned subsidiary of the applicant.

(5) An application under subsection (4) must be made in writing to the

(a) the name of the subsidiary;

(b) documentary proof sufficient to establish that the subsidiary is wholly owned by the applicant;

(c) a description of the type of trust business being, or to be, carried on by the subsidiary; and

(d) any other information or documentation that the Commission considers necessary.

(6) The Commission may, upon granting a general trust company licence to the applicant, extend the licence to include the subsidiary referred to in subsection (4), subject to such terms and conditions as it thinks fit.

(7) The licence is automatically suspended if the subsidiary becomes no longer wholly owned by the applicant and the Commission may revoke the licence on further review.

Maintenance of capital

18. (1) A holder of a general trust company licence, other than a domestic bank, must ensure that its paid up share capital is maintained in an amount not less than $250,000, or the equivalent in another currency, or such greater sum as may be ordered under subsection (3).

(2) A holder of a restricted trust company licence must ensure that its fully paid up share capital is maintained in an amount not less than the amount prescribed by the Commission as being the minimum capital for a restricted trust company, or such greater sum as may be ordered under subsection (3).

(3) The Commission may order a licensee to increase its fully paid up capital to such greater amount than that required under subsection (1) or (2) as it may determine having regard to the nature of the general or restricted trust business being, or sought to be, undertaken.

(4) A company that contravenes subsection (1) or (2) commits

an offence and is liable on conviction to a fine of $25,000 per week for each week that it contravenes the subsection.

(5) Where an offence under this section is committed by a company, a director or officer of the company who knowingly authorized, permitted or acquiesced in the commission of the offence also commits an offence and is liable on conviction to a fine of $25,000 or to a term of imprisonment for 6 months or to both.

PART 4

MATTERS APPLICABLE TO INTERNATIONAL BANKING BUSINESS AND TRUST BUSINESS

Interpretation

19. In this Part;

"licence" means an international banking licence or a trust company licence;

"licenced business" means the international banking business or the trust business, as the case may be, that the licensee is licensed to carry on;

"licensee" means a person holding an international banking licence or holding a trust company licence.

Revocation, Suspension and Surrender of Licence and Variation of Terms of Licence

20. (1) The Commission may at any time suspend or revoke a licence if it appears;

(a) that the licensee;

(i) is not a fit and proper person in accordance with the criteria as set out in regulation 3 of the regulations or is not qualified to carry on the licenced business,

(ii) is carrying on the licenced business in a manner detrimental to the public interest or to the interests of any of its creditors or, in the case of a holder of an international banking licence, of any depositors or, in the case of a holder of a trust company licence, of any beneficiary of a trust of which it is a trustee,

(iii) has failed to maintain sufficient capital or liquidity to meet its liabilities or is insolvent,

(iv) has contravened or is in contravention of any provision of this Act, the Code of Practice or Guidelines issued under section 51 or of the Practice Code of the Prevention of Money Laundering or the Money Laundering Regulations,

(v) has breached or is in breach of any term or condition of its licence,

(vi) failed to commence operations within a period of 12 months following the granting of the licence or has ceased to carry on the licensed business, or

(vii) has furnished the Commission with false, inaccurate or misleading information whether on making application for a licence or subsequent to the issue of the licence; or

(b) that any person having a share or interest in the licensee, whether equitable or legal, or any director or officer of the licensee is not a fit and proper person to have an interest in or to be concerned with the management of a licensee, as the case may be; or

(c) that the licensee has merged or amalgamated with another company and the licence is no longer required.

(2) The Commission shall revoke a licence if the licensee fails to pay the prescribed annual fee together with the appropriate late payment penalty in full on or before 7 months of the date the fees were due or 31st December in the year in which the annual fee was due, whichever comes first.

(3) Subject to subsections (4) and (5), the period of suspension of a licence under subsection (1), except subsection (1)(a)(iii), shall not exceed 90 days.

(4) Subject to subsection (5), if it is satisfied that it is in the public interest to do so the Commission may extend, the period of suspension as set out in subsection (3), of a licence under this section for one or more further periods not exceeding 90 days each.

(5) Where the Commission suspends a licence under subsection (1)(a)(iii), the period of suspension of a licence shall continue for such period of time as the condition therein continues or until such time as the Commission decides to revoke the licence.

Appointment of administrator by the Court

21. (1) If a licence is or is about to be suspended or revoked under section 20, the Commission may apply to the Court;

(a) for the appointment of an administrator to take over and manage the licensed business then carried on by the licensee or carried on by it immediately prior to the revocation or suspension of its licence, as the case may be; or

(b) for an order that the licensee be wound up by the Court or subject to the supervision of the Court under the Companies Act, or the International Business Companies Act, as the case maybe.

(2) An application made under subsection (1) may be made on an ex parte basis.

(3) On an application made under subsection (1), the Court may make such order as it considers necessary to safeguard;

(a) in the case of a holder of an international banking licence, the interests of any depositors; or

(b) in the case of a holder of a trust company licence, the interests of any beneficiary of a trust of which the licensee is a trustee.

(4) Without limiting subsection (3), an order made under that subsection may;

(a) grant an administrator the powers of a licensee under this Act;

(b) require the administrator to provide security;

(c) fix the remuneration of the administrator;

(d) require such persons as it considers necessary to appear before the Court for the purposes of giving information concerning the licenced business; and

(e) make any order that could be made by the Magistrate on an application made under section 37.

Surrender of licence

22. (1) A licensee that ceases to carry on the licenced business may apply to the Commission to surrender its licence.

(2) An application under subsection (1) must;

(a) contain the information and be in the form prescribed in the regulations to this Act; and

(b) be accompanied by the documentation prescribed in the regulations to this Act.

(3) If the Commission is satisfied that;

(a) the licensee has ceased to carry on the licenced business and that;

(i) the licensee has repaid all deposits accepted by it, or

(ii) the licensee has properly distributed, transferred or otherwise dealt with all trust assets that were held or administered by it; or

(b) the licensee being wound up, is solvent and is able on demand;

(i) in the case of a company holding an international banking licence, to repay all deposits accepted by it, or

(ii) in the case of a person holding a trust company licence, to properly distribute, transfer or otherwise deal with all trust assets that are or were held or administered by it: the Commission may approve the surrender.

(4) In the case of a surrender of a licence under paragraph (3) (b), the Attorney General or the Commission may apply to the Court for an order that the licensee be wound up by the Court or subject to the supervision of the Court under the Companies Act or the International Business Companies Act as the case maybe.

Variation of terms or conditions of licence

23. The Commission may, upon giving reasonable notice to the licensee;

(a) vary or cancel any terms or conditions imposed on the issue of a licence or under the extension of a licence under section 17(4) or imposed thereafter; or

(b) impose new terms or conditions.

Principal Office and Authorised Agent

24. (1) A licensee must have;

(a) a principal office in Montserrat being a place of business; and

(b) 2 authorised agents who comply with subsection (2): Providing that where the licensee is a bank, "place of business" means any bank (other than a subsidiary or branch of a bank licenced in a country or territory outside Montserrat) having such resources (including staff and facilities) and such books and records as the Commission considers appropriate having regard to the nature and scale of business.

(2) Each authorised agent;

(a) must be an individual resident in Montserrat; or a general trust company licenced under this Act; and

(b) must, prior to his appointment;

(i) have consented in writing to act as an authorised agent, and

(ii) be approved in writing as an authorised agent by

the Commission under the Company Management Act or as a general trust company under this Act;

(c) if he is an individual, may be a principal or a senior officer of a Company licensed under the Company Management Act or 20 CAP. 11.04 International Banking and Trust Companies as a general trust company under this Act and approved as in (b)(ii) herein.

(3) The licensee must appoint its first authorised agents not later than the day of the issue of its licence and shall forthwith notify the Commission that the approved appointments have been made.

(4) A licensee may not change the address of its principal office or appoint an authorised agent without the prior written approval of the Commission.

(5) An agent whose licence has been suspended or cancelled under sections 8 and 9 respectively of the Company Management Act or whose trust licence has been suspended or cancelled under this Act cannot continue as an agent under this section.

(6) Subject to subsection (7), a licensee that contravenes this section commits an offence and is liable on summary conviction;

(a) in respect of a breach of subsection (1), to a fine of $25,000; and

(b) in respect of a breach of subsection (3) or subsection (4), to a fine of $10,000.

(7) A licensee does not contravene subsection (1) when an authorised agent dies or resigns or has his licence suspended or cancelled as set out under subsection (5) if;

(a) the licensee forthwith submits to the Commission

the name of a person to replace the authorised representative; and

(b) appoints an authorised agent forthwith after he is approved; so long as the licensee has at least 1 authorised agent.

(8) This section does not apply to a domestic bank but does apply to a subsidiary of a domestic bank.

(9) The Authorised Agents of a licensee shall in their capacity as representatives of the licensee ensure compliance with all statutory requirements under this Act.

Operation outside Montserrat

25. (1) A licensee, unless it is a foreign bank must not operate a subsidiary, branch, agency or office outside Montserrat without the prior approval of the Commission.

(2) A licensee must keep the Commission informed at all times of the location addresses, telephone numbers, fax numbers and e-mail addresses of any subsidiary, branch, agency or office of the licensee and the Commission must be notified immediately of any change.

(3) A licensee who contravenes subsection (1) or subsection (2) commits an offence and is liable on summary conviction to a fine of $25,000 for each week or part thereof that the contravention continues.

Restrictions on and Change of Names

Restrictions on use of certain terms

26. (1) No person other than a licensee shall, except with the authority of the Commission or under the authority of any other written law;

(a) use, whether in the name under which he is registered or in the description or title under which he carries on business in or from within Montserrat and whether in English or in any language;

(i) the words "bank", "fund", "mutual", "savings" or "trust" or any derivative, or

(ii) any word that, in the opinion of the Commission, suggests international banking business or trust business; or

(b) make any representation in any document or in any other manner that is likely to suggest that he is carrying on international banking business or trust business.

(2) The Commission may, by written notice, require a licensee who carries on international banking business or trust business under a name that is;

(a) identical to that of any other person, whether within or outside Montserrat, or which so nearly resembles that name as to be likely to deceive;

(b) likely to suggest falsely the patronage of or connection with some person whether within or outside Montserrat; or

(c) likely to suggest falsely that it has special status in relation to or derived from the Government or has the official approval of, or acts on behalf of, the Government or of any of its departments or officials; forthwith to change the name and in default of compliance may suspend or revoke the licence.

(3) A person who contravenes subsection (1) commits an offence and is liable on summary conviction to a fine of $25,000 or to a term of imprisonment of 1 year or to both.

(4) A licensee who fails to change his name within 7 days of the date of receipt of a written notice under subsection (2) commits an offence and is liable on summary conviction to a fine of $10,000 and to a daily default fine of $500.

Change of name

27. A licensee shall not change its name without the prior written approval of the Commission.

Transfer of Shares and Appointment of Directors

28. (1) No share or other interest, whether legal or equitable, in a licensee shall be issued, transferred or otherwise disposed of without the prior written approval of the Commission.

(2) The Commission may grant written approval of the transfer provided that it is satisfied that the new shareholder is a fit and proper person in accordance with the criteria set out in regulation 3 of the regulations.

(3) Where the company is a publicly listed company, or as otherwise determined by the Commission, such company may be exempted from the provisions of subsection (1), subject to such terms and conditions as the Commission thinks fit.

Number and appointment of directors

29. (1) A licensee shall have not less than 2 directors.

(2) Subject to subsection (3), no appointment of a director or other senior officer of a licensee shall be made without the prior written approval of the Commission.

(3) Subsection (2) does not apply to a licensee that is exempted in writing by the Commission.

(4) An exemption under subsection (3) may be granted subject to such terms and conditions as the Commission considers fit and may be revoked by the Commission in writing.

Exemption for domestic bank

30. Sections 28 and 29 do not apply to a domestic bank but it does apply to a subsidiary of a domestic bank.

Obligations of Licensee

31. (1) A licensee shall pay the prescribed annual licence fee each year in advance, on or before 15th January of that year.

(2) If a licensee fails to pay the annual fee in full on or before 15th January in any year, it is liable to pay a late payment penalty calculated as prescribed.

(3) A licensee that fails to pay the prescribed annual fee on or before 15th January in any year is deemed not to have contravened subsection (1) if;

(a) it pays the annual fee and the appropriate late payment penalty in full on or before 14th March of the year due; and

(b) at the time of payment his licence has not been revoked or suspended.

(4) The annual fee and any late payment penalty payable by a licensee remains payable notwithstanding that his licence has been suspended.

Display of licence

32. A licensee must prominently display its licence on the premises where its licensed business is carried on.

Returns and Accounts

33. (1) Every licensee shall in relation to its operations submit, within 30 days of the end of each quarter, to the Commission in English, in such form as the Commission may from time to time approve, a statement of its assets and liabilities in such detail as the Commission may require, as at the close of the last business day of each quarter.

(2) The Commission may require a licensee to submit such further information as it may deem necessary for the proper understanding of any statement or return furnished by that licensee under subsection (1) of this section and such information shall be submitted within such a period and in such manner as the Commission may require.

(3) Every licensee shall have its accounts audited annually or at such other periods as the Commission may require.

(4) The licensee shall forward the audited accounts to the Commission within 3 months from the end of the financial year of the licensee unless the Commission has granted prior written approval for an extension.

Audit requirements

34. (1) A licensee shall appoint an Approved Auditor.

(2) The Auditor's duties are set out in regulation 5 of the regulations.

(3) Where a licensee changes its Auditor, the licensee shall authorize the former Auditor to disclose the circumstances that gave rise to the change, and when so authorised, the Auditor shall disclose such circumstances and if the Commission so requires, the Auditor shall provide such further information with regard to the circumstances as the Commission may request.

Directions for the reporting of information

35. (1) The Commission may issue directions to licensees for the making of returns, or the furnishing of documentation, for regulatory purposes.

(2) A notice under subsection (1) must specify the period within which returns must be made or documentation filed.

(3) Directions issued under subsection (1) may make different provision in relation to different persons, circumstances or cases.

(4) A licensee that fails, within the period specified, to make a return or furnish documentation to the Commission in accordance with directions issued under subsection (1) commits an offence and is liable on summary conviction to a fine of $5,000.

Administration

Commissioner

36. (1) The Commission, by its Commissioner, shall ensure the proper administration of this Act.

(2) The functions of the Commissioner include;

(a) supervising international banking business and trust business;

(b) advising the Commission on all matters concerning the regulation and supervision of international banking business and trust business;

(c) examining and evaluating all applications for;

(i) international banking licences, and

(ii) trust licences, and making recommendations to the Commission concerning such applications;

(d) examining and, if he thinks fit, reporting to the Commission upon returns made and documents filed by licensees under this Act;

(e) where he thinks fit or when required by the Commission, to examine in such manner, including an on-site examination, as he considers necessary, the affairs or business of any licensee for the purpose of satisfying himself that the provisions of this Act, the Code of Practice or Guidelines issued under section 51, the Practice Code on the Prevention of Money Laundering and the Money Laundering Regulations and any similar Acts and Regulations are being complied with and that the licensee is in a sound financial position and is carrying on its business in a satisfactory manner;

(f) the provision of assistance in the investigation of any offences under the laws governing banking and other commercial activities committed by the licensee, its directors, agents or officers; and

(g) reporting to the Commission where he thinks fit, regarding the examination of any documents produced to him in the course of the performance of his functions.

(3) For the purposes of performing his functions under subsection (2) the Commissioner shall be entitled;

(a) to have access to and take copies of such books, records, vouchers, documents, cash and securities and all other financial instruments and business records of any licensee and its subsidiary and shall be entitled to ask questions of any person employed by or engaged by the licensee;

(b) to request such information, matter or thing from any person who, he has reasonable grounds to believe, is carrying on international banking business or trust business in contravention of any part of this Act; and

(c) to call upon the authorised agent, or manager, of the licensee for such information or explanation; as the Commissioner may reasonably require for the purpose of enabling him to perform his functions under this Act.

(4) The Commission may assess a licensee for the reasonable expenses of conducting an examination under subsection 2(e).

(5) The Commissioner may authorize in writing any person to assist him in the performance of his functions under this Act.

(6) Where an appraisal of any loan or asset held by a bank or its subsidiaries has been made by the Commissioner to the Commission and the value varies materially from the value placed by the bank on the asset, the Commission shall send to the bank and auditor a written notice of the appropriate value of the asset as determined by the Commission.

(7) If the Commission is satisfied that there is reasonable ground for suspecting that an offence against this Act has been or is being committed by a licensee, the Commission shall issue an order as the Commission may consider necessary in the interest of the depositors or of the beneficiaries of any trust or other creditors of the licensee and to preserve any assets of the licensee.

Power of search

37. (1) If a Magistrate is satisfied by information on oath or affirmation given by the Commissioner or by a person authorised by him;

(a) that a licence has been revoked or suspended under section 20;

(b) that there are reasonable grounds for believing that an offence under this Act has been or is being committed and that evidence of the commission of the offence is to be found on any premises or in any vehicle, vessel or aircraft specified in the information; or

(c) that any document that ought to have been produced under section 35 and has not been produced is to be found at any premises or in any vehicle, vessel or aircraft specified in the information; he may grant a search warrant authorising the Commissioner, together with any other person named in the warrant, to enter the premises or any premises upon which the vehicle, vessel or aircraft may be located at any time within 1 month from the date of the warrant and to search the premises or the vehicle, vessel or aircraft.

(2) The Commissioner or any other person authorised by a warrant to search any premises or any vehicle, vessel or aircraft;

(a) may search every person who is found in or whom he has reasonable grounds to believe to have recently left, or to be about to enter, those premises or that vehicle, vessel or aircraft; and

(b) may seize any document found on the premises or in the vehicle, vessel or aircraft that he has reasonable grounds for believing ought to have been produced under section 36(3).

(3) Where under this section a person has any power to enter any premises or a vehicle, vessel or aircraft, he may use such force as is reasonably necessary for the purpose of exercising that power.

Attorney General may apply to Court

38. Where a licensee or a person who has at any time been a licensee

is being wound up voluntarily the Attorney General may, when requested by the Commissioner apply to the Court for leave to intervene on behalf of any interested party if he considers that the winding up is not being conducted in the best interests of its depositors, the beneficiaries of any trust, or other creditors and the Court shall make such order as it shall consider appropriate.

Measures to be taken by the Commissioner

39. (1) The Commissioner may require one or more measures to be taken by the licensee where in the opinion of the Commissioner an examination conducted under sections 36(2)(d) and 36(2)(e) shows the licensee or any affiliate, director, officer, employee or shareholder of the licensee to be;

(a) engaging in unsafe or unsound practices in conducting the business of the licensee; or

(b) violating any provision of this Act, or any Regulation or Guideline issued.

(2) The measures to be taken under subsection (1) are set out in regulation 6 of the regulations.

Corporate Governance
Removal and disqualification of directors

40. (1) Any person who is a director, a manager or other officer concerned with the management of a licensee shall cease to hold office if any of the events set out in regulation 7 of the regulations occur or have occurred.

(2) A person who contravenes subsection (1) commits an offence and is liable on summary conviction to a fine of $5,000 or to imprisonment for a term of 1 year or to both.

Declaration and registration of related interest and conflicts of interest by directors

41. (1) Every director of a licensee who is in any manner, whether directly or indirectly, interested in loans, advances, contracts or transactions from that licensee shall as soon as possible declare the nature of his interest to the board or other body responsible for the management of the licensee and shall cause such declaration to be minuted and circulated forthwith to all of the members of the board.

(2) Every director of a licensee who holds any office or possesses any property whereby, whether directly or indirectly, duties or interests might be created in conflict with his duties or interests as such director shall declare the fact, nature, character and extent of such duties and interests at the first meeting of the board held;

(a) after he becomes a director of the licensee, or

(b) if already a director, after he commences to hold office or to possess the property.

(3) A director who contravenes subsections (1) and (2) commits an offence and is liable on summary conviction to a fine of $5,000 or to imprisonment for a term of 1 year or to both.

Responsibility for deceptive statements and obstruction of audit or examination

42. (1) Any director, manager, secretary, employee or agent of a licensee, who;

(a) with intent to deceive;

(i) makes any false or misleading statement or entry, or

(ii) omits any statement or entry that should be made in any book, account, report or statement of the licensee, or

(b) obstructs or endeavours to obstruct;

(i) the proper performance by an auditor of his duties in accordance with the provisions of this Act, or

(ii) a lawful examination of the licensee by a duly authorized examiner, commits an offence and is liable on summary conviction to a fine of $10,000 or to imprisonment for a term of 1 year or to both.

Management's duty of compliance with the requirements of the laws

43. Any director, manager, secretary or other officer concerned in the management of a licensee, who fails to take all reasonable steps to secure compliance by the licensee with the requirements of this Act commits an offence and is liable on summary conviction to a fine of $5,000 or to imprisonment for a term of 1 year or to both.

Advertising

44. (1) No licensee shall engage in advertising or promotion practices which are in the opinion of the Commissioner likely to mislead the public.

(2) Any licensee that contravenes subsection (1) commits an offence and is liable on summary conviction to a fine of $5,000 for each contravention.

Miscellaneous

45. (1) The Commissioner may by written notice require a licensee to effect a policy of insurance with an approved insurance company and maintain it.

(2) The policy of insurance shall insure against;

(a) losses arising out of claims of negligence or breach of duty by the licensee or by an employee;

(b) the dishonesty of employees or of the licensee;

(c) the loss of documents; and

(d) such other risks as the Commissioner may stipulate; in such amount and of such nature as the Commissioner determines having due regard to the nature and type of business carried on by the licensee.

(3) The licensee shall effect the policy of insurance within the time specified in the notice or any extension of the time given by the Commissioner.

(4) The licensee shall without delay give notice to the Commissioner in writing if;

(a) it is unable to obtain insurance as required by the Commissioner; or

(b) it ceases to maintain the insurance.

(5) A licensee who contravenes this section commits an offence and is liable on summary conviction to a fine of $10,000, to a term of imprisonment of 1 year or to both.

Confidentiality

46. (1) For the purposes of this section, "protected person" means;

(a) a person who has applied for a licence under this Act;

(b) a licensee;

(c) a customer of a licensee;

(d) a settlor or beneficiary of a trust of which the licensee is a trustee; or

(e) a company managed by a licensee.

(2) Subject to subsection (3), the Commissioner, a person acting under the Commissioner's authority, and a person appointed by the Commissioner under section 36(5) to assist the Commissioner must not disclose to any person information concerning the affairs of a protected person that he has acquired in the course of his duties or in the exercise of his functions under this Act.

(3) Subsection (2) does not apply to a disclosure;

(a) required or permitted by any Court of competent jurisdiction in Montserrat;

(b) to the Commission;

(c) to any person for the purpose of discharging any duty or exercising any power under this Act;

(d) in respect of the affairs of a protected person made with the consent of that person;

(e) if the information disclosed is or has been available to the public from any other source;

(f) where the information disclosed is in a summary or in statistics expressed in a manner that does not enable the identity of a protected person to which the information relates to be determined; or

(g) made by the Commissioner to a foreign regulatory authority upon the written request of that authority.

(4) The Commissioner may not disclose information concerning the affairs of a protected person to a foreign regulatory authority under paragraph (3)(g) unless he is satisfied;

(a) that the foreign regulatory authority is subject to adequate legal restrictions on further disclosure; and

(b) that the information disclosed is reasonably required by the authority for the purposes of its regulatory functions.

(5) The Commission may issue guidelines to the Commissioner concerning the discharge of his functions under this section.

(6) Any person who contravenes the provisions of this section commits an offence and is liable on summary conviction to a fine of $10,000 and to imprisonment for one year, and on conviction on indictment to a fine of $50,000 and imprisonment for three years.

Immunity

47. No liability, including any costs incurred or to be incurred in defending an action, attaches to the Commission, the Commissioner or any person acting under the authority of the Commission or the Commissioner for an act done in good faith in the discharge or purported discharge of his functions under this Act.

Gazette notices

48. (1) The Commission shall cause notice of the issue, revocation or suspension of a licence to be published in the Gazette.

(2) A notice of issue of a licence published in the Gazette must specify the terms and conditions, if any, to which the licence is subject.

Appeals

49. (1) A decision of the Commission under sections 7, 16, 17, 18 or 23 is final and conclusive and shall not be called into question in any court of law.

(2) An appeal lies to the Court from a decision of the Commission to suspend or revoke a licence under section 20.

(3) Unless the Court otherwise orders, an appeal made under subsection (2) does not operate to suspend the decision of the Commission.

Regulations

50. The Governor in Council may make regulations generally for giving effect to the provisions of this Act and specifically but not limited to;

(a) requiring the payment of fees under this Act and prescribing them, including;

(i) fees for filing an application;

(ii) fees for the issuance of a licence;

(iii) annual fees;

(iv) penalty fees for late submission of documents required under this Act;

(v) administrative fees;

(vi) administrative penalties;

(b) prescribing the documents to be submitted in an application for a licence;

(c) prescribing anything required or permitted to be prescribed by this Act;

(d) exempting any trust company from this Act or any provision of this Act, subject to such conditions, if any, as are imposed in respect of the exemption;

(e) relating to loan concentrations, related party transactions and matters relating to self-dealing.

Code of Practice or Guidelines

51. (1) The Commissioner may issue a Code of Practice or Guidelines with respect to the procedures to be followed by and the conduct expected of a licensee in the operation of its licensed business.

(2) The Code of Practice or Guidelines may include;

(a) due diligence procedures;

(b) record keeping requirements;

(c) accounting standards;

(d) policies, procedures and systems for identifying, monitoring and controlling country risk, transfer risk, market risk, liquidity risk, interest rate risk, operational risk and such other risks as may from time to time be specified;

(e) treatment of investments, loans and other assets and credit facilities;

(f) anti-money laundering and combating the financing of terrorism matters.

(3) The Code of Practice or Guidelines may make different provision in relation to different persons, circumstances or cases.

(4) The Commissioner must publish a notice of the creation of a Code of Practice or Guidelines and any amendments thereto in the Gazette.

Offences

52. (1) A person who with intent to deceive, or for any purpose of this Act makes any representation that he knows, or

would reasonably be expected to know, to be false or does not believe to be true commits an offence and is liable on summary conviction to a fine of $25,000 or to imprisonment for a term of 1 year or to both.

(2) A person who;

(a) assaults or obstructs the Commissioner or other person in the performance of his functions under this Act;

(b) uses any insulting language to a Commissioner or other person in the performance of his functions under this Act;

(c) by the offer of any gratuity, bribe or other inducement prevents or attempts to prevent a Commissioner or other person from performing his functions under this Act; or

(d) contravenes any provision of this Act or regulations, for which no penalty is specifically provided; commits an offence and is liable on summary conviction to a fine of $10,000 or to imprisonment for a term of 1 year or to both.

(3) A licensee that carries on business contrary to the terms or conditions of its licence or, in the case of the holder of a restricted trust company licence, in contravention of the restriction, commits an offence and is liable on summary conviction to a fine of $25,000.

(4) Where an offence under this Act is committed by a company, a director or officer of that company who knowingly authorised, permitted or acquiesced in the commission of the offence also commits the offence and is liable on summary conviction to;

(a) a fine of the amount specified for the offence; or

(b) to a term of imprisonment as specified for the offence, if any; or

(c) to both a fine and imprisonment.

(5) Notwithstanding that the offence is punishable only on summary conviction, the Proceeds of Crime Act applies to the offences created by and punishable under the following sections;

(a) section 5(2);

(b) section 9(3);

(c) section 9(4);

(d) section 14(3);

(e) section 18(4);

(f) section 18(5);

(g) section 25(2);

(h) section 45(5);

(i) section 52(1) and 52(3);

(j) section 52(4), where the offence committed by the company is an offence referred to in paragraphs (a) to (f).

Transitional provisions

53. (1) A person holding a licence under the Offshore Banking Act immediately before the commencement of this Act is deemed to have been granted a licence under this Act subject to such terms and conditions as may have been imposed on the granting of the licence under that Act.

(2) The Governor-in-Council may make regulations providing for such further savings and transitional provisions to have effect in connection with the coming into operation of this Act as he considers necessary or expedient.

(3) Regulations made under subsection (2) may be given retrospective operation to a day not earlier than the date that this Act comes into operation.

INTERNATIONAL BANKING AND TRUST COMPANIES REGULATIONS

ARRANGEMENT OF REGULATIONS

Short title

1. This Order may be cited as the International Banking and Trust Companies Regulations.

Application for licence

2. In considering an application for a licence, the Commission may review and investigate the;

   (a) validity of the documents submitted by the applicant;

   (b) financial condition and history of the applicant, including its owners and directors;

   (c) nature and reputation of the business of the applicant, including its owners and directors;

   (d) legal and management structure of the applicant;

   (e) experience of the person or persons who are to constitute its management;

(f) adequacy of its capital structure;

(g) business plan, which should include; the applicant's proposed products and services, marketing and operational plans, including policies and procedures to monitor and control major risk areas and 3 year financial projections covering capital, investments, deposits and loans and income and expenditure;

(h) references supplied by the owners and directors of the applicant;

(i) prior written consent (or a statement of "no objection") of the home country supervisor and its written assurance that it will carry out consolidated supervision; in the case of a foreign bank establishing a subsidiary or branch.

Fit and Proper criteria

3. In conducting a test as to whether a person is a fit and proper person, the Commission shall have regard to the following minimum criteria;

(a) the skills and experience in the relevant financial activity being applied for;

(b) that person's probity, competence and soundness of judgement for fulfilling the responsibilities of that position;

(c) the diligence with which that person is fulfilling or likely to fulfill the responsibilities of that position;

(d) whether the interests of depositors, or potential depositors of the licensee or settlors and beneficiaries and potential settlors and beneficiaries are, or likely to be, in any way threatened by that person holding that position;

(e) the previous conduct and activities in business or financial matters of that person;

(f) whether there is evidence that that person has committed an offence involving fraud or other dishonesty or violence;

(g) whether there is evidence that that person has contravened any provision under any enactment designed for protecting members of the public against financial loss due to dishonesty, incompetence or malpractice or from financial loss due to the conduct of a discharged or undischarged bankrupt;

(h) whether there is evidence that that person has been engaged in any business appearing to be deceitful or improper (whether lawful or not) or which otherwise reflects on that person's method of conducting business;

(i) whether there is evidence of an employment record, which leads to the belief that that person carried out an improper act in the handling of his employer's or client's business ;

(j) whether there is evidence that that person has been associated with any other business practices or otherwise conducted himself in such a way as to cast doubt on his competence and soundness of judgment.

Restrictions and requirements on banking business

4. (1) A licensee shall not directly or indirectly, except with the written approval of and subject to such terms and conditions, as the Commission may determine;

(a) grant to any person, any member of a borrower group or to any borrower group any advances or credit facilities or make any guarantee so that the total value of the advances, credit facilities, or guarantee in respect of such person, member or borrower group, is at any time more than 25% of the aggregate amount of the licensee's unimpaired capital and reserves;

(b) grant any advance against the security of its own shares, the shares of its holding company, or the shares of its affiliates;

(c) grant or permit to be outstanding to its officers and employees unsecured advances which in aggregate amount for any one officer or employee exceeds the annual remuneration of such officer or employee;

(d) engage in trade, except insofar as may be temporarily necessary in the conduct of its business or in the course of the satisfaction of debts due to it;

(e) acquire or continue in the acquisition of any ownership interest in any financial, commercial, agricultural, industrial or other undertaking except such interest as a licensee may acquire for the satisfaction of debts due to it which shall, however, be disposed of as soon as possible thereafter, but this paragraph shall not prevent the purchase and sale of shares or stocks for trust account or upon the order and for the account of a customer without recourse; but a licensee may;

(i) hold shares in any company set up for the purpose of promoting the development of a money market or securities market;

(ii) hold shares in another company the aggregate value of which does not at any time exceed 10% of the sum of the unimpaired capital and reserves of that licensee, and where there is no established market value for such shares the value of such shares shall be established on the basis of a valuation approved by the Commissioner: Provided that the total amount of a licensee's holdings under this paragraph may not exceed 60% of the sum of the unimpaired capital and reserves of the licensee;

(f) purchase, acquire or lease real or immovable property except as may be necessary for the purpose of conducting its business as a licensee including provision for future expansion and housing its officers and employees;

Provided that;

(i) in respect of any real or immovable property held or leased by it prior to the commencement of this Act for purposes other than those referred to herein, it shall be allowed a period of 3 years in which to comply with this paragraph; and

(ii) it may secure a debt on any property immovable or movable and in default of repayment may acquire such property for resale as soon as possible thereafter, but not later than 5 years thereafter.

(2) A licensee shall not directly or indirectly grant or permit to be outstanding unsecured advances, unless such advances have been approved by its board and the Commissioner has been provided with prior notification thereof, to;

(a) the members of its board whether such advances are obtained by them jointly or severally;

(b) any person in which it or any one or more of its directors have any interest as a director, partner, manager, agent, member or otherwise;

(c) any person who owns, controls or has the power to vote more than 10% of any class of voting securities of the licensee;

(d) any person serving as an auditor under section 34 or conducting an examination under section 36;

(e) any person, whose relationship to another financial institution in which a correspondent account is maintained, is within any of the categories described in paragraphs (a) to (d).

(3) The total of all unsecured advances made to any person within any of the categories described in paragraphs (a) to (d) of subsection (2) shall not exceed 5% of the sum of the paid-up (or, as the case may be, assigned) capital and reserves of the licensee.

(4) Where the total value of advances, extensions or guarantees of credit granted under paragraph (a) of subsection (1) is at any time more than 15% of the aggregate amount of the licensee's unimpaired capital and reserves the transaction shall be secured by collateral, fully covered by insurance, having an ascertainable market value or otherwise having such a value as collateral found in good faith by an officer of such licensee, of at least 20% more than the amount of the obligations secured thereby.

(5) The maximum amount of advances permitted under paragraph (a) of subsection (1) may be varied from time to time by the Commissioner.

(6) Any advances, extensions or guarantees of credit made to any person under paragraph (a) of subsection (1) or within any of the categories described in paragraphs (a) to (d) of subsection (2) shall be made on substantially the same terms, including interest rates and collateral, as applicable, as those prevailing for comparable transactions with other persons.

(7) In determining whether any approval referred to in paragraph (e) of subsection (1) should be granted, the Commissioner shall take into account whether;

(a) acquisition of the shares is likely to prejudice the;

(i) financial condition of the licensee;

(ii) capitalisation of the licensee;

(iii) interest of depositors of the licensee; or

(b) the corporate affiliations and structure of the licensee exposes it to undue risks or hinders its effective supervision.

(8) A licensee shall submit a report quarterly to the Commissioner, in such form as the Commissioner shall determine, on all exposures that are equal to or are in excess of 10% of the unimpaired capital and reserves of the licensee.

(9) The aggregate of exposures in excess of 10% incurred by a licensee shall not exceed 400% of its unimpaired capital and reserves, or such other percentage as the Commission may prescribe.

(10) A licensee shall maintain information systems to identify loans to connected or related parties. A licensee shall record the amount of such loans and monitor and report on such loans to the Commissioner at such times as the Commissioner shall specify.

(11) In applying paragraph (a) of subsection (1) and subsection (2), if the Commissioner shall determine that the interests of 2 or more persons are connected or related, the total indebtedness of such persons shall be aggregated and deemed to be the indebtedness of a single person; and a licensee shall not be deemed to have violated paragraph (a) of subsection (1) or subsection (2) solely by reason of the fact

that the aggregated indebtedness exceeds the limitation at the time of the determination, but the licensee shall dispose of the indebtedness of such persons in the amount in excess of the limitation within such reasonable time as shall be determined by the Commissioner.

(12) Any licensee to which subsections (1) and (2) are applicable that, prior to the commencement of this Act, entered into any transactions incompatible with paragraphs (a), (b), (c), (d), or (e) of subsection (1) and subsection (2) shall, within 12 months after the commencement of this Act, or within such further period as the Commissioner may determine, submit a statement thereof to the Commissioner and shall in respect of such transactions, take such corrective action, and within such reasonable time, as shall be determined by the Commissioner.

(13) Unless the approval of the Commission is first obtained, no licensee shall be an affiliate or subsidiary of a company that does not conduct banking business or business of a financial nature.

Auditor's duties

5. (1) A licensee shall appoint annually an auditor acceptable to the Commissioner whose duties shall;

(a) be to examine the books and records and to make a report upon the annual financial statements and financial position, and in every such report the auditor shall state whether in the auditor's opinion the balance sheet and profit and loss account give a true and fair view of the state of affairs of the licensee and of its results for the period then ended; and

(b) be to conduct the audit in accordance with internationally accepted auditing standards; and

(c) include all or any of the following duties as may from time to time be imposed on the auditor by the licensee at the request of the Commissioner to;

(i) submit such additional information in relation to the audit of the licensee as the Commissioner considers necessary;

(ii) carry out any other examination or establish any procedure in any particular case;

(iii) submit a report on any of the matters referred to in subparagraphs (i) and (ii);

(iv) submit a report on the financial and accounting systems and risk management controls of the licensee;

(v) submit a report on whether prudent credit–granting and investment criteria, policies, practices and procedures are approved and reviewed by the management and board and communicated to all credit officers and whether major credits and investments are decided at board level;

(vi) certify whether the systems of loan classification, provisioning and write-offs determined by the Commissioner are being adhered to; and

(vii) certify whether suitable measurers to counter money laundering and to combat the financing of terrorism have been adopted by the licensee and are being implemented in accordance with the applicable laws.

(2) A licensee shall remunerate the auditor in respect of the discharge by the auditor of all or any of the duties set out in subsection (1).

(3) If in the course of the performance of an auditor's duties an auditor is satisfied that;

(a) there has been a serious breach of or non-compliance with the provisions of this Act or any, regulations, notice, order, guidelines or directions issued under this Act;

(b) there is evidence that a criminal offence involving fraud or other dishonesty may have been committed;

(c) losses have been incurred which reduce the paid up or assigned capital, as the case may be, of the licensee by 25% or more;

(d) serious irregularities have occurred, including those that affect the interest of depositors; or

(e) the claims of depositors covered by the assets cannot be confirmed; the auditor shall report the matter forthwith to the licensee and the Commissioner.

(4) The Commissioner may request copies of reports submitted to the board of a licensee by both its internal and external auditors.

(5) An auditor shall report to the Commissioner any matter it is required to report on any licensee to any investigative, regulatory or other institution, within a reasonable time of reporting to that licensee.

(6) An auditor who is required to make any disclosure to the Commissioner or to a person authorised by the Commission shall not by reason of the disclosure be regarded as being in breach of duty to the licensee.

(7) The report of the auditor made in accordance with subsection (1) shall be presented with the report of the board and the financial statements of the licensee at the annual

meeting of shareholders. A copy of the financial statements and reports shall be sent to the Commissioner within 3 months of the end of the financial year.

(8) The Commissioner may appoint an auditor to conduct an independent audit of a licensee and to report the findings or results thereof to him.

(9) The Commission may in writing, require that the auditor make a particular examination relating to the adequacy of procedures adopted by the licensee for the safety of its creditors or shareholders, or any other examination, where in the Commission's opinion, the public interest may require and report to the Commission thereon. Expenses of the audit examination are payable by the bank.

(10) No person having an interest in any licensee otherwise than as a depositor and no director, manager, secretary, employee or agent of a licensee shall be eligible for appointment as auditor for such licensee.

(11) Any person appointed as auditor who shall, after an appointment, acquire any interest, otherwise than as a depositor, or become a director, manager, secretary, employee or agent of such licensee shall forthwith cease to be such auditor.

Measures to be undertaken by the Commissioner

6. (1) If in the opinion of the Commissioner an examination authorised under section 36(2)(e) of the Act shows that the licensee concerned or any affiliate, director, officer, employee, or significant shareholder of the licensee is;

(a) engaging in unsafe or unsound practices in conducting the business of the licensee;

(b) violating any law, regulation or guideline issued by the Commissioner to which the licensee or person is subject; or the Commissioner has reasonable cause to believe that the practices or violations referred in paragraphs (a) and (b) are likely to occur, the Commissioner may take one or more of the following measures;

(i) issue a written warning as is deemed necessary;

(ii) conclude a written agreement with the licensee providing for a program of remedial action which may be in any form as provided for in subparagraphs (3) (a), (b), (c) and (d);

(iii) issue a cease and desist order that requires the licensee, the affiliate and/or the person responsible for the management of the licensee to cease and desist from the practice or violations specified in the order; or

(iv) issue such directions as it deems necessary in relation to the persons comprising the management of the licensee.

(2) Where in the opinion of the Commissioner any of the circumstances in subparagraphs (a) or (b) of paragraph (1) exists, the Commissioner may, after exhausting all the measures under paragraph (1), recommend that the Commission;

(a) restrict or vary any restriction of a licence; or

(b) revoke or suspend the licence to do banking business or trust business pursuant to section 20.

(3) An agreement made under subparagraph (ii) of paragraph (1) may require the licensee to;

(a) increase the paid-up share capital of its affiliate;

(b) sell or otherwise dispose of the affiliate or part of its business;

(c) make advances or grant credit facilities to the affiliate; or

(d) make special provisions for any potential losses which in the opinion of the Commissioner, the affiliate is likely to incur where such affiliate has credit facilities with the licensee.

(4) (a) A cease or desist order issued under subparagraph (iii) of paragraph (1) may require that the licensee take action to correct the condition resulting from any unsound practices or violation of any law.

(b) Any person served with a cease and desist order under subparagraph (iii) of paragraph (1) may apply to the High Court for an order setting aside, varying, or suspending the operation of the cease and desist order.

(5) A licensee, its affiliate, or any director, officer, employee or significant shareholder of a licensee who fails to comply with any requirement or contravenes any prohibition imposed on the licensee under this section shall be guilty of an offence and is liable on summary conviction;

(a) in the case of the licensee or its affiliate, to a fine of $100,000, and in the case of a continuing offence, to a further penalty of $10,000 for each day on which the offence is continued after conviction therefor;

(b) in the case of any individual specified in this section, to a fine of $50,000 and in the case of a continuing offence, to a further penalty of $5,000 for each day on which the offence is continued after conviction therefore.

(6) Any order, warning, agreement, or direction issued by the Commissioner under paragraph (1) shall be deemed to take effect from the date specified therein.

Surrender of Licence

7. A licensee wishing to surrender its licence in accordance with the provisions of section 22 of the International Banking and Trust Companies Act, 2006 shall apply to the Financial Services Commission, in writing in the form set out in Schedule 1 hereto, stating in full, its reasons for the request, and the Financial Services Commission shall within 60 days of receipt of such application inform the applicant of its decision, in the form set out in Schedule 2 hereto.

Disqualification of Directors

8. (1) Any person who is a director, manager or other officer concerned with the management of a licensee shall cease to hold office;

(a) upon notification by the board of a finding by two-thirds of its Members;

(i) of that person's permanent incapacity or serious neglect of, or misconduct in, office; or

(ii) that the person is not a fit and proper person in accordance with the criteria specified in regulation 3.

(b) if that person;

(i) is or was convicted of an offence under this Act;

(ii) has been declared bankrupt or has compounded with, or suspended payment to, that person's creditors; or

(iii) has been convicted in a court of law of any offence involving fraud, dishonesty, or violence.

(2) Any person who;

(a) has been sentenced for an offence involving a term of imprisonment of or exceeding 6 months or for default of payment of a fine;

(b) has been a director or manager of a company which has been wound up by a court or has been placed in receivership;

(c) has been a director or manager of, or directly or indirectly concerned in the management of a former licensee, the licence of which has been revoked, unless such revocation was due to;

(i) its amalgamation with another licensee or company; or

(ii) its voluntary winding up; shall not, without the express approval of the Commission, act or continue to act as a director or manager of, or be directly or indirectly concerned in any way in the management of any licensee.

(3) A person who contravenes paragraph (1) or (2) commits an offence and is liable on summary conviction to a fine not exceeding $10,000 or to imprisonment for a term not exceeding 1 year or to both such fine and imprisonment.

SCHEDULE 1

(Regulation 7)
(Inserted by S.R.O. 47/2007)

APPLICATION FOR SURRENDERING AN INTERNATIONAL BANKING OR TRUST LICENCE

Applicant:

____

(Name of institution)

1. In compliance with section 22 of the International Banking and Trust Companies Act, we hereby give notice of the intention to surrender the licence of the above-named bank.

2. The surrender of the licence as approved by our Board Resolution Number ___________

   dated ___________

The reason(s) for surrendering the licence being:

____

____

____

____

____

____

____

3. We submit with this application, the following information:

   i) Schedule of deposits and other liabilities;

   ii) Schedule, certified by the bank's external auditors, confirming that the bank's assets exceed its liabilities;

iii) Schedule of assets held in trust;

iv) A list of the current Board members and principal officers together with both their current and forwarding addresses;

v) The physical location where the books and records detailing the activities of bank for at least the past 6 years* will be maintained;

vi) The original licence issued by the Financial Services Commission. [where the original licence is lost or misplaced, an affidavit to swear/affirm that it is lost or misplaced].

4. We hereby declare that:

a) the institution has ceased to carry on its business and;

i) produces evidence that it has repaid all deposits held by it, or

ii) it has transferred all trust assets held or administered by it; or

b) the institution being wound up, is solvent and is able on demand:

i) to repay all deposits accepted by it; or

ii) in the case of an institution holding a trust company licence, to properly distribute, transfer or otherwise deal will all trust assets that are or were held or administered by it.

____________________ Date

____

Chairman/Chief Executive

Name of institution

____

* To comply with Anti-Money Laundering Regulations

SCHEDULE 2

APPROVAL TO AN APPLICATION FOR SURRENDERING OF AN INTERNATIONAL BANKING OR TRUST LICENCE

Name of Applicant:

____ Bank Limited

Date of receipt of application:

____

The Financial Services Commission has considered your application and confirm:

Approval for surrender of licence has been granted

____

Approval for surrender of licence has been refused

____

Approval for surrender of the licence has been granted subject to the following conditions:

____

Commissioner

____

INTERNATIONAL BANKING AND TRUST COMPANIES (FEES) REGULATIONS

Short title

1. These Regulations may be cited as the International Banking and Trust Companies (Fees) Regulations.

Fees

2. The fees and penalties payable under the Act are prescribed as follows:

   (a) the non-refundable fees payable under section 15 for processing an application to commence a banking business or banking and trust business: US$ 3,000

   (b) the annual licence fees payable under section 31 in respect of a licence to carry on banking business: US$ 19,000

   (c) the annual licence fees payable under section 31 and section 7 in respect of a licence to carry on banking business and trust business: US$ 21,000

   (d) application for approval of mergers or reorganization of a licenced Financial Institution; US$ 200

   (e) application for approval of the appointment of a new director of an existing licensee: US$ 200

   (f) (i) letter confirming licenced status of a Financial Institution: US$ 100

      (ii) certificate of good standing of licensee: US$ 250

(g) approval for voluntary surrender of the licence by Financial Institution including those in run-off status: US$ 200

(h) penalty for late submission of returns and accounts;

  (i) seven (7) days late: US$ 50

  (ii) over seven (7) days to thirty (30) days late: US$ 200

  (iii) after 31 days to 60 days late: US$500

  (iv) after 60 days late: US$ 1,000

(i) copies of any documents, per page: US$ .50¢

(j) certified true copies of documents, per page: US$ 1

St. Vincent & the Grenadines

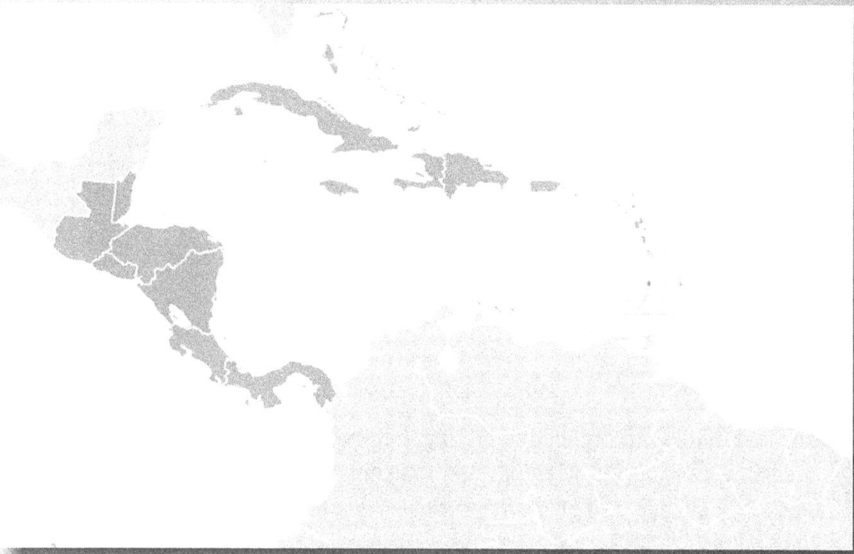

Background

Resistance by native Caribs prevented colonization on Saint Vincent until 1719. Disputed between France and the United Kingdom for most of the 18th century, the island was ceded to the latter in 1783. Between 1960 and 1962, Saint Vincent and the Grenadines was a separate administrative unit of the Federation of the West Indies. Autonomy was granted in 1969 and independence in 1979.

Population

103,537 (July 2012 est.)

Capital

Kingstown

Official Language

English, French Patois

Regulatory Authority

International Financial Services Authority
NIS Headquarters - Upper Bay Street
P.O. Box 356 - Kingstown
St. Vincent West Indies
Phone: +1 784 456 2577
Fax: +1 784 457 2568
Email: info@svgifsa.com
Web: www.svgifsa.com

License Types

Offshore banks are regulated by the International Banks Act 2004. Class A licensees can offer services to non-residents without further restrictions and Class B licensees can only offer services to a limited number of pre-identified customers.

Capital Requirements

Class A licensees are required to maintain a paid up capital of USD 1,000,000.00 and invest USD 500,000.00 of this capital in a manner prescribed by the regulator. Class B licensees are required to maintain USD 500,000.00 in paid up capital and invest USD 100,000.00 of this capital in a manner prescribed by the regulator.

Offshore Bank License Fees

Application Fee Class A/B:	USD 1,000.00
License Issuing Fee Class A/B:	USD 10,000.00
License Renewal Fee Class A:	USD 10,000.00
License Renewal Fee Class B:	USD 5,000.00

ST. VINCENT AND THE GRENADINES INTERNATIONAL BANKS ACT, 2004

ARRANGEMENT OF SECTIONS

PRELIMINARY

PART I

LICENCES

PART II

ACCOUNTS

PART III

RESTRICTIONS BUSINESS

14. Number and approval of directors
15. Use of the word "bank, trust" etc.
16. Shares not to be issued or transferred without approval
17. Restriction on business activities
18. Limits on equity acquisitions

PART IV

ADMINISTRATION

19. Functions of the Authority and the Executive Director
20. Remedial powers
21. Powers of the Authority
22. Attorney General may apply to court
23. Authority responsible for monitoring compliance
24. Preservation of confidentiality

PART V

EXEMPTION FROM TAXATION AND DUTIES

25. Exemption from taxation, duties and certificate

PART VI

MISCELLANEOUS

26. Power of the Authority to require insurance
27. Offences
28. Appeals
29. Immunity
30. Regulations
31. Guidelines
32. Non-application of Banking Act, Exchange Control Act and Interest Act

SAINT VINCENT AND THE GRENADINES
ACT NO. 40 OF 2004

I ASSENT

DR. FREDRICK BALLANTYNE
Governor-General 24 th December, 2004

AN ACT to repeal and replace the International Banks Act, 1996; to provide for better licensing procedures and regulation of international banking business in accordance with the generally accepted principles of banking; to provide incentives for international banking business carried on from within the State, and relate matters.

[28th December, 2004]

BE IT ENACTED by the Queen's Most Excellent Majesty by and with the advice and consent of the House of Assembly of Saint Vincent and the Grenadines and by the authority of the same as follows:

PRELIMINARY

1. This Act may be cited as the International Banks Act, 2004.

2. (1) In this Act "affiliate" includes an affiliated corporation and for the purposes of this Act;

   (a) one body corporate is affiliated with another body corporate if one of them is the subsidiary of the other, or both are subsidiaries of the same body corporate, or each of them is controlled by the same person or group of persons; and

(b) if two bodies corporate are affiliated with the same body corporate at the same time, they are affiliated with each other;

"auditor" means a person who is licensed and in good standing as a member of an approved accounting body listed in Schedule 2.

"Authority" means the Saint Vincent and the Grenadines International Financial Services Authority created pursuant to the Saint Vincent and the Grenadines International Financial Services Authority Act;

"bank" means any financial institution whose operations include the acceptance of deposits subject to transfer by the depositor by cheque or other means of payment transfer;

(a) the business of receiving funds through

(i) the acceptance of monetary deposits that are repayable on demand or after notice or any similar operation; and

(ii) the sale or placement of bonds, certificates, notes or other securities and the use of them, either in whole or in part, for loans or investment for the risk of the customer; and

(b) any other activity recognized by the Central Bank or the Authority as customary banking practice and which a financial institution may additionally be authorized to do;

"Central Bank" means the Eastern Caribbean Central Bank established under Article 3 of the Agreement set out in the Schedule to the Eastern Caribbean Central Bank Act;

"connected or related persons or groups" means where the interest of two or more persons or groups of persons are so interrelated that they should be considered as a single unit or borrower group;

"controller" is a person who effectively controls or directs the activities of the bank other than by virtue of being a shareholder or director;

"Court" means the High Court

"eligible company" means

(a) a body corporate

(i) having at least one director who is a resident,

(ii) that is incorporated, subsisting, continued or registered as an external company under the Companies Act; or

(iii) that is incorporated, subsisting or continued under the International Business Companies Act, does not issue bearer shares and all the shares are registered shares and the names of all the shareholders and the beneficial owners are lodged with Authority; and

(iv) whose objects or business activities are restricted to international banking business;

"Executive Director" means the Executive Director of the Saint Vincent and the Grenadines International Financial Services Authority appointed pursuant to the International Financial Services Authority Act;

"financial year" means, in relation to a licensee under this Act, a period not exceeding fifty-two weeks;

"group" means

(a) in relation to a company, that company and

(i) any other company which is its holding company or subsidiary;

(ii) any other company which is a subsidiary of its holding company;

(iii) any company which directly or indirectly controls or is controlled by any company referred to in subparagraph (i) or (ii);

(iv) any company in which connected persons have a controlling interest;

(b) in relation to a person other than a company,

(i) a group of relatives where each member of the group is substantially dependent upon the same income source;

(ii) any other group of person in which one member has power directly or indirectly to control the other members;

(iii) any other group of person that may be prescribed by the Authority;

"international banking business" means banking business that does not involve

(a) conducting banking business with residents;

(b) investing in any asset that represents a claim on any resident, except a claim resulting from

(i) a loan to an international business company or any international trust;

(ii) a loan by way of mortgage to a member of the licensee's staff for the purchase or construction of a residence in the State to be owner occupied; or

(iii) a transaction with another licensee under this Act;

(c) the purchase of bonds or other securities issued by the

State, a statutory corporation or a company where the Government is the sole or majority beneficial owner; or

(d) acting as trustee of trust assets, for persons not resident, where trust assets are to be administered, managed, or invested or otherwise dealt with for the benefit of persons not Resident, and includes any incidental or ancillary related activities;

"international business company" means a company incorporated or subsisting under the International Business Companies Act;

"internationally established bank" means a baking institution incorporated overseas that is subject to consolidated supervision and deemed by the Authority to be reputable banking institution;

"licensee" means a body corporate that holds a subsisting valid licence under this Act to carry on international banking business from within the State;

"Minister" means the Minister of Finance;

"prescribed" means prescribed by this Act or Regulations made under this Act;

"registered agent" means a person licensed to carry on the business of international representation under the Registered Agent and Trustee Licensing Act;

"regulatory capital" means paid up capital as set out in section 10 together with retained earnings;

"resident" means, for the purpose of this Act,

(a) a natural person who is ordinarily resident and subject to income tax in the State under general principles of State income taxation;

(b) a trust company, partnership, limited partnership or other body under the laws of the State, the majority of shares or other ownership of which is legally or beneficially owned, directly or indirectly, by persons who are resident under the provisions of paragraph (a) or (c), or by the State; and

(c) any other trust, corporation, partnership, limited partnership, or other entity who or which is a resident of, or ordinarily resident or domiciled in, the State under general principles of State income taxation, provided that for these purpose the term "resident" shall not include

(i) an international trust registered under the International Trusts Act;

(ii) an international business company incorporated under the International Business Companies Act;

(iii) an international insurance company licensed under the International Insurance (Amendment and Consolidation) Act;

(iv) mutual funds licensed under the Mutual Funds Act; or

(v) a bank which is licensed under this Act; so long as and to the extent that the registration, incorporation or compliance continues under the provisions of the applicable Act;

"subsidiary" means a body corporate that is controlled by another body corporate; and

"State" means the State of Saint Vincent and the Grenadines.

(2) For the purposes of this Act, "associate" means, when used to indicate a relationship with any person,

(a) a company in which that person beneficially owns or controls, directly or indirectly, shares or securities convertible into shares carrying more than twenty per cent of the voting rights under all circumstances or by reason of the occurrence of an event that has occurred and is continuing, or a currently exercisable option or right to purchase those shares or convertible securities;

(b) a partner of that person acting on behalf of the partnership of which they are partners;

(c) a trust or estate in which that person has a substantial beneficial interest or in respect of which he serves a trustee or in a similar capacity.

(3) For the purposes of this Act

(a) a company is the holding company of another if that other company is its subsidiary;

(b) a company is a subsidiary of another company if it is controlled by that other company.

(4) For the purposes of this Act, a licensee is controlled by another company or by an individual, trust or government if at the relevant time it is effectively controlled directly or indirectly by that other company, individual, trust or government

(a) through being an associate of that other company, individual, trust or government;

(b) through being an affiliate of that other company;

(c) through the holding of shares of incorporated or unincorporated body, but subject to subsection (5);

(d) through the holding of membership in an unincorporated body;

(e) through voting trusts or other agreements relating to the voting of shares;

(f) through the holding by an unincorporated body of a substantial portion of the licensee's borrowings;

(g) through management or control of an unincorporated body; or

(h) through any other means.

(5) For the purpose of this Act, a company is controlled by a person if shares of the company that carry voting rights sufficient to elect a majority of the directors of the company, are held directly or indirectly, other than by way of security only, by or on behalf of that person.

(6) In this Act any reference to "dollar" or "$" shall unless otherwise stated, be to the lawful currency of the United States of America.

Part I

LICENCES

3. (1) No international banking business may be transacted from within the State, in whole or in part, including banking business transacted outside the State except by an eligible company in possession of a licence granted under this Act to carry on international banking business.

(2) A person who contravenes this section commits an offence and is liable on summary conviction to a fine not exceeding one hundred thousand dollars or to imprisonment for a term not exceeding two years or to both, and in the case of a continuing offence to a fine not exceeding ten thousand dollars for each day that the offence continues.

4. (1) An eligible company desirous of carrying on international banking business from within the State must apply to the Authority for the grant of a licence.

(2) An application under subsection (1) must

(a) be filed with the Executive Director;

(b) contain the particulars set out in Schedule 1; and

(c) be accompanied by the fee prescribed in the Regulations.

(3) The Executive Director shall

(a) review the application to ensure that it contains the required information and is accompanied by the proper fee;

(b) submit the application to the Central Bank for its review;

(c) in conjunction with the Central Bank, conduct any inquires that may be considered necessary, and in particular to ascertain

(i) the authenticity of the documents submitted;

(ii) the financial condition and history of the applicant and, where the applicant is a newly formed entity, the viability of its business plan;

(iii) the nature of the proposed business of the applicant;

(iv) whether the proposed directors, shareholders, controllers, officers and senior managers are fit and proper persons to carry on the business of international banking;

(v) the sources of initial capital and the adequacy of its capital structure;

(vi) the suitability of the significant shareholders;

(vii) the transparency of the ownership structure, and

(viii) whether the proposed legal and managerial structures will allow for effective supervision of the financial institution.

(d) communicate with any persons, bodies or authorities as required; and

(e) forward completed applications to the Authority.

(4) If the Authority is satisfied that an application to carry on international banking business is complete and that the applicant is an eligible company qualified to carry on international banking business, it may, with the written approval of the Minister, grant the application and issue to the applicant a licence subject to the terms and conditions it finds necessary.

(5) A decision to issue or to refuse to issue a licence under this Act to an applicant shall be made within a reasonable time of the receipt of the completed application.

(6) A decision to refuse to grant a licence, other than with respect to a renewal or continuation of an existing licence, is final and is not subject to any appeal, and no reason for the refusal need be given.

(7) The Authority shall cause notice of the grant of a licence and all subsequent annual renewals under this Act to be published in the Gazette.

(8) A licence issued under this Act shall be prominently displayed on each premises where the international banking business is carried on.

(9) The Minister acting on the advice of the Authority may amend Schedule 1.

5. (1) An internationally established bank or a subsidiary thereof desirous of opening a branch for carrying on international

banking business from within the State must apply in writing to the Authority for the grant of international banking licence.

(2) An application under subsection (1) shall be filed with the Executive Director in terms set out in section 4 and include consent, in writing, from the home country supervisor to establish the branch.

(3) If the Authority is satisfied that an application in this section is complete and the applicant is an eligible company qualified to carry on international banking through the establishment of a branch, it may, with the approval of the Minister, issue the applicant with a licence subject to the following conditions:

(a) confirmation by way of evidence satisfactory to the Authority that it is subject to comprehensive supervision on a consolidated basis by the appropriate authorities in its home country; and

(b) an undertaking by the applicant to submit audited financial statements of the parent bank in addition to and accompanying its returns under section 13 and upon request by the Authority or any person authorized by the Authority.

6. (1) A licence issued under this Act is valid until the 31 st day of December of the year it is issued and is renewable for the following year upon payment of the fee prescribed in the Regulations on or before the 15th day of January of the following year.

(2) A licensee who fails to pay the prescribed renewal fee by that date may have its licence revoked by the Authority, but in any event shall pay a surcharge not exceeding one-twelfth of that fee for every month or part of a month that the annual fee is not paid.

(3) Subject to subsection (5) a licensee shall at any time within fifteen working days of a written request issued by the Executive Director provide the following information:

(a) a list of the current shareholders, directors and officers of the licensee presented in the form of an affidavit sworn by each shareholder and director and where the shareholder or director is a company by an officer of the company

(i) detailing the actual beneficial ownership of the shares of the company; and

(ii) identifying the relevant natural persons involved with details of their current and former names, dates and places of birth, nationally and current residential addresses;

(b) the most recent audit report of the company prepared by an auditor;

(c) current statement of assets and liabilities;

(d) analysis of total loans classified by size and maturity;

(e) report of large loans;

(f) analysis of total loans classified by country and currency;

(g) analysis of total deposits classified by size and maturity;

(h) analysis of total deposits classified by country and currency;

(i) report of large deposits;

(j) analysis of total investments classified by type and currency;

(k) reports on unsatisfactory assets;

(l) current income statement; or

(m) any other information the Executive Director may require.

(4) The licensee shall provide, on the request of the Executive Director, any of the returns required under section 13 (4) (5) and (6).

(5) Where a licensee is publicly traded on a stock exchange, an authorized officer of the licensee, together with the Secretary, shall swear affidavits detailing the identity of persons owning in excess of ten per cent of the issued share capital of the licensee.

7. Where a material change occurs in the particulars of a licensee as set out in the application for the licence or in the records filed with the Authority or any material adverse development, the licensee shall, as soon as possible and in any event not later than seven days after such change, inform the Authority in writing of the nature and circumstances of the change or material adverse development.

8. (1) A licensee shall have a physical presence in the State which shall include the following:

(a) a physical place of business in the State where all books and records are kept;

(b) a minimum of two employees, one of whom shall be of senior management level;

(c) a designed registered agent, that the Authority has received notification of and who is not an officer of the licensee.

(2) A licensee that does not have a physical presence in the State at the commencement of this Act must within six months of this Act coming into force or any further period

the Authority may in writing allow, establish a physical presence.

(3) It shall be a condition of every licence granted under this Act that the licensee shall immediately notify the Authority, in writing of any change in the location of its office in the State and of any change of its registered agent.

(4) Where the Authority has approved a person under subsection (1) as a registered agent, it may in writing revoke the approval if the person ceases to hold a licence to act as a registered agent.

(5) If the Authority revokes its approval of a registered agent or if a registered agent resigns, the licensee shall ensure that a new registered agent is appointed within fifteen days.

(6) By accepting a licence granted under this Act, the licensee appoints its registered agent as its agent for the acceptance of service of documents in any action arising out of the operations of the licensee.

9. (1) A licence granted under this Act shall be in the following categories:

(a) a Class A International Banking Licence for the purpose of carrying on international banking business generally;

(b) a Class B International Banking Licence for the purpose of carrying on international banking business subject to the restriction that the licensee shall not offer or provide its international banking business services, or otherwise receive or solicit funds by way of trade or business, except for non-resident persons specifically named and described in an undertaking accompanying the application for the licence and the undertaking shall, without further notice, constitute a condition to the Class B licence, if and when the licence is granted.

(2) No Class B licensee shall do business with persons other than those described in the undertaking accompanying the application for the license except with the prior written approval of the Authority.

10. (1) No Class A International Banking Licence shall be granted to or maintained by a Requirement company unless it remains an eligible company and

(a) has and maintains a fully paid-up capital of not less than one million dollars or its equivalent in another currency, or any greater sum the Authority may reasonably determine; and

(b) has deposited or invested the sum of five hundred thousand dollars or its equivalent in another in currency, in a manner the Authority may reasonably prescribe; and

(c) maintains the ratios and deposits that the Authority may from time to time prescribe in consultation with the Central Bank using a risk weighted approach to enable the Authority to determine the additional capital that a bank is required to maintain.

(2) No Class B International Banking Licence shall be granted to or maintained by a company unless it remains an eligible company and

(a) has and maintains a fully paid-up capital of not less than five hundred thousand dollars or its equivalent in another currency, or any greater sum the Authority may reasonably determine; and

(b) has deposited or invested the sum of one hundred thousand dollars or its equivalent in another currency in a manner the Authority may reasonably prescribe.

(3) A branch of an internationally established bank subject to consolidated supervision shall be granted a Class A or

a Class B International Banking Licence but will not be subject to the requirements of the statutory deposit or capital requirements under subsections (1) and (2)

(4) The Authority may require a licensee to increase its fully paid-up capital to any greater amount it may determine to be reasonable for the nature of the international banking being, or sought to be, undertaken.

(5) A licensee must comply with an order from the Authority to increase its paid up capital under subsection (4) or comply with the capital requirements of this section within the time frame set by the Authority.

(6) When the Authority makes an appraisal of an asset held by a licensee or its subsidiary and the value varies materially from the value placed on it by the licensee or its subsidiary, the Authority shall send to the licensee and the auditor written notice of the appropriate value of the asset as determined by the Authority.

11. (1) A licensee that has ceased to carry on the business in respect of which its licence was granted may apply to the Authority to surrender its licence if the licensee

(a) produces evidence that it has repaid all deposits held or administered by it; or

(b) is being wound up voluntarily and produces evidence that it is solvent and is able on demand to repay all its depositors and all other creditors, the Authority may then approve the surrender of the licence and publish a notice of the surrender in the official Gazette or any other publication it finds necessary.

(2) When a licence is surrendered, the licence or previous licensee shall appoint a liquidator that meets the approval of the Authority.

(3) In the case of an application under subsection (1) (b), where the Authority considers that the winding up is not being conducted in the best interests of the depositors or other creditors it may, request the Attorney General apply to apply to the Court for an order that the licensee be wound up, either by the Court or subject to the supervision of the Court, and where the Court so orders the provisions of the International Business Companies Act or the Companies Act relating to the winding up of the company by or subject to the supervision of the Court shall apply mutatis mutandis.

(4) Where the holder of a Class A licence seeks to surrender that licence, the Class A licensee may apply for a Class B licence, provided that the Class A licensee meets the requirements of a Class B licence.

12. A licensee shall not, without the prior written approval of the Authority, Required

(a) change its name; or

(b) acquire, open or operate outside the State any subsidiary, agency, representative office or branch.

Part II

ACCOUNTS

13. (1) A licensee shall appoint an audit recognized by the Authority as listed in Schedule 2 who shall audit the accounts of the licensee annually or at any other periods the Authority may require.

(2) The audited accounts shall be filed with the Authority within three months from the end of the financial year of the licensee, unless prior written approval for an extension has been granted by the Authority.

(3) A licensee who fails to file annual accounts, as they become due shall pay a fine of five hundred dollars for each day the licensee is in default.

(4) A licensee must file quarterly returns with the Authority in the format provided by the Authority within fifteen days of the end of a quarter and must contain the following:

(a) current statement of assets and liabilities;

(b) analysis of total loans classified by size and maturity;

(c) report of large loans;

(d) analysis of total loans classified by country and currency;

(e) analysis of total deposits classified by size and maturity;

(f) analysis of total deposits classified by country and currency;

(g) report of large deposits;

(h) analysis of total investments classified by type and currency; and

(i) reports on unsatisfactory assets;

(j) report on past due loans;

(k) current income statement;

(l) schedule of different income sources; and

(m) any other information the Executive Director may require.

(5) A licensee who fails to file the quarterly returns within the stipulated time shall pay a fine of two hundred and fifty dollars a day until the returns are filed.

(6) If a licensee changes its auditor, the licensee shall, when required by the Authority, authorized the former auditor to disclose the circumstances that gave rise to the change, and when so authorized, the auditor must disclose the circumstances.

(7) The Authority may appoint an auditor at the expense of the licensee to conduct an independent audit of the licensee and to report their findings to the Authority.

(8) Where the licensee fails to appoint an auditor satisfactory to the Authority, the Authority may appoint an auditor for the licensee, the remuneration of the auditor so appointed shall be determined by the Authority in accordance with going market rate and paid by the licensee.

(9) If in the course of the performance of an auditor's duties an auditor is satisfied that

(a) there has been a serious breach of or non-compliance with the provisions of this Act or any, regulations, notice, order, guidelines or directions issued under the Act;

(b) there is evidence that a criminal offence involving fraud, money laundering or other dishonesty may have been committed;

(c) losses have been incurred that reduce the regulatory capital, to a level below that which is required;

(d) serious irregularities have occurred, including those that affect the interest of depositors;

(e) the claims of depositors cannot be confirmed; or

(f) the assets of depositors cannot be confirmed, the auditor must report the matter immediately to the licensee and the Authority.

(10) No liability shall attach to the auditor, the members or employees of the auditor, for breach of confidentiality for an act done in good faith and in the proper discharge of their official duties under the functions described in this Act.

Part III

RESTRICTIONS ON BUSINESS

14. (1) A licensee shall at no time have fewer than two directors who shall each be a natural person and one of whom shall be a Resident.

(2) A licensee shall, prior to the appointment of a director, general manager or other senior officer, apply to the Authority for its written approval of the appointment.

(3) The directors of a bank shall manage or supervise the management of the business and affairs of the bank, and in particular establish

(a) investment and lending policies;

(b) anti-money laundering policies; and

(c) internal controls and procedures.

(4) The directors of a bank must disclose any interests in transactions, loans or other arrangements of the licensee that may arise during his term in office as a director.

(5) A director and officer of a bank in exercising any of the powers of a director or an officer shall

(a) act honestly and in good faith with a view to the best interests of the bank; and

(b) exercise the care, diligence and skill that a reasonably prudent person would exercise in comparable circumstances.

(6) A director, officer and employee of a bank shall comply with this Act, its Regulations, the bank's incorporating instrument and the by-laws of the bank.

(7) No provision in any contract, in any resolution or in the by-laws of a bank relieves a director, officer or employee of the bank from the duty to act in accordance with this Act and its Regulations or relieves a director, officer or employee from liability for breach of duty.

15. (1) No person or entity, other than a licensee shall

(a) use or continue to use the words "bank", "financial institution", "deposit" or any of their derivatives, whether in English or in any other language, in the name, description or title under which that person or entity is carrying on international banking business from within the State, whether or not the international banking business is carried on within or outside the State; or

(b) make or continue to make a representation in any advertisement, billhead, circular, letter, letterhead, notice, paper or in any other manner that the person or entity is carrying on international banking business.

(2) A person or entity who contravenes subsection (1) except with the written approval of the Authority on the advice of the Minister, or under the authority of another law of the State, commits an offence and is liable on summary conviction to a fine of one hundred thousand dollars or to a term of imprisonment for two years or both, and in the case of a continuing offence to a fine of ten thousand dollars for each day the offence continues.

(3) Except where provided elsewhere in the laws of the State, the Minister may refuse to grant a license to a company or, if the company is already in possession of a licence, it may

revoke the licence if, in its opinion, the company is carrying on or intends to carry on international banking business under a name that is

(a) identical with that of another person or entity, whether within or outside the State, or that so nearly resembles that name as to be likely to deceive or mislead;

(b) likely to falsely suggest the patronage of or connection with some person or entity, whether within or outside the State; or

(c) likely to falsely suggest that the person or entity

(i) has special status in relation to or derived from the Government;

(ii) has the official approval of or acts on behalf of the Government or of any department, branch, agency or organization of Government, or any office of Government; or

(iii) is recognized in the State as a national or central bank.

(4) Whenever the Minister revokes a license under subsection (3), it shall cause notice of the revocation to be published in the Gazette, and may cause notice to be published, whether within the State or elsewhere, in a newspaper or other publication it may think fit in the circumstances.

(5) Where a licensee is or intends to carry on business under a name that contravenes subsection (1) the Minister may direct the company to change its name.

16. (1) No shares or other interests, whether legal or equitable, in a licensee shall be issued, Issued or transferred or otherwise disposed of without the prior written approval of the Authority and the application may be treated in the same

manner as a first time application for a Without licence under section 4 of this Act.

(2) Notwithstanding subsection (1) a licensee may dispose of his shares by will without prior written approval of the Authority.

(3) The Authority may exempt from the provisions of subsection (1) a licensee whose shares are publicly traded on a stock exchange recognized by the Authority, and any exemption shall be subject to

(a) a condition that the licensee shall as soon as reasonably practicable notify the Authority of

(i) any change in control of the licensee;

(ii) the acquisition by any person or group of shares representing more than ten per cent of the licensee's issued share capital or total voting rights; or

(iii) the acquisition by any person or group of shares representing more than ten per cent of the issued share capital or total voting rights of the licensee's parent company;

(b) a condition that the licensee shall, as soon as reasonably practicable, provide information to the Authority and within a period of time the Authority may require for the purpose of enabling an assessment as to whether persons acquiring control or ownership of the licensee in the circumstances set out in paragraph (a) are fit and proper persons to have control or ownership; and

(c) any other terns and conditions the Authority may deem necessary.

(4) In subsection (1) the reference to legal or equitable shares or other interests being transferred or disposed of

includes ownership through one or more trustees, legal representatives, agents, companies or other intermediaries.

17. (1) The holder of a Class A licence shall not

(a) grant to the shareholders and the directors of the bank any loan or advance that exceeds in aggregate five per cent of paid up capital;

(b) grant unsecured advances or unsecured credit of an aggregate amount in excess of two thousand five hundred dollars or of one per cent of the paid up capital of the licensee whichever is the greater or give any financial guarantee in excess of the amount without security, or incur any other liability in excess of that amount without security,

(i) to or on behalf of its directors whether or not the advances, credit, guarantees or other liabilities are obtained by or on account of the directors jointly or severally;

(ii) to or on behalf of any person in whom it or any of its directors is interested as a director, partner, manager or agent or as guarantor; or

(iii) to its holding company, a subsidiary or affiliate or a director of the company, subsidiary or affiliate;

(c) grant credit facilities on terms and conditions more favourable than the terms and conditions generally applicable to borrowers to

(i) its holding company or a subsidiary or affiliate;

(ii) a firm in which a director or officer or the relative of the officer or director has an interest or controls twenty per cent or more of the voting shares;

(iii) a person, if the credit facilities are guaranteed by an officer, director, or any relative of the officer or director;

(iv) a person who controls more than twenty per cent of the licensee's shares;

(d) grant to its officers or employees unsecured advances or unsecured credit that exceed in aggregate for any one officer or employee, one year's emoluments of that officer or employee; except in so far as may be necessary with respect to the interests or shareholding that a licensee may require in satisfaction of debts due to it,

(i) engage, whether on its own account or on a commission basis, in the wholesale or retail trade, including the business of import and export, or otherwise have a direct interest in any commercial, agricultural, industrial or other undertaking; or

(ii) acquire or hold in an aggregate amount exceeding twenty-five per cent of the paid up capital of the licensee, any part of the share capital of any commercial, agricultural, industrial or other undertaking.

but all the interests or shareholding, as the case may be, shall be disposed of within a period not exceeding five years unless permission to extend this period has been given by the Authority;

(f) without the approval of the Authority, invest in the shares of an entity so that the value of the investment at any time exceeds ten per cent of the paid up capital and published reserves of the licensee.

(2) The holder of a Class A licence shall not

(a) purchase, acquire or lease real estate unless

(i) the real estate is necessary for the purpose of conducting its business or providing housing or amenities for its staff, having regard to any reasonable requirements for future expansion of its business or staff; and

(ii) the purchase prices of the real estate does not exceed the paid up capital of the licensee, except that where the licensee exercises its legal right in respect of any property which is the security for any debt, the licensee may acquire the property, but in that case the property shall not be retained for a period in excess of five years without the permission of the Authority;

(b) acquire, deal in or underwrite its own shares or the shares of its holding company;

(c) grant an advance against the security of its own shares, or the shares of its holding company or a subsidiary of the licensee.

(3) Where prior to the commencement of this Act, a licensee has given to any person an advance, credit or financial guarantee or incurred any liability referred to in subsection (1)or (2), no action shall be taken under this Act against the licensee in respect of advance, credit, guarantee or liability for a period of one year after the commencement of this Act.

(4) Subsection (3) does not apply where the licensee has within the period specified in that subsection, increased the amount of advance, credit, guarantee or liability or where the licensee fails to comply with the conditions given by the Authority.

18. A licensee shall not, or allow its subsidiaries to,

(a) purchase or otherwise acquire any participating shares of a body corporate or any ownership interests in an unincorporated entity that the licensee has, or by virtue of the acquisition would have, a substantial investment, or

(b) acquire control of a body corporate that holds shares or ownership interests referred to in paragraph (a),

if the aggregate value of all participating shares and all ownership interests in unincorporated entities beneficially owned by the licensee and its subsidiaries exceeds, or the purchase or acquisition would cause the aggregate value to exceed, seventy per cent of the paid up capital of the licensee.

PART IV

ADMINISTRATION

19. (1) The Authority, under the supervision of the Minister, shall be responsible for ensuring the proper administration of this Act.

(2) The functions of the Authority in administering this Act include but are not limited to the following:

(a) to examine by way of the receipt of regular return, on-site inspections or in any other manner it thinks fit the affairs or business of a licensee carrying on business within or outside the State for the purpose of determining that the licensee is in a sound financial position and is carrying on its business in a satisfactory manner;

(b) in respect of a holding company, parent company or any other company that holds shares in a licensee

(i) to inspect the books of the company;

(ii) to request any information from the appropriate authorities in any country where the company is located;

(c) to assist in the investigation of any contravention of the laws of the State or the laws of another state which has requested assistance on the basis that it has reasonable grounds to believe that an offence has or may have been committed by a licensee or by any of the licensee's directors or officers;

(d) to examine accounts, audited annual accounts and quarterly returns forwarded to it under section 13; and

(e) to examine and approve or deny the applications for licences under this Act.

(3) The Authority may, in the exercise of its powers under subsection (2), call upon an auditor, director, officer or employee of a licensee

(a) to produce all books, minutes, cash, securities, vouchers and other documents and records relating to its assets, liabilities and business generally at a time fixed by the Authority or the Executive Director; and

(b) to give the Authority or the Executive Director any information concerning its affairs and business as may be requested.

(4) An auditor director, officer, or employee of a licensee who is required under this Part to make any disclosure to the Authority shall not by reason of making the disclosure be regarded as being in breach of his duty to the licensee.

(5) In the performance of its functions under this Act and subject to the confidentiality provisions in this Act and elsewhere under the laws of the State, the Authority shall at all reasonable times

(a) have access to the books, records, vouchers, documents, cash and securities of any licensee;

(b) request any information, matter or thing from any person who the Authority has reasonable grounds to believe is carrying on international banking business without a licence;

(c) examine or cause an examination to be made of a licensees affiliates aboard to the same extent that an examination may be made of the licensee, for the purpose of enabling the Authority to perform its functions under the Act.

(6) The Executive Director or the Authority or any person or entity acting under or with either of them may remove, communicate, send or in any manner transmit any of the information, document or related material to another State in accordance with the Mutual Assistance in Criminal Matters Act and any other enactment.

(7) The Executive Director or the Authority or any person or entity acting under or with either of them may remove, communicate, send or in any manner transmit any of the information, document or related material to an approval agency of the government as listed in Schedule 3.

(8) For the purposes of subsection (5) the Executive Director shall have access to the name or title of an account of a customer and any other confidential information about the customer that is in the possession of a licensee and any account established by a licensee on behalf of a customer shall state the name and address of the customer and or the beneficiary of the account.

(9) The Authority may, if it appears that there are reasonable grounds for suspecting that there is a contravention of this Act or that a contravention is likely, petition the court for an order authorizing it to take any action it considers necessary in the interest of the depositors or other creditors and to

preserve any assets of the bank that is the subject of the order.

(10) The Authority shall examine or cause to be examined the affairs of each licensee or previous licensee from time to time or whenever in its judgment an examination is necessary or expedient in order to determine that the licensee or previous licensee is in a sound financial condition and that the requirements of this Act have been complied with in the conduct of its business.

(11) For the purposes of determining the condition of a licensee or previous licensee and its compliance with this Act, the Authority may at any time examine or cause to be examined any of its affiliates to the same extent that an examination may be made of the licensee or previous licensee.

20. If the Authority is satisfied that the licensee is engaging in unsafe or unsound practices in conducting the business of the licensee or is violating the laws, regulations or guidelines issued by the Authority, the Authority may take one or more of the following actions:

(a) issue a written warning as is deemed necessary;

(b) make a written agreement with the licensee providing for a programme of remedial action;

(c) issue a cease or desist order that requires the licensee, director or officer to cease or desist from the practice or violations specified in the order; or

(d) issue any directions it deems necessary to the licensee.

21. (1) If the Authority is satisfied that a licensee

(a) has ceased to carry on international banking business or fails to commence international banking business within one year of the grant of the licence without the written approval of the Authority;

(b) has gone into liquidation, is wound up or is in the process of being wound up, or is otherwise dissolved;

(c) has made any arrangement or composition with its creditors that is prejudicial to the safety and soundness of the bank;

(d) is unable or appears likely to become unable to meet its obligations as they fall due;

(e) is carrying on business in a manner detrimental to the public interest, the interests of its depositors, or the interests of other creditors;

(f) has knowingly provided false information to the Authority upon application for license or as a licensee;

(g) has contravened any provision of this Act;

(h) has failed to comply with a condition of its licence;

(i) or a person holding a position as director, manager or officer of a licensee is not a fit an proper person to hold the respective position; or

(j) has not conducted the direction and management of the business in a fit and proper manner, it may, with the advice of the Minister, take one or more of the actions set out in subsection (2).

(2) The actions that the Authority may take in pursuance of subsection (1) are as follows:

(a) revocation of the licence;

(b) imposition of new or additional conditions upon the licensee;

(c) the substitution of any director or officer of the licensee;

(d) the appointment, at the expense of the licensee, of a person to advise the licensee on the proper conduct of its affairs and to report to the Authority within three months of the appointment;

(e) the appointment, at the expense of the licensee, of a person to assume control of the licensee's affairs who shall mutatis mutandis have all the powers of a person appointed as a receiver or manager of a business appointed under the Companies Act and any other power conferred by the Authority;

(f) to require the licensee to take any other action the Authority considers necessary;

(g) the appointment, where a licence has been revoked, at the expense of the previous licensee, of a person to assume control of the previous licensee's affairs who shall have all the powers of a person appointed as a receiver or manager of a business appointed under the Company Act.

(3) Before ordering any of the actions authorized in subsection (2), the Authority shall give the opportunity to the licensee to show cause against the action, whether in person or by representative, except where the Authority determines that it is in the public interest that it shall not give the licensee the opportunity to show cause and a licensee may pursuant to section 28 appeal to the court against any action ordered under subsection (2).

(4) A person appointed under subsection (2) (d), (e) or (g) or whose appointment has been extended under subsection (5) (b) shall from time to time and in any case within three months from the date of his appointment or of the extension of his appointment, as the case may be, prepare and furnish

a report to the Authority of the affairs of the licensee and may make recommendations.

(5) The Authority, acting on the device of the Minister, may, on receipt of a report under subsection (4),

(a) revoke the appointment of the person appointed under subsection (2) (d), (e) or (g);

(b) extend to period of appointment of the person appointed under subsection (2) (d), (e) or (g);

(c) subject to any conditions that the Authority may impose, allow the licensee to reorganize its affairs in a manner approved by the Authority; or

(d) revoke the licence and request the Attorney General to apply to the court for an order that the licensee be forthwith wound up by the Court pursuant to the provisions of the International Business Companies Act or the Companies Act.

(6) Whenever the Authority revokes a licence under subsection (2) (a) or subsection (5) (d), it shall cause notice of the revocation to be published in the Gazette and may also cause notice to be published, whether within the State or elsewhere, in the newspaper or other publication as it may think fit in the circumstances.

(7) Whenever a licence has been revoked, the licensee or previous licensee must appoint a liquidator that meets the approval of the Authority to ensure that the company is properly liquidated in keeping with the procedure outlined in the Companies Act.

(8) The Authority may use any funds deposited pursuant to section 10 to secure the liquidation of the company or any other expenses.

22. Where a current or former licensee is being wound up voluntarily, the Attorney General may, upon request of the Authority, apply to the Court for leave to intervene on behalf of any interested party if he considers that the winding up is not being conducted in the best interests of its depositors or other creditors, and the Court may make such order as it considers appropriate.

23. The Authority shall be responsible for monitoring compliance, by a licensee, with the requirements of section 46 of the Proceeds of Crime and Money Laundering (Prevention) Act.

24. Subject to section 19 (6) neither the Minister nor the Authority nor any person or entity acting under the authority of either including the Executive Director, shall disclose, or in any way remove from or transmit out of the State any information relating to the identity or affairs of a customer of a licensee, that the Minister, the Authority or any person or entity acting on behalf of the Minister or the Authority has acquired in the course of their duties or the exercise of their functions under this Act.

PART V

EXEMPTION FROM TAXATION AND DUTIES

25. (1) No income tax, capital gains tax or other direct tax shall be levied by the State upon the profits, gains or earnings of a licensee in respect of its international banking business.

(2) No income tax, capital gains tax or other direct tax shall be levied by the State in respect of any dividends or earnings attributable to the shares, debt or securities of a licensee that are beneficially owned by another licensee or by a person who is not a resident.

(3) No estate, inheritance, succession or similar duties or impost shall be levied by the State in respect of any shares, securities or assets of a licensee that are beneficially owned by a person

who is not a resident, and the transfer of those shares, securities or assets shall likewise be exempt from the tax if the transferee is a licensee or otherwise not a resident.

(4) No income tax, capital gains tax or other direct tax or impost shall be levied, withheld or collected in or by the State in respect of any dividends, interest or other returns from any shares, securities, deposits or other borrowings of a licensee or any assets managed by the licensee if the dividends interest or other returns are in respect of shares, securities, deposits or other borrowings or assets beneficially owned by a person who is not a Resident; but the burden of establishing the ownership lies on the licensee.

(5) Notwithstanding any provision of the Stamp Act to the contrary

(a) all instruments relating to transfers of any property to or by a company licensed under this Act;

(b) all instruments relating to transactions in respect of the shares, debt obligations or other securities of a company licensed under this Act; and

(c) all instruments relating in any way to the assets or activities of a company licensed under this Act, are exempt from the payment of stamp duty.

(6) The exemption from taxes and duties conferred by this section may be evidenced by a certificate issued by the Authority on behalf of the State confirming that the licensee shall be exempt from the taxes described in this section for a minimum period of twenty-five years from the date a license is first granted under this Act to the licensee; provided that the provisions of this Part shall not be constructed or applied so as to provide any guarantee or assurance that the license will be renewed or so as to exempt a licensee under this Act from increases in fees charged under or pursuant to this Act

or to exempt any resident from the provisions of any law of the State imposing any tax.

(7) The Minister may by order exempt a licensee from all or so much of any duty payable under the Customs (Control and Management) Act in respect of goods imported by the licensee as the Minister considers expedient, if the licensee satisfies the Minister that:

(a) the goods are not being made or manufactured in the State;

(b) the goods are essential as equipment or fixtures for conducting international banking business in the State and

(c) the goods will exclusively be used for international banking business in the State; and the licensee shall notify the Minister prior to the sale, transfer or disposal of the goods either in or out of the State following the importation of the goods into the State.

Part VI

MISCELLANEOUS

26. (1) The Authority may require a licensee to effect a policy of insurance with a reputable insurance company against

(a) losses arising out of claims of negligence or breach of duty by the licensee or any of its directors or employees;

(b) the dishonesty of employees of the licensee;

(c) loss of documents; and

(d) any other risks as the Authority may from time to time stipulate, in an amount and of a nature as the

Authority may determine to be fit and proper having regard for the nature and type of business carried on by the licensee; and in the event that the insurance is withdrawn, cancelled or not renewed, the licensee shall immediately notify that Authority and shall cease to carry on its business until the insurance has been reinstated or replaced.

(2) A person who contravenes this section commits an offence and is liable on summary conviction to a fine not exceeding ten thousand dollars or to imprisonment for two years or both.

(3) The penalty imposed under subsection (2) shall not preclude the Authority from taking any remedial action under this Act.

27. (1) A licensee or applicant for a licence under this Act or any director, shareholder or officer of a licensee or applicant who knowingly or willfully supplies false or misleading information to the Authority commits an offence and is liable on summary conviction to a fine of one hundred thousand dollars or to imprisonment for two years or both.

(2) A licensee who advertises inviting either directly or indirectly other parties to commit breaches of the laws of the country where the advertisement appears or where the advertisement is directed commits an offence and is liable on summary conviction to a fine of one hundred thousand dollars or to imprisonment for two years or both.

(3) If a licensee is convicted of an offence pursuant to subsection (2), every director and every officer concerned with the management of the company is liable to be convicted for that offence unless he satisfies the Court that the offence was committed without his knowledge or consent or if the director or officer had knowledge of the offence, that he took all reasonable steps to prevent the commission of the offence.

(4) A person who

(a) fails to comply with a request made to him by the Authority;

(b) assaults or willfully obstructs an officer of the Authority in the performance of his duties under this Act;

(c) by the offer of any gratuity, bribe or any other inducement prevents or attempts to prevent the Authority, the Minister or the Executive Director from performing their duties under this Act; or

(d) contravenes any provision of this Act or its Regulations where no punishment is specifically provided, commits an offence and is liable on summary conviction to a fine of one hundred thousand dollars or to imprisonment for two years or both.

28. (1) An appeal from a decision of the Authority

(a) not to renew or continue a licence under section 6;

(b) to revoke a licence under section 6 (2) or section 21 (2) (a) or (5) (d); or

(c) to withdraw an approval, lies directly to the Court.

(2) An appeal against the decision of the Authority must be started by fixed date claim from in accordance with Form 2 of the Eastern Caribbean Supreme Court Civil Procedure Rules with annexed grounds of appeal within twenty-eight days of receiving the decision by the Authority.

(3) The appellant must serve the claim form and grounds of appeal on the Authority and the Attorney General.

(4) In accordance with Part 60 of the Eastern Caribbean Supreme Court Civil Procedure Rules the date for the first

hearing shall not be less than twenty-eight days nor more than fifty-six days after the issue of the claim form.

(5) At the hearing of the appeal the appellant shall be governed by the rules set down in Part 60 of the Eastern Caribbean Supreme Court Civil Procedure Rules.

(6) The Court may, upon the hearing of the appeal confirm, reverse, vary or modify the decision of the Authority or remit the matter with the opinion of the Court to the Authority.

(7) An appeal against a decision of the Authority shall not operate as a suspension of the decision of the Authority.

29. No liability attaches to the Minister, the Authority, the members or employees of the Authority, the Executive Director or any other person acting on behalf of the Authority for an act done in good faith.

30. (1) The Minister, acting on the advice and recommendation of the Authority, may make Regulations generally for the purpose of carrying out or giving effect to the provisions of this Act.

(2) In particular and without prejudice to the generality of the powers conferred by subsection (1) the Minister may make Regulations in respect of

(a) capital adequacy;

(b) risks and large exposures;

(c) major acquisitions or investments by licensees;

(d) classification and concentrations of loans and other assets;

(e) the treatment of interest;

(f) the extent and control of advertising by licensees;

(g) records to be kept at the principal office;

(h) the forms to be used for the purposes of this Act;

(i) fees applicable under this Act;

(j) any other matters required by this Act to be prescribed.

31. Without limiting or affecting section 30 the Authority may from time to time issue guidelines for the purpose of carrying out and giving effect to the provisions of this Act.

32. (1) Except as expressly provided in this Act, the Banking Act shall not apply to any company carrying on an international banking business and this Act shall have no application to companies licensed to carry on banking business under the Banking act.

(2) Neither a company licensed under this Act, nor the dividends, royalties, interest, foreign securities, funds, gains or assets generated or managed by a licensee in the course of its international banking business shall be subject to the provisions of the Exchange Control Act or any order or regulation made under that Act, or to any other exchange or currency control legislation or regulations of the State.

(3) Neither the Interest Act nor any other law of the State regulating the charging of interest on loans by financial institutions or banks shall apply to a licensee or its international banking business.

33. Nothing in this Act shall apply to the Caribbean Development Bank.

34. (1) The International Bank Act 1996 is repealed.

(2) Notwithstanding any other provision of this Act to the contrary a former Act licence which is in force at the

commencement of this Act shall remain in force and have effect as from the commencement of this Act for the remaining period of the current licence.

(3) The licence referred to in subsection (2) may, at the first applicable renewable date, be renewed subject to such conditions as the Authority may impose for the renewal and grant of a licence under this Act.

(4) For the purpose of this section, "former Act licence", means a licence granted under the International Banks Act, 1996.

SCHEDULE 1

PARTICULARS TO BE SPECIFIED IN APPLICATIONS

[Section 4]

A company applying for a licence under this Act shall furnish in writing to the Authority the following particulars, which shall accompany and form part of the form of application prescribed by the Authority for use under this Act:

(1) Name of applicant.

(2) Address in the State of its place of business and the name and address of the registered agent in the State.

(3) The names, addresses, citizenship and residency of all directors, shareholders, officers, managers and in the case of a publicly traded company only the names and addresses of shareholders owing ten per cent of the issued share capital or more.

(4) Names and addresses of solicitors, if any, to the applicant together with a letter from the solicitors confirming that they act for the applicant.

(5) Names and addresses of auditors of the applicant, together with a letter from the auditors confirming that they consent to act for the applicant.

(6) Evidence of a proper application for incorporation of the company in the State and that the company is an "eligible company".

(7) Evidence in writing that the applicant itself or some person directly or indirectly connected with the applicant is possessed of solid and practical experience in banking business.

(8) An undertaking in writing to provide and set apart a fully paid-up capital fund before or at the time it commences business, that the Authority may in its determination require, based upon the class of licence for which the application is being made.

(9) Police record certifying no criminal convictions or alternatively a police record approved by the Authority.

(10) Annual accounts of its holding company, if any, for the proceedings three years and subsequently annually duly audited and certified by an independent auditor.

(11) Names of all subsidiary companies of the applicant with addresses of their registered offices.

(12) A copy of the articles of incorporation and by-laws of the applicant company verified by an affidavit sworn by the Resident director of the applicant.

(13) One character reference and two bank references.

(14) Statement of assets and liabilities, and certified statement of net worth of the applicant shareholder; where the applicant is an existing company, basic financial statements and where the applicant is a group of companies, the audited financial statements from all the members of the group.

(15) Statement of capital of any company held directly or through a subsidiary as an asset of the applicant.

(16) If application is being made for a Class B licence the list and description of the proposed customers of the licensee.

(17) The applicant must provide a business plan containing the following:

(a) a description of the objectives of the company;

(b) proposed customer base;

(c) opening balance sheet and three year projections as certified by an auditor;

(d) management structure;

(e) anti money laundering policies and provision

(f) a feasibility study; (g)the economic need that the company intend to meet;

(h) the nature and source of capital financing;

(i) proof of applicants ability to meet statutory requirements for minimum paid up capital and statutory deposits;

(j) a description of internal systems and controls; and

(k) copy of the ownership structure including group member and affiliated companies

(18) All directors, managers, senior office and shareholders must complete a fit and proper questionnaire.

SCHEDULE 2

(Section 2 and 13 (1)

LIST OF APPROVED ACCOUNTING BODIES

United Kingdom
The Institute of Chartered Accountants in England and Wales
The Institute of Chartered Accountants in Ireland
The Institute of Chartered Accountants of Scotland
The Association of Chartered Certified Accountants
The Chartered Institute of Management Accountants

United States
The American Institute of Certified Public Accountants

Canada
The Canadian Institute of Chartered Accountants
The Certified General Accountants Association of Canada
The Certified Management Accountants of Canada

Caribbean
Institute of Chartered Accountants of the Eastern Caribbean
Institute of Chartered Accountants of Trinidad and Tobago
Institute of Chartered Accountants of Barbados
Institute of Chartered Accountants of Jamaica
Institute of Chartered Accountants of Guyana
Institute of Chartered Accountants of Belize
The Bahamas Institute of Chartered Accountants

Or any other such body of accountants as may from time to time be approved by the Institute of Chartered Accountants of the Eastern Caribbean.

SCHEDULE 3

(Section 19 97)

LIST OF APPROVED GOVERNMENT AGENCIES

1. The Royal Saint Vincent and the Grenadines Police Force.
2. The Office of the Director of Public Prosecutions.
3. The Financial Intelligence Unit.
4. The Office of the Attorney General.
5. The Customs and Excise Department.
6. The Ministry of Foreign Affairs.
7. Any other body the Authority may in its own discretion approve.

Passed in the House of Assembly this 16th of November, 2004.

Republic of Vanuatu

Background

Multiple waves of colonizers, each speaking a distinct language, migrated to the New Hebrides in the millennia preceding European exploration in the 18th century. This settlement pattern accounts for the complex linguistic diversity found on the archipelago to this day. The British and French, who settled the New Hebrides in the 19th century, agreed in 1906 to an Anglo-French Condominium, which administered the islands until independence in 1980, when the new name of Vanuatu was adopted.

Population

256,155 (July 2012 est.)

Capital

Port Vila

Official Language

Pidgin (known as Bislama or Bichelama), English, French plus more than 100 local unofficial languages.

Regulatory Authority

Reserve Bank of Vanuatu
PMB 9062 - Port Vila
Republic of Vanuatu
Phone: +678 23333
Fax: +678 24231
Email: rbvinfo@rbv.gov.vu
Web: www.rbv.gov.vu

License Types

Offshore Banks are regulated by the International Banking Act No 4 of 2002. There are no restricted Class B Licenses.

Capital Requirements

Offshore banks are subject to a USD 500,000.00 paid up capital requirement.

Offshore Bank License Fees

License Issuing Fee	USD 8,000.00
Annual License Renewal Fee:	USD 8,000.00

INTERNATIONAL BANKING

INTERNATIONAL BANKING ACT NO 4 OF 2002

Arrangement of Sections

PART 1

PRELIMINARY

PART 2

LICENSING OF INTERNATIONAL BANKING BUSINESS

PART 3

SUPERVISION AND ENFORCEMENT

Part 4

OBLIGATIONS AND RESTRICTIONS ON LICENSEES

Division 1 – Obligations on licensees

Division 2 – Restrictions of licensees

Part 5

DISCLOSURE AND TAX EXEMPTIONS

Part 6

MISCELLANEOUS

INTERNATIONAL BANKING

To provide for the licensing, regulation and supervision of international banking business and for related purposes.

Be it enacted by the President and Parliament as follows:

Part 1

PRELIMINARY

1. Interpretation

In this Act unless the contrary intention appears:

accounting records includes the working papers and other documents as are necessary to explain the methods and calculations by which financial statements are made up and includes data held electronically or in any other form of non-paper based system.

administrator means a person appointed as administrator under subsection 17(2).

approved auditor means an auditor appointed under subsection 34(1).

banking business has the meaning given by section 2.

company means a body corporate incorporated, formed or constituted under the laws of Vanuatu or any other country.

compliance inspection means the activities referred to in subsection 14(1).

Court means the Supreme Court of Vanuatu.

director means an individual who exercises management and policy-making functions at the highest level of a company, and includes an individual who is a member of the board of directors, committee, council or other governing body of a company.

disqualified person means a person referred to in subsection 24(3).

dollars and $ means dollars of the currency of the United States of America.

eligible capital of a company means the capital of that company that qualifies as eligible capital under international adequacy standards in accordance with the Basel Capital Accord.

examiner means a person appointed as an examiner under subsection 18(1).

exempted company has the same meaning as in the Companies Act [CAP191].

financial statements means profit and loss accounts, and balance sheets, and includes notes (other than directors' reports) attached to, or intended to be read with, any of the profit and loss accounts or balance sheets and also includes if applicable, a consolidated profit and loss account and balance sheet.

foreign bank means a company, other than a company incorporated or continued under the Companies Act [CAP 191], that is licensed to carry on banking business in a jurisdiction outside Vanuatu.

foreign incorporated licensee means a licensee that is not a locally incorporated licensee.

foreign regulatory authority means an authority or body outside Vanuatu that exercises functions corresponding or similar to the functions exercised by the Reserve Bank.

holding company has the same meaning as in the Companies Act [CAP191].

international banking business means banking business that is conducted in a currency other than the legal currency of Vanuatu and with a person who is not a resident of Vanuatu.

international company means a company incorporated or continued under the International Companies Act No. 32 of 1992.

law enforcement authority means an authority or body, within or outside Vanuatu, dealing with the investigation of suspected criminal activity and includes the Financial Intelligence Unit established by the Financial Transactions Reporting Act No. 33 of 2000.

licence means a licence issued under section 7.

licensee means a company licensed under this Act to carry on international banking business.

locally incorporated licensee means a licensee that is incorporated or continued under the Companies Act [CAP 191].

manager of a licensee means:

(a) an individual who occupies the position of chief executive (however described) of the licensee; or

(b) any other individual who under the immediate authority of the chief executive or a director exercises management functions for the licensee.

Minister means the minister responsible for finance.

officer of a licensee includes a director, manager or company secretary.

prescribed means prescribed by regulations made under this Act.

prudential matters in relation to a licensee includes matters relating to the conduct by the licensee of its affairs, with integrity, prudence and professional skill, in such a way as to keep itself in a sound financial position and not to cause or promote instability in the financial system.

prudential supervision means the supervision of prudential matters and includes:

(a) the collection and analysis of information in respect of prudential matters relating to licensees; and

(b) the encouragement and promotion of licensees to carry out sound practices in relation to prudential matters; and

(c) the evaluation of the effectiveness and carrying out of such practices.

records include:

(a) accounting records;

(b) books, registers, documents and vouchers;

(c) securities and financial instruments;

(d) any record of information or date;

whether stored in paper, on disk or tape, or in electronic or any other non-paper based form.

regulations mean regulations made under this Act.

Reserve Bank means the Reserve Bank established under the Reserve Bank Act [CAP 125].

resident of Vanuatu means;

(a) an individual who ordinarily resides in Vanuatu; or

(b) a company incorporated or continued under the Companies Act [CAP 191]; but does not include:

(c) an exempted company; or

(d) a trust company if the settlors and beneficiaries are not residents of Vanuatu; or

(e) a company incorporated under the International Companies Act No. 32 of 1992.

relevant person means a licensee, a former licensee or a subsidiary or holding company of a licensee or of a former licensee.

significant interest has the meaning given by subsection 1(2).

subsidiary has the same meaning as in the Companies Act [CAP 191].

trust company means a company licensed under the Trust Companies Act [CAP 69].

(2) A person has a significant interest in a company if:

(a) the person has a legal or equitable interest in that company or in a holding company of that company; and

(b) the interest, directly or indirectly:

(i) enables the person to control 10 percent or more of the voting rights of the company at a general meeting of the company; or

(ii) entitles the person to a share of 10 percent or more in dividends declared and paid by the company; or

(iii) entitles the person to a share of 10 percent or more in any distribution of the surplus assets of the company; whether or not the person holds the interest alone or with one or more other persons.

2. Banking business

(1) A person is carrying on banking business if the person:

(a) accepts deposits of money that are withdrawable, or payable upon demand, after a fixed period or after notice; or

(b) undertakes the frequent sale or placement of bonds, certificates or other securities; and uses such deposits or the proceeds of such sales or placements, either in whole or in part, for loans or investments for the account and at the risk of the person.

(2) A person is taken to be carrying on banking business if the person:

(a) advertises for or solicits deposits of money, or offers to sell or place bonds, certificates or other securities; and

(b) uses or intends to use the funds so acquired, either in whole or part, for making loans or investments, or any other activity authorised by law or customary banking practice, for the account and at the risk of the person.

(3) Banking business does not include the acceptance of a deposit of money which is paid by a company ("the paying company") to another company if:

(a) the paying company is a subsidiary of the other company; or

(b) the paying company and the other company are both subsidiaries of a third company.

3. Application of Act

(1) This Act does not apply to financial institutions licensed under the Financial Institutions Act No. 2 of 1999.

(2) This Act has effect despite the Companies Act [CAP 191] and the International Companies Act No. 32 of 1992 and if there is any conflict between the provisions of this Act and the provisions of the Companies Act [CAP 191] or the International Companies Act No. 32 of 1992, the provisions of this Act prevail.

(3) However, nothing in this Act exempts a licensee from complying with the provisions of the Companies Act [CAP 191] or the International Companies Act No. 32 of 1992.

PART 2

LICENSING OF INTERNATIONAL BANKING BUSINESS

4. Licence needed to carry on international banking business

(1) A person must not carry on international banking business unless the person is licensed under this Act.

(2) If a person contravenes subsection (1), the person is guilty of an offence punishable on conviction:

(a) if an individual by a fine not exceeding $150,000 or imprisonment for a term not exceeding 10 years or both;

(b) if a body corporate a fine not exceeding $750,000.

5. Existing exempted banks and exempted financial institutions

(1) On 1 January 2003 each exempted entity is taken to have been issued with a licence under this section to carry on international banking business and the Reserve Bank must as soon as possible after that date issue each exempted entity with the licence.

(2) A licence under this section is to be in such form as is approved by the Reserve Bank and the licensee must pay to the Reserve Bank on or before 31 January 2003 the prescribed annual licence fee.

(3) While a licence under this section remains in force an exempted entity is subject to the provisions of this Act, other than sections 20, 21 and 22.

(4) A licence under this section ceases to be in force on 31 December 2003.

(5) If an exempted entity wishes to carry on international banking business after 31 December 2003, the exempted entity must before 1 August 2003 apply to the Reserve Bank under section 6 for a licence to carry on international banking business.

(6) To avoid doubt, an application by an exempted entity under section 6 is an application for a new licence and the fact that the exempted entity has a licence under this section is not to be taken into account by the Reserve Bank in determining the application for a licence under section 6.

(7) Despite the provisions of any other Act, an exempted entity ceases to be subject to the Banking Act [CAP 63] on 1 January 2003 and any licence issued under that Act to the exempted entity ceases to be in force on 1 January 2003.

(8) In this section, exempted entity means a company that on 31 December 2002 was licensed as an exempted bank or exempted financial institution under the Banking Act [CAP 63].

6. Application for licence to carry on international banking business

(1) A company must apply in writing to the Reserve Bank for a licence to carry on international banking business.

(2) An application under subsection (1) must:

(a) be in such form as is specified by the Reserve Bank; and

(b) be accompanied by:

(i) a statement disclosing the ultimate and intermediate, if any, beneficial ownership of the applicant; and

(ii) such documents as are specified by the Reserve Bank; and

(iii) the prescribed application fee and the prescribed annual licence fee.

(3) The Reserve Bank may in writing request that an applicant provide such additional information and documents as the Reserve Bank considers necessary to determine the application.

(4) If a request has been made under subsection (3), the applicant must provide such additional information and documents to the Reserve Bank within the time specified by the Reserve Bank.

(5) If an application is refused, the Reserve Bank is to refund the annual fee to the applicant. However, the application fee is not refundable.

(6) An applicant must not furnish any information or document

that is false or misleading in any material particular in connection with an application.

(7) If an applicant contravenes subsection (6), the applicant is guilty of an offence punishable on conviction by a fine not exceeding $250,000.

7. Reserve Bank to issue or refuse licence within 4 months

(1) The Reserve Bank must within 4 months after receiving an application for a licence and all other information and documents requested by the Reserve Bank under subsection 6(3):

(a) issue a licence to the applicant subject to such terms and conditions as the Reserve Bank considers fit; or

(b) refuse the application and inform the applicant of the refusal.

(2) The Reserve Bank must advise an applicant in writing of the reasons for its refusal to issue a licence under this section.

(3) As soon as practicable after a licence has been issued, the Reserve Bank must publish a notice to this effect in the Gazette.

8. Criteria for the issue of a licence

(1) The Reserve Bank must not issue a licence unless it is satisfied that:

(a) the ownership spread, financial capacity and financial history (if any) of the applicant are satisfactory; and

(b) each director and manager of the applicant is a fit and proper person and has sufficient experience in international banking to be involved with operations or management of an international bank; and

(c) each associate of the applicant is a fit and proper person to have an interest in an international bank; and

(d) the risk management, accounting and internal control systems of the applicant are satisfactory; and

(e) the capital structure of the applicant is adequate and the amount of unimpaired paid up capital of the applicant is at least $500,000; and

(f) the applicant if issued with a licence intends to carry on international banking business and the kind of international banking business that the applicant intends to carry on is acceptable; and

(g) a written undertaking has been given by the applicant to the Reserve Bank that the applicant will provide the Reserve Bank with any information that the Reserve Bank may require for it to carry out its prudential supervision functions under this Act; and

(h) a written statement has been given by the applicant to the Reserve Bank that the applicant will keep the Reserve Bank informed of any significant developments adversely affecting its financial soundness or reputation and the financial soundness or reputation of its holding company (if any); and

(i) the applicant upon the issue of the licence will comply with this Act and the regulations; and

(j) the relationship between the applicant and its associates will not prejudice the effective supervision of the banking business of the applicant; and

(k) if a foreign bank is an associate of the applicant - the applicant and the foreign bank will be effectively supervised on a consolidated basis; and

(l) issuing the licence is not against the public interest and would not be detrimental to the reputation of Vanuatu.

(2) In subsection (1), a person is an associate if the person:

(a) has a significant interest in the applicant; or

(b) is a subsidiary of the applicant; or(c) is a holding company of the applicant.

(3) If a person has a significant interest in the applicant and a significant interest in another company, that other company is an associate of the applicant for the purposes of subsection (1).

9. Criteria for issue of licence to foreign banks

(1) This section applies to an application for a licence to carry on international banking business made by a foreign bank.

(2) The Reserve Bank must not issue a licence unless satisfied:

(a) of the matters set out in subsection 8(1); and

(b) the international reputation of the foreign bank is satisfactory; and

(c) the relevant law and regulatory requirements relating to the licensing and supervision of banking business in the foreign bank's home country is acceptable; and

(d) there is sufficient evidence that the foreign bank is subject to comprehensive supervision and regulation on a consolidated basis by relevant authorities in the foreign bank's home country; and

(e) the foreign bank has provided written confirmation from the supervisory banking authority in the foreign bank's home country that the authority has no objection to the foreign bank carrying on international banking business; and

(f) the foreign bank has provided a statement from the supervisory banking authority in the foreign bank's home country that it is supervised on a basis consistent with the guidelines established by the Basel Committee on Banking Supervision, and the authority is willing to cooperate in the supervision of the foreign bank; and

(g) the foreign bank has provided a written acknowledgment that the Reserve Bank may discuss its conduct and status with the supervisory banking authority in its home country; and

(h) the foreign bank has provided written confirmation that it will comply with the relevant laws of Vanuatu in respect of the employment and training of Ni-Vanuatu citizens.

10. Conditions of a licence including annual fees

(1) A licence issued under this Act must not be assigned or transferred and any purported assignment or transfer is null and void.

(2) A licence is subject to such terms and conditions as are determined by the Reserve Bank.

(3) The Reserve Bank may:

(a) vary or revoke a condition of a licence; or

(b) impose further conditions on a licence.

(4) A licence issued under this Act remains in force until it is revoked by the Reserve Bank under section 11.

(5) A licensee must pay to the Reserve Bank the prescribed annual licence fee on each anniversary of the licence being issued.

(6) A licensee that fails to pay the fee by the due date is liable to a surcharge equal to the amount of the annual licence fee payable to the Reserve Bank within 7 days after the due date for payment of the annual licence fee.

(7) An annual licence fee and any surcharge are debts due to the Reserve Bank and are recoverable in a court of competent jurisdiction.

(8) All annual licence fees and surcharges received by the Reserve Bank must be paid by the Reserve Bank to the Public Fund within the meaning of the Public Finance and Economic Management Act No. 6 of 1998.

(9) If a licensee fails to pay:

(a) an annual licence fee by the due date; or

(b) a surcharge referred to in subsection (6) by the due date; and continues to transact international banking businesses, the licensee is guilty of an offence punishable on conviction by a fine not exceeding $250,000.

11. Revocation of licence

(1) The Reserve Bank may revoke the licence of a licensee if:

(a) the Reserve Bank is entitled to take enforcement action against the licence under section 16; or

(b) the licensee has failed to commence carrying on international banking business within 3 months after the issue of its licence; or

(c) the licensee has ceased to carry on international banking business for a period exceeding 3 months; or

(d) the licensee has made a written request to the Reserve Bank for its licence to be revoked.

(2) If the Reserve Bank intends to revoke a licence, under paragraph (1)(a), (1)(b) or (1)(c), the Reserve Bank must give notice in writing to the licensee stating that the Reserve Bank intends to revoke the licence and the grounds upon which it intends to revoke the licence.

(3) The licensee may within 14 days after receiving the notice under subsection (2) submit in writing reasons why its licence should not be revoked.

(4) The Reserve Bank may revoke a licence:

(a) if the licensee does not make a submission under subsection (3); or

(b) having taken into account the submission made by the licensee, the Reserve Bank is of the opinion that the licensee has failed to show good reason why its licence should not be revoked.

(5) The Reserve Bank must give a licensee written notice of a revocation.

(6) A revocation takes effect:

(a) on the date the notice referred to in subsection (6) is given to the licensee; or

(b) such later date as is specified by the Reserve Bank in the notice.

(7) If a licence is revoked under this section, the licensee must:

(a) cease to carry on international banking business on and from the date the revocation takes effect; and

(b) return to the Reserve Bank the original licence and all copies of the licence in its custody or control.

12. Appeals against revocation

(1) A person may appeal to the Court against a decision of the Reserve Bank to revoke a licence.

(2) An appeal must be made to the Court within 21 days after the date the licence was revoked or within such further time as the Court may allow.

(3) Unless the Court otherwise orders, an appeal does not operate to suspend the decision of the Reserve Bank.

(4) In determining an appeal, the Court may confirm, vary, or revoke the decision of the Reserve Bank.

(5) A person aggrieved by the decision of the Court may appeal to the Court of Appeal against that decision.

Part 3

SUPERVISION AND ENFORCEMENT

13. Banking supervision

(1) The functions of the Reserve Bank include:

(a) to undertake in accordance with the provisions of this Act and the regulations the prudential supervision of the international banking business of licensees;

(b) to review international banking business and implement internationally accepted standards for the prudential supervision of international banking business;

(c) to recommend to the Minister such amendments to this Act and the regulations as the Reserve Bank considers necessary to enable it to supervise international banking business in accordance with internationally accepted standards.

(2) In carrying out the functions under subsection (1) in relation to a licensee, the Reserve Bank must have regard to the following matters:

(a) the capital adequacy of the licensee in relation to the size and nature of its international banking business;

(b) the asset concentration and risk exposure of the licensee;

(c) the separation of international banking business of the licensee from the financial interests of any person having a significant interest in the licensee;

(d) the adequacy of the liquidity of the licensee in relation to its liabilities;

(e) the quality of the licensee's assets and the adequacy of its loss provision;

(f) the internal controls, risk management and accounting systems of the licensee;

(g) the quality of the management of the licensee; and

(h) such other matters as the Reserve Bank considers relevant.

(3) The Reserve Bank may formulate in writing guidelines and issue directives for the purpose of the prudential supervision of the international banking business of:

(a) all licensees; or

(b) a specified class of licensees; or

(c) one or more specified licensees or classes of licensees.

(4) The directives issued by the Reserve Bank must be published in the Gazette.

(5) The Reserve Bank may vary or revoke a directive or guideline.

14. Compliance inspection

(1) The Reserve Bank may, for the purposes of the prudential supervision of the international banking business of licensees, do all or any of the following;

(a) inspect the premises and the business, within or outside Vanuatu, including the systems and controls, of a relevant person;

(b) inspect the assets, including cash, belonging to or in the possession or control of a relevant person;

(c) examine and make copies of records belonging to or in the possession or control of a relevant person, being records that in the opinion of the Reserve Bank relate to the carrying on of international banking business by the relevant person.

(2) If, after a compliance inspection, the Reserve Bank is satisfied that a person is or has been an officer, employee or agent of a relevant person or holds or has held a significant interest in a relevant person, the Reserve Bank may, by notice in writing, require the person:

(a) to produce any records in the person's possession or control, or

(b) to provide any information within the person's knowledge or belief; concerning the international banking business carried on or formerly carried on by the relevant person.

(3) A notice issued under subsection (2) must state the time period within which and the place where the records must be produced or the information provided.

(4) A person who fails to comply with a notice issued under subsection (2) is guilty of an offence punishable on conviction by a fine not exceeding $50,000 or a term of imprisonment of not more than 2 years, or both.

15. Participation of a foreign regulatory authority

(1) Subject to subsection (2), the Reserve Bank may, upon the request of a foreign regulatory authority, permit that authority to take part in a compliance inspection undertaken by the Reserve Bank under section 14.

(2) The Reserve Bank must not permit a foreign regulatory authority to take part in a compliance inspection unless it is satisfied that:

(a) the compliance inspection is necessary for the effective consolidated supervision of the licensee; and

(b) the foreign regulatory authority is subject to adequate legal restrictions on further disclosure of information obtained during the compliance inspection; and

(c) the foreign regulatory authority will not, without the written permission of the Reserve Bank:

(i) disclose information obtained during the compliance inspection to any person other than an officer or employee of the authority engaged in prudential supervision; or

(ii) take any action on information obtained during the compliance inspection.

16. Enforcement action

(1) The Reserve Bank may take enforcement action against a licensee, if:

(a) in the opinion of the Reserve Bank, the licensee:

(i) has contravened this Act or the regulations; or

(ii) carries on international banking business in a manner detrimental to the public interest or to the interest of any depositors or creditors; or

(iii) is or is likely to become insolvent; or

(iv) has failed to comply with a directive given to it by the Reserve Bank within the time specified; or

(v) is in breach of any term or condition of its licence; or

(vi) has furnished the Reserve Bank with any false, inaccurate or misleading information; or

(b) the licensee:

(i) is compulsorily wound up; or

(ii) has passed a resolution for voluntary winding up; or

(iii) is dissolved; or

(c) the licensee, or an officer or shareholder of the licensee is convicted of any offence by any court in Vanuatu or in a jurisdiction outside Vanuatu; or

(d) a receiver and/or manager has been appointed, in respect of the licensee's banking business; or

(e) possession has been taken of any of the licensee's property by or on behalf of the holder of a debenture secured by a registered charge; or

(f) in the opinion of the Reserve Bank, a person:

(i) who has a share or interest in the licensee, either equitable or legal; or

(ii) who is an officer of the licensee; is not a fit and proper person to have an interest in or to be concerned with the management of the licensee; or

(g) in the opinion of the Reserve Bank, the licensee or a subsidiary or holding company of the licensee has refused or failed to co-operate with the Reserve Bank on a compliance inspection conducted by the Reserve Bank.

(2) If the Reserve Bank is of the opinion that an enforcement action must be taken against a licensee, such action may consist of all or any of the following:

(a) revocation of the licence of the licensee under section 11;

(b) appointment of an examiner to carry on an investigation under section 18;

(c) appointment of a qualified person to audit the licensee on the conduct of its international banking business.

17. Protection order

(1) The Reserve Bank may apply to the Court for a protection order to protect or preserve:

(a) the business or property of a licensee; or

(b) the interests of its depositors, creditors or the public.

(2) The Court may make a protection order providing for all or any of the following:

(a) an order preventing a licensee or any other person from transferring, disposing or otherwise dealing with property belonging to it or in its custody or control;

(b) an order appointing a person as an administrator to take over and manage the international banking business of the licensee;

(c) an order that the licensee be wound up in accordance with the Companies Act [CAP 191];

(d) an order granting the Reserve Bank a search warrant on such terms as the Court determines.

(3) If the Court makes an order under paragraph (2)(b) in respect of a licensee, it may extend the appointment of the administrator to include any subsidiary of the licensee.

(4) An order referred to in paragraph (2)(b) may:

(a) specify the powers of the administrator, which may include the powers of a licensee under this Act or of a liquidator under the Companies Act (CAP 191); or

(b) require the administrator to provide security to the satisfaction of the Court; or

(c) fix and provide for the remuneration of the administrator; or

(d) require such persons as it considers necessary to appear before the Court for the purposes of giving information or producing records concerning the licensee or the international banking business carried on by the licensee.

(5) An order made under paragraph (2)(b) must make provision

for reports to be submitted by the administrator to the Court and to the Reserve Bank.

(6) The Court may on its own motion or on the application of the Reserve Bank or the administrator:

(a) give directions to the administrator concerning the exercise of his powers; or

(b) vary the powers of the administrator; or

(c) terminate the appointment of the administrator.

(7) An application under subsection (1) may be made ex parte or upon such notice as the Court may require.

18. Appointment of examiner

(1) The Reserve Bank may by notice in writing appoint an examiner to investigate and report to the Reserve Bank on a licensee if:

(a) the Reserve Bank intends to take enforcement action under section 16; or

(b) a written request for an investigation is made to the Reserve Bank by:

(i) shareholders holding not less than one third of the total number of issued shares in the licensee; or

(ii) depositors holding not less than one tenth of the gross amount of the deposit liabilities of the licensee.

(2) If a request for an investigation is made under paragraph (1)(b), the Reserve Bank may refuse to appoint an examiner until the shareholders or depositors, have provided security for the costs of the investigation to the satisfaction of the Reserve Bank.

(3) An investigation referred to in subsection (1) may be made in respect of:

(a) the nature, management, conduct or state of the licensee's international banking business or any aspect of it; and

(b) the ownership and control of the licensee.

(4) An examiner appointed under subsection (1) may exercise any of the powers conferred upon the Reserve Bank under this Part.

(5) As soon as practicable after the conclusion of an investigation under this section, the examiner must submit a full report of the investigation to the Reserve Bank.

(6) The Reserve Bank may direct that the costs and expenses of and incidental to the investigation are paid by the licensee.

19. Investigation of suspected contravention

(1) The Reserve Bank may investigate the affairs of a person that the Reserve Bank suspects is carrying on or has carried on international banking business without a licence.

(2) For the purposes of this section, the Reserve Bank may exercise the powers available to the Reserve Bank under this Part as if the person were a licensee.

Part 4

OBLIGATIONS AND RESTRICTIONS ON LICENSEES

Division 1 – Obligations on licensees

20. Physical presence of licensees and employees in Vanuatu

(1) Subject to subsections (2) and (3), a licensee must occupy premises in Vanuatu within 30 days, or such longer period as the Reserve Bank allows, after being issued with a licence under section 7.

(2) A licensee must not occupy premises in Vanuatu unless it has obtained the prior written approval of the Reserve Bank.

(3) The Reserve Bank must not give its approval under subsection (2) to any premises unless it is satisfied that:

(a) the premises are located at a fixed address in Vanuatu; and

(b) the licensee will carry on international banking business under its licence from those premises; and

(c) the licensee will maintain at those premises operating records including financial statements relating to the international banking business conducted under its licence; and

(d) the employee or employees of the licensee will operate full time from those premises; and

(e) those premises adequately symbolize the physical presence of the licensee in Vanuatu.

(4) A licensee must within 30 days, or such longer period as the Reserve Bank allows, after being issued with a licence under section 7, appoint such employees, and have in place such facilities, as the Reserve Bank considers appropriate having regard to the nature and scale of the international banking business to be carried on by the licensee under its licence.

(5) At least one employee of a licensee must have a day-to-day of the international banking business conducted by the licensee under its licence and sufficient authority within the licensee to participate in the management of that day-to-day international banking business.

(6) A licensee must not change the address of its premises in Vanuatu unless it has obtained the approval of the Reserve Bank in writing for the change.

(7) If a licensee contravenes subsection (2), (4) or (6), the licensee is guilty of an offence, punishable on conviction by a fine not exceeding $250,000.

21. Maintenance of minimum capital

(1) A locally incorporated licensee must maintain at all times eligible capital:

(a) in such minimum proportion in relation to its assets, liabilities or risk exposures; and

(b) subject to subsection (2), in such amount; as the Reserve Bank determines in writing.

(2) A locally incorporated licensee must maintain at all times paid up capital of not less than $500,000.

(3) If a locally incorporated licensee contravenes subsection (1) or (2), the licensee is guilty of an offence punishable on conviction by a fine not exceeding $250,000.

(4) If the capital of a locally incorporated licensee is reduced below its minimum capital requirement, the licensee must, within 7 days after becoming aware of the reduction, advise, the Reserve Bank in writing of the reduction.

22. Computation and form of minimum capital

(1) The Reserve Bank must determine in writing the computation and form of capital required to be maintained under section 21 by a locally incorporated licensee after consultation with the licensee.

(2) Without limiting subsection (1), the Reserve Bank may in making a determination have regard to the following:

(a) the scale and nature of the locally incorporated licensee's financial liabilities, including its deposits;

(b) the nature of the locally incorporated licensee's assets and the degree of risk associated with them; and

(c) the nature of the international banking business carried on by the locally incorporated licensee.

(3) A locally incorporated licensee must comply with a determination made by the Reserve Bank within one month, or such longer period as the Reserve Bank allows, after the determination is made.

(4) The Reserve Bank may in writing vary or revoke a determination.

(5) The Reserve Bank may under subsection (1) determine different requirements for the computation and form of capital for different classes of locally incorporated licensees.

23. Keeping of accounting records

(1) A licensee must keep and maintain accounting records that are necessary to disclose with reasonable accuracy the financial position of the licensee at intervals not exceeding three months or such other interval as the Reserve Bank may require in writing.

(2) A licensee that contravenes subsection (1) is guilty of an offence punishable on conviction by a fine not exceeding $250,000.

24. Appointments

(1) A locally incorporated licensee must have at least two directors who are individuals one of whom must be a resident of Vanuatu and must not appoint:

(a) a disqualified person as an officer; or

(b) any other person as an officer, unless the Reserve Bank has given prior written approval for the appointment in accordance with subsection (4).

(2) A foreign incorporated licensee must not appoint in relation to the licensee's international banking business conducted under its licence:

(a) a disqualified person as an officer; or

(b) any other person as an officer unless the Reserve Bank has given prior written approval for the appointment in accordance with subsection (4).

(3) A person is a disqualified person if, at any time:

(a) the person has been convicted of an offence against or arising out of this Act; or

(b) the person is or has been a director, or is or has been directly or indirectly concerned in the management of a licensee or a bank or other financial institutions in Vanuatu or any other country which has had its licence revoked or has been wound up by a court in any jurisdiction; or

(c) the person has been convicted by a court for an offence involving dishonesty; or

(d) the person is or becomes bankrupt; or

(e) the person has applied to take the benefit of a law for the relief of bankrupt or insolvent debtors; or

(f) the person has compounded with his or her creditors.

(4) The Reserve Bank must not give its approval to the of a person as an officer of a licensee unless it is satisfied that the person concerned meets all of the criteria for fitness and propriety set out in the prudential guidelines. An approval

may be given on such terms and conditions as the Reserve Bank considers appropriate.

(5) A disqualified person must:

(a) not accept an appointment as an officer; or

(b) if the person is already an officer, continue as an officer.

(6) A licensee that contravenes subsection (1) or (2) is guilty of an offence punishable on conviction by a fine not exceeding $250,000.

(7) An individual who contravenes subsection (5) is guilty of an offence punishable on conviction by a fine not exceeding $50,000 or imprisonment for a term not exceeding 2 years, or both.

25. The Reserve Bank may remove officers

(1) The Reserve Bank may direct in writing a licensee to remove a person who is an officer of the licensee (other than a director of a foreign incorporated licensee) if the Reserve Bank is satisfied that the person:

(a) is a disqualified person; or

(b) does not meet one or more of the criteria for fitness and propriety set out in the prudential guidelines.

(2) Before directing the licensee to remove a person, the Reserve Bank must give written notice to the person and the licensee giving each of them a reasonable opportunity to make submissions on the matter.

(3) A direction takes effect on the day specified in it, which must be at least 7 days after it is made.

(4) If the Reserve Bank directs a licensee to remove a person, the Reserve Bank must give a copy of the direction to the person and the licensee.

(5) If a licensee fails to comply with a direction under this section, the licensee is guilty of an offence punishable on a conviction by a fine not exceeding $250,000.

26. Operations outside Vanuatu

(1) A locally incorporated licensee must not create a subsidiary or operate a branch, agency or office in any place outside of Vanuatu unless it obtains the prior written approval of the Reserve Bank.

(2) The Reserve Bank must not give its approval under subsection (1) unless it is satisfied that:

(a) the authority responsible for banking supervision in the jurisdiction in which the branch, agency or office will be located consents to the establishment of the branch, agency or office; and

(b) the branch, agency or office will be subject to adequate banking supervision; and

(c) the Reserve Bank will have access to the information and documents it considers necessary to supervise the international banking business of the licensee in accordance with this Act.

(3) The Reserve Bank may give an approval on such terms and conditions as it considers appropriate.

(4) If a licensee contravenes subsection (1) or fails to comply with a term or condition of an approval, the licensee is guilty of an offence punishable on conviction by a fine not exceeding $250,000.

27. Banking business name

(1) A licensee must not without the prior written approval of the Reserve Bank carry on business under a name, description

or title that is different to the name, description or title under which it is licensed.

(2) If the Reserve Bank is of the opinion that a licensee is carrying on business under a name, description or title that:

(a) is identical to the name title or description of any other person or so closely resembles the name title or description that it is likely to mislead or deceive; or

(b) is likely to suggest falsely the patronage of or a connection with some person of authority within or outside Vanuatu ; or

(c) is likely to suggest falsely that the licensee has special status in relation to or derived from the Government of any country or has the official backing of any Government, or acts on behalf of, any Government; the Reserve Bank may, by notice in writing, direct the licensee to change or cease using the name, title or description within such time specified in the notice.

(3) A licensee that contravenes subsection (1) or fails to comply with a directive under subsection (2) is guilty of an offence punishable on conviction by a fine not exceeding $250,000

Division 2 – Restrictions on Licencees

28. Restriction on disposition of significant interest

(1) A person owning or holding a significant interest in a locally incorporated licensee must not sell, transfer, charge or otherwise dispose of the person's interest or any part of the person's interest, unless the person has obtained the prior written approval of the Reserve Bank.

(2) A locally incorporated licensee must not, unless it has obtained the prior written approval of the Reserve Bank:

(a) cause, permit or acquiesce in a sale, transfer, charge or other disposition referred to in subsection (1); or

(b) issue or allot any shares or cause, permit or acquiesce in any other reorganization of its share capital that results in:

(i) a person acquiring a significant interest in the licensee; or

(ii) a person who already owns or holds a significant interest in the licensee, increasing or decreasing the size of the person's interest.

(3) The Reserve Bank may give an approval under subsection (1) or (2) on such terms and conditions as it considers appropriate.

(4) If a person contravenes subsection (1), the person is guilty of an offence punishable on conviction:

(a) if an individual by a fine not exceeding $50,000 or imprisonment for a term not exceeding 2 years; or both; or

(b) if a body corporate by a fine not exceeding $250,000.

(5) If a locally incorporated licensee contravenes subsection (2), the licensee is guilty of an offence punishable on conviction by a fine not exceeding $250,000.

29. Restrictions on carrying on banking business

(1) A locally incorporated licensee must not:

(a) carry on any banking business other than international banking business; or

(b) carry on international banking business in contravention of:

(i) a term or condition of its licence; or

(ii) a provision of this Act or the regulations; or

(iii) a directive issued by the Reserve Bank, whether generally or specifically to the licensee.

(2) If a locally incorporated licensee contravenes subsection (1), the licensee is guilty of an offence punishable on conviction by a fine not exceeding $250,000.

30. Restrictions on advances exceeding 25 percent of capital

(1) A locally incorporated licensee and each subsidiary must not:

(a) make any advance or credit facility to:

(i) any person or body (whether corporate or unincorporate); or

(ii) any group of bodies that is under the control of a particular individual (see subsection (2)); or

(b) give any financial guarantee or incur any other liability on behalf of that person, body or group; if to do so would result in the total value of the advances, credit facilities, financial guarantees and other liabilities made or given to that person, body or group exceeding 25 percent of the value of the licensee's eligible capital.

(2) For the purposes of subsection (1), a group of bodies is under the control of a particular individual if that individual:

(a) holds, or has the power to vote for, at least 51 percent of the voting shares or stock of each of the bodies in the group; or

(b) exercises practical control over the policies of each of the bodies in the group.

(3) Subsection (1) does not apply to the following:

(a) transactions between banks or between branches of a bank;

(b) the purchase of telegraphic transfers;

(c) any advance or credit facility made to, or guaranteed by, the government;

(d) the purchase of bills of exchange or documents of title to goods if the holder of those bills or documents is entitled to:

(i) payment on those bills or documents outside Vanuatu for exports from Vanuatu; or

(ii) advances made against those bills or documents;

(e) any advance or credit facility that is fully secured by cash or a deposit redeemable in cash if:

(i) there is a written agreement that is legally binding in all relevant jurisdictions between the licensee and the person lodging the cash or deposit as collateral; and

(ii) the written agreement establishes the direct and unconditional right of the licensee to the cash or deposit.

(4) For the purposes of paragraph (3)(e), a common law or bankers' right of set off is insufficient on its own to satisfy that paragraph.

(5) For the purposes of paragraph (3)(e), the currency in which the collateral is lodged may differ from that of the exposure against which it is held. However, it must be valued at current market exchange rates with a margin approved by the Reserve Bank.

(6) The Reserve Bank may approve in writing an exposure for a licensee under subsection (1) that exceeds the 25 percent limit in that subsection, if the licensee agrees to reduce the exposure to within that limit within a period of time specified by the Reserve Bank.

(7) If a licensee contravenes subsection (1), the licensee is guilty of an offence punishable on conviction by a fine not exceeding $250,000.

31. Restrictions on advances without security

(1) A locally incorporated licensee and each subsidiary must not:

(a) make, or permit to be outstanding, unsecured advances or unsecured credit facilities which in total exceed $200,000 or one percent of the value of the licensee's eligible capital (whichever is the higher); or

(b) give any financial guarantees exceeding that amount without security; or

(c) incur any other liability related to the business of banking exceeding that amount without security; to, or on behalf of, all or any of the following:

(d) a director of the licensee or subsidiary whether the unsecured advances or credit facilities, or guarantees or other liabilities, are obtained by or on account of the director jointly or severally;

(e) any partnership, body corporate or other body in which the licensee or subsidiary, or any one or more of its directors, is a partner, director, manager, officer or agent;

(f) any partnership, body corporate or other body of

which any one or more of the licensee's or subsidiary's directors is a guarantor.

(2) If a locally incorporated licensee contravenes subsection (1), the licensee is guilty of an offence punishable on conviction by a fine not exceeding $250,000.

(3) In this section:

director includes a spouse, father, mother, son or daughter of a director; unsecured advances or unsecured credit facilities means:

(a) advances or credit facilities made without security; or

(b) if an advance or credit facility has been made with non-marketed securities – any part of that advance or credit facility which at any time exceeds four fifths of the licensee's valuation; or

(c) if an advance or credit facility has been made with any other security - any part of that advance or credit facility which at any time exceeds four fifths of the market value of the assets constituting that security.

32. Other restrictions on advances

(1) A locally incorporated licensee and each subsidiary must not make any advance or credit facility against the security of its own shares.

(2) A licensee and each subsidiary must not grant to any of its directors or shareholders in Vanuatu any advance, credit facility or guarantee unless granted on substantially the same terms, including interest rates and security, as those prevailing at the time for comparable transactions by the licensee or subsidiary with members of the public.

(3) A licensee and each subsidiary must not make, or permit to be outstanding, to any of its officers or employees in

Vanuatu unsecured advances or unsecured credit facilities, the total amount of which for that officer or employee exceeds his or her salary for one year.

(4) If a locally incorporated licensee contravenes subsection (1), the licensee is guilty of an offence punishable on conviction by a fine not exceeding $250,000.

(5) If a licensee contravenes subsection (2) or (3), the licensee is guilty of an offence punishable on conviction by a fine not exceeding $250,000.

33. Other restrictions on international banking business

(1) A licensee must not:

(a) acquire any shares issued by any company incorporated or continued under the Companies Act [CAP 191], other than an exempted company or a trust company; or

(b) acquire any interest in any business or undertaking in Vanuatu; or

(c) trade or do business in Vanuatu, other than with a person who or entity which is not a resident of Vanuatu or in furtherance of its international banking business.

(2) A locally incorporated licensee must not:

(a) make any invitation to the public in Vanuatu or outside Vanuatu to subscribe for any of its shares or debentures;

(b) issue bearer shares or share warrants; or

(c) transact any international banking business with a person, unless the licensee has carried out a due diligence investigation into that person and is satisfied that the person is a fit and proper person to transact international banking business with.

(3) A locally incorporated licensee must not, unless it has obtained the approval of the Reserve Bank in writing:

  (a) issue a cheque book to any depositor; or

  (b) provide any cheque account facility; or

  (c) provide any credit card facility; for the transaction of international banking business.

(4) A locally incorporated licensee must not for its own account acquire or hold share capital in a financial, commercial, agricultural, industrial or other undertaking if to do so would result in the combined value of all of those shares exceeding 25 percent, or such higher percentage as the Reserve Bank approves in writing, of the value of the licensee's eligible capital.

(5) Subsection (4) does not apply to:

  (a) the acquisition and disposal of shares by a licensee as a trustee or nominee; or

  (b) the purchase and sale of shares by a licensee upon the order and for the account of a customer; or

  (c) any shareholding that a licensee acquires in the course of the satisfaction of debts due to it, however, any such shareholding must be disposed of within such reasonable period as is determined by the Reserve Bank after consultation with the licensee taking into account relevant commercial factors; or

  (d) any part of the share capital of any company held or acquired by a licensee under an underwriting or sub-underwriting contract for a period not exceeding 3 months or such other period as the Reserve Bank may approve in writing in any particular case.

(6) For the purposes of subsections (4) and (5), a shareholding acquired or held by a licensee includes share capital acquired or held by a subsidiary of the licensee for the subsidiary's own account, whether or not the subsidiary is licensed under this Act.

(7) If a licensee contravenes subsection (1), the licensee is guilty of an offence punishable on conviction by a fine not exceeding $250,000.

(8) If a locally incorporated licensee contravenes subsection (2), (3) or (4), the licensee is guilty of an offence punishable on conviction by a fine not exceeding $250,000.

PART 5

AUDIT, DISCLOSURE AND TAX EXEMPTIONS

34. Appointment of approved auditor

(1) A licensee must for each financial year appoint an auditor whose duty is to report:

(a) on the financial statements of the licensee examined by the auditor; and

(b) on all financial statements prepared by the licensee in relation to that year.

(2) An appointment of an auditor by a licensee is subject to the prior written approval of the Reserve Bank which must not be given unless:

(a) the auditor is qualified to act as an auditor under section 166 of the Companies Act [CAP 191]; and

(b) the Reserve Bank is satisfied that the auditor is sufficiently experienced in auditing banking business; and

(c) the auditor has no financial interest in the licensee, other than as a depositor; and

(d) the auditor is not a shareholder, director, officer, agent or employee of the licensee.

(3) If a licensee fails to appoint an approved auditor or at any time fails to fill a vacancy for an auditor with an approved auditor, the Reserve Bank may appoint an auditor and fix the remuneration to be paid by the licensee to that auditor.

(4) A licensee must give notice in writing to the Reserve Bank if the licensee proposes to terminate the appointment of an approved auditor.

(5) If a person appointed as an auditor to a licensee:

(a) subsequently acquires a financial interest in the licensee, other than as a depositor; or

(b) becomes a shareholder, director, officer, agent or employee of the licensee; the person ceases by force of this section to be the auditor of the licensee.

(6) If a licensee contravenes subsection (1), the licensee is guilty of an offence punishable on conviction by a fine not exceeding $50,000.

35. Duties of auditor

(1) The following documents must be presented at the annual general meeting of the shareholders of a licensee:

(a) the licensee's financial statements;

(b) the licensee's auditor's report;

(c) the licensee's directors' report.

(2) The licensee must provide to the Reserve Bank copies of its financial statements and its auditor's report within four months after the close of the licensee's financial year or within such further time as the Reserve Bank approves in writing.

(3) The approved auditor of a licensee must report as soon as practicable to the Reserve Bank information relating to the affairs of the licensee obtained in the course of an audit if the auditor is of the opinion that:

(a) the licensee is insolvent or is likely to become insolvent or is likely to be unable to meet its obligations or is in serious financial difficulties; or

(b) a criminal offence involving fraud or dishonesty may have been committed; or

(c) serious irregularities have occurred, including irregularities that may place at risk the interest of depositors and creditors; or

(d) losses incurred that substantially reduce the capital of the licensee; or

(e) the licensee is unable to confirm that the claims of creditors are adequately covered by the licensee's assets; or

(f) the licensee has failed to comply with a directive or guideline issued by the Reserve Bank under Part 3.

(4) If an auditor contravenes subsection (3), the auditor is guilty of an offence punishable on conviction by a fine not exceeding $50,000.

(5) No civil, criminal or disciplinary proceedings lie against an auditor arising from the disclosure in good faith of information to the Reserve Bank pursuant to this section.

36. Licensee to provide Reserve Bank with report

(1) After consultation with a licensee including about costs, the Reserve Bank may, by notice in writing, require the licensee to provide the Reserve Bank with a report, prepared by its approved auditor or a person nominated by the Reserve Bank on all or any of the following:

(a) an opinion on asset quality;

(b) adequacy of provisions for losses;

(c) adequacy of the accounting and control system;

(d) such other matters as the Reserve Bank determines.

(2) No civil, criminal or disciplinary proceedings lie against an auditor arising from the disclosure in good faith of information to the Reserve Bank pursuant to this section.

37. Audit conducted in accordance with international standards

A foreign incorporated licensee is exempt from sections 34 and 35 if:

(a) the licensee obtains a report on the annual financial statements of the licensee made by a duly qualified auditor in accordance with the laws of the country in which the licensee is incorporated; and

(b) a copy of that report, the audited financial statements of the licensee and the report of the directors of the licensee is provided to the Reserve Bank as soon as practicable; and

(c) the Reserve Bank is satisfied that the audit has been carried out in accordance with international auditing standards.

38. Disclosure of information by Reserve Bank and persons authorised by it

(1) Subject to subsections (2) and (3), each of the following:

(a) the Reserve Bank;

(b) an employee or officer of the Reserve Bank;

(c) an examiner;

(d) any other person acting under the authority of the Reserve Bank; must not disclose any information relating to a protected person if the information has been acquired in the discharge of duties or in the performance of functions or in the exercise of powers under this Act.

(2) Subsection (1) does not apply to a disclosure if:

(a) the disclosure is required or authorised by a court; or

(b) the disclosure is made to the Minister; or

(c) the disclosure is made to the Attorney General or the Public Prosecutor; or

(d) the disclosure is made to the Vanuatu Financial Services Commission; or

(e) the disclosure is made to a law enforcement authority in Vanuatu; or

(f) the disclosure is made for the purpose of discharging any duty, performing any function or exercising any power under this or any other Act; or

(g) the disclosure is made with the express or implied consent of the protected person; or

(h) the person making the disclosure does so as a witness summoned to give evidence or produce documents; or

(i) the disclosure is made as required by or under a warrant; or

(j) the information disclosed is or has been available to the public from another source; or

(k) the information disclosed is in a form of a summary or in statistics expressed in a manner that does not enable identification of the protected person to whom the information relates; or

(l) subject to subsection (3), the disclosure is made to a foreign law enforcement authority or a foreign regulatory authority; or

(m) the disclosure is otherwise required or authorised by or under any law.

(3) The Reserve Bank or any other person referred to in subsection (1) must not disclose information concerning the affairs of a protected person to a foreign law enforcement authority or a foreign regulatory authority under paragraph (2)(l) unless the Reserve Bank is satisfied:

(a) that the foreign regulatory authority or the foreign law enforcement authority is subject to adequate legal restrictions on further disclosure; and

(b) that the information disclosed is reasonably required by the foreign authority for the purpose of its regulatory or law enforcement functions.

(4) If information concerning the affairs of a protected person is disclosed to a person in accordance with any paragraph of subsection (2), that person may disclose that information, subject to any applicable restrictions on further disclosure

contained in any law, for the purpose of discharging any duty, performing any function or exercising any power under this or any other Act.

(5) If a person contravenes any of the provisions of this section, the person is guilty of an offence punishable on conviction:

(a) if an individual by a fine not exceeding $50,000; or imprisonment for a term not exceeding 2 years, or both; or

(b) if a body corporate to a fine not exceeding $250,000.

(6) In this section, protected person means:

(a) a person who has applied for a licence under this Act; or

(b) a licensee; or

(c) a depositor or other customer of a licensee.

39. Disclosure of protected and other information generally

(1) Subject to subsection (2), a person must not disclose protected information or any other information relating to:

(a) the international banking business of a licensee; or

(b) a depositor or other customer of the licensee.

(2) Subsection (1) does not apply to a disclosure if:

(a) the disclosure is required or authorised by a court; or

(b) the disclosure is made for the purpose of discharging any duty, performing any function or exercising any power under this or any other Act; or

(c) the disclosure is made as part of a suspicious transaction report under the Financial Transactions Reporting Act No. 33 of 2000; or

(d) the disclosure is made to the Reserve Bank; or

(e) the disclosure is made to a law enforcement authority in Vanuatu and the person making the disclosure believes on reasonable grounds that the disclosure is reasonably necessary for the investigation or prosecution of a criminal offence; or

(f) the disclosure is made with the express or implied consent of the licensee or person concerned; or

(g) the person making the disclosure does so as a witness summoned to give evidence or produce documents; or

(h) the disclosure is made as required by or under a warrant; or

(i) the information disclosed is or has been available to the public from another source; or

(j) the information disclosed is in a form of a summary or in statistics expressed in a manner that does not enable identification of any depositor or other customer of a licensee; or

(k) the disclosure is otherwise required or authorised by or under any law of Vanuatu.

(3) If information is disclosed to a person in accordance with any paragraph of subsection (2), that person may disclose that information, subject to any applicable restrictions on further disclosure contained in any law, for the purpose of discharging any duty, performing any function or exercising any power under this or any other Act.

(4) If a person contravenes a provision of this section, the person is guilty of an offence punishable on conviction:

(a) if an individual by a fine not exceeding $50,000 or

imprisonment for a term not exceeding 2 years, or both; or

(b) if a body corporate by a fine not exceeding $250,000.

(5) Subsection (1) does not apply to the Reserve Bank or any other person referred to in subsection 38(1).

(6) In this section, protected information means:

(a) whether or not a person has an account with a licensee; or

(b) the name in which an account of a depositor or other customer of a licensee stands; or

(c) the balance of any such account; or

(d) the amount of any individual transaction undertaken by any licensee for a depositor or other customer of the licensee.

40. Exemption from taxes and stamp duty

(1) Despite anything contained in any other Act:

(a) no income tax, or any other direct or indirect tax or impost is payable in Vanuatu upon the income, profits, gains interest or dividends earned or paid in respect of the international banking business of a licensee; and

(b) no estate, inheritance, succession or gift tax, rate, duty, levy or other charge is payable in Vanuatu with respect to any shares, debt obligations or other securities of a licensee.

(2) The international banking business of a licensee is zero rated for the purposes of the Value Added Tax Act No. 12 of 1998.

(3) Despite any provision of the Stamp Duties Act [CAP 68], the following instruments are exempted from stamp duty:

(a) a bill of exchange, promissory note and every other document, instrument or certificate executed by, or for or in connection with the international banking business of, a licensee;

(b) an instrument in relation to:

(i) a transfer of property, other than real property, situated in Vanuatu, to or by a licensee; and

(ii) a transaction and declaration in respect of shares, debt obligations or other securities of a licensee; and

(iii) any other transaction of the international banking business of a licensee.

PART 6

MISCELLANEOUS

41. Offences

(1) A person who with intention to deceive makes any representation that the person knows to be false or does not believe to be true is guilty of an offence punishable on conviction:

(a) if an individual by a fine not exceeding $50,000 or imprisonment for a term not exceeding 2 years or both;

(b) if a body corporate to a fine not exceeding $250,000.

(2) An officer or employee, or a former officer or employee, of a licensee or a person who holds information on behalf of the licensee who knowingly:

(a) makes a false or misleading entry in any book, or record; or

(b) makes or provides any false or misleading statement, report, return, document or information; or

(c) omits an entry or alters or conceals an entry in any book or record so as to mislead; or

(d) conceals or destroys within six years of its creation any information, book, voucher, record, report, return, minutes or document relating to the accounts, transactions, affairs, or a business of the licensee so as to mislead; is guilty of an offence punishable on conviction by a fine not exceeding $50,000 or imprisonment for a term not exceeding 2 years or both.

(3) An officer or employee, or a former officer or employee, of a licensee or a person who holds information on behalf of a licensee who obstructs or endeavours to obstruct:

(a) an approved auditor in the proper performance of the auditor's duties; or

(b) the Reserve Bank or an examiner in an examination of the licensee, or any branch, agency, office or subsidiary of the licensee; or

(c) an examiner or administrator in the proper performance of his or her duties; is guilty of an offence punishable on conviction by a fine not exceeding $50,000 or imprisonment for a term not exceeding 2 years or both.

42. Protection of the term 'bank' etc

(1) A person (other than a licensee) must not use in the name, description or title under which the person is carrying on business in Vanuatu:

(a) the term "bank" or a derivative of the word "bank" in any language; or

(b) any other word that indicates that the person is conducting international banking business; unless the Reserve Bank has given its prior written approval to the use.

(2) If a person contravenes subsection (1), the person is guilty of an offence punishable on conviction:

(a) if an individual by a fine not exceeding $50,000; or imprisonment for a term not exceeding 2 years, or both;

(b) if a body corporate by a fine not exceeding $250,000.

43. Indemnity from liability

No action lies against the Reserve Bank, an employee or officer of the Reserve Bank, an examiner or any other person acting under the authority of the Reserve Bank in respect of any act done in good faith in the discharging of any duty, the performance of any function or the exercise of any power under this Act.

44. Variation of terms and conditions

If the Reserve Bank has under this Act or the regulations granted an approval or an exemption subject to terms and conditions, the Reserve Bank may upon giving 21 days' notice to a licensee vary or cancel any of the terms or conditions, or impose new terms or conditions.

45. Court proceedings

(1) Civil proceedings under this Act to which a licensee is a party or which relate to a licensee are to be heard in camera, unless the Court otherwise orders.

(2) Any documents produced or evidence given in civil proceedings under this Act must not be disclosed to a person

if that person is not a party to those proceedings unless the Court otherwise orders.

(3) If a notice of legal proceedings is served on a licensee, a copy of the notice must be served on the Reserve Bank.

(4) This section does not apply to criminal proceedings under this Act.

46. Directives by the Reserve Bank

If any act is required or permitted to be done under this Act and no form is prescribed or procedure laid down in this Act or the regulations, the Reserve Bank may, in response to an application made to it or on its own motion, issue written directives as to the manner in which the act should be done, and an act done in accordance with a directive is valid.

47. English or French the authentic text

(1) All documents filed with the Reserve Bank and all accounting records required to be kept under this Act must be in either the English or French language.

(2) If such document or record is not in the English or French language, it must be accompanied by an authentic English or French translation and in the event of any conflict in meaning between the foreign language and the English or French version; the English or French version prevails.

48. Regulations

The Minister may, on the advice of the Reserve Bank, make regulations prescribing all matters:

(a) required or permitted by this Act to be prescribed or provided; or

(b) is necessary or convenient to be prescribed for the carrying out or giving effect to this Act and its due administration.

49. Commencement

This Act commences on 1 January 2003.

Table of Acts

International Banking Act No. 4 of 2002. Assented to on 31.12.2002. Date of commencement, 01.01.2003. (ref: Gaz # 2, 20.01.2003)

License Application

The offshore regulatory authorities mentioned in this book will generally be happy to provide you with an application package for an offshore banking license including all the relevant forms and check lists. Belize is an exception, where the first step of the application process is always to schedule an appointment for an interview with the Central Bank. No application forms or other paperwork related to the application will be provided prior to the initial interview.

The Due Diligence requirements are fairly uniform in the jurisdictions included in this book. All principals including directors, senior officers, shareholders and other key individuals are required to be deemed "fit and proper" and are required to provide Police clearance certificate (or register extract), character and banking references, documentation demonstrating net worth and any previous experience from the banking/financial services industry. The proposed bank would also need to provide a Business Plan including financial projections and detailed descriptions of the planned banking products and services to be offered, customer types to be targeted and their geographic location, anti-money laundering measures and anticipated customer identification procedures (KYC).

A successful application requires the assistance of accountants, lawyers and possibly a licensing consultant who can coordinate contact with the required professionals and authorities in the relevant jurisdiction and assist throughout the entire application process.

Here is an example of information and documentation required to accompany an application for an international banking license, in this case in St. Vincent and the Grenadines:

(1) Name of applicant.

(2) Address in the State of its place of business and the name and address of the registered agent in the State.

(3) The names, addresses, citizenship and residency of all directors, shareholders, officers, managers and in the case of a publicly traded company only the names and addresses of shareholders owing ten per cent of the issued share capital or more.

(4) Names and addresses of solicitors, if any, to the applicant together with a letter from the solicitors confirming that they act for the applicant.

(5) Names and addresses of auditors of the applicant, together with a letter from the auditors confirming that they consent to act for the applicant.

(6) Evidence of a proper application for incorporation of the company in the State and that the company is an "eligible company".

(7) Evidence in writing that the applicant itself or some person directly or indirectly connected with the applicant is possessed of solid and practical experience in banking business.

(8) An undertaking in writing to provide and set apart a fully paid-up capital fund before or at the time it commences business, that the Authority may in its determination require, based upon the class of licence for which the application is being made.

(9) Police record certifying no criminal convictions or alternatively a police record approved by the Authority.

(10) Annual accounts of its holding company, if any, for the proceedings three years and subsequently annually duly audited and certified by an independent auditor.

(11) Names of all subsidiary companies of the applicant with addresses of their registered offices.

(12) A copy of the articles of incorporation and by-laws of the applicant company verified by an affidavit sworn by the Resident director of the applicant.

(13) One character reference and two bank references.

(14) Statement of assets and liabilities, and certified statement of net worth of the applicant shareholder; where the applicant is an existing company, basic financial statements and where the applicant is a group of companies, the audited financial statements from all the members of the group.

(15) Statement of capital of any company held directly or through a subsidiary as an asset of the applicant.

(16) If application is being made for a Class B licence the list and description of the proposed customers of the licensee.

(17) The applicant must provide a business plan containing the following:

(a) a description of the objectives of the company;

(b) proposed customer base;

(c) opening balance sheet and three year projections as certified by an auditor;

(d) management structure;

(e) anti money laundering policies and provision

(f) a feasibility study;

(g) the economic need that the company intend to meet;

(h) the nature and source of capital financing;

(i) proof of applicants ability to meet statutory requirements for minimum paid up capital and statutory deposits;

(j) a description of internal systems and controls; and

(k) copy of the ownership structure including group member and affiliated companies

(18) All directors, managers, senior office and shareholders must complete a fit and proper questionnaire.

The personal questionnaires are also quite similar from jurisdiction to jurisdiction. Below is an example of questions that each principal of a proposed bank would be required to answer, in this case in Vanuatu:

Personal Questionnaire for Directors, Shareholders, Managers, Officers and Controllers

1. Name of the institution in connection with which this questionnaire is being completed

2. Surname

   Forename(s)

   Any previous name(s) by which you have been known.

   Gender (Male/Female)

3. Are you completing this questionnaire as a Director, Shareholder, Manager, Officer or Controller?

4. Private address

5. Previous private addresses during the last ten years (with relevant dates)

6. Date of Birth

   Place of birth (including town, state and country)

7. Nationality and how it was acquired (e.g. birth, naturalization, marriage)

8. Identification number

9. Present occupation or employment and occupations and employment during the last ten years, including the name of the employer, the nature of business, the position held and relevant dates, leaving no period unaccounted for, and including for each employment;

    i. the title of your position,

    ii. the dates of employment,

    iii. the name and address of your employer, and

    iv. the name, position and telephone number of a reference.

10. Of what bodies corporate –

    (a) are you now a director or controller?

    (b) have you been a director or controller at any time during the last ten years? (specify the country of incorporation in each case & nature of business)

11. Details of shareholding interest in financial institutions (current and last ten years)

    (a) name of company

    (b) country of incorporation

    (c) percentage holding

    (d) nature of business

12.

    (a) Professional qualifications and year in which they were obtained.

    (b) Academic qualifications

13. Have you at any time been involved with an application for regulatory approval in any other jurisdiction where that application has been refused or withdrawn?

14. Have you at any time been charged or convicted of any offence other than

    (a) an offence committed when you were under the age of 18 years unless the same was committed within the last ten years, or

    (b) an offence in connection with the use or ownership of a motor vehicle which was tried in a court of summary jurisdiction) by any court, whether civil or military, in any jurisdiction? If so, give full particulars of the charge and if convicted, the date of conviction, the offence and the penalty imposed.

15. Have you ever, at any time, been the subject of an investigation in relation to a financial institution? If so, give full particulars.

16. Have you, anywhere, been censured, disciplined or criticised by any professional body to which you belong or have belonged, or have you ever held a practising certificate subject to conditions? If so, give full particulars.

17. Have you ever been required to give evidence in any trial or proceedings involving fraud, dishonesty or similar matters, other than as an expert witness? If so, give full particulars.

18. Have you, or any body corporate, partnership or unincorporated institution with which you are, or have been associated as a director, shareholder, manager, officer or controller, been the subject of an investigation, anywhere, by a governmental, professional or other regulatory body? If so, give full particulars.

19. Have you, anywhere, been dismissed from any office or employment or barred from entry to any profession or occupation? If so, give full particulars

20. Have you been adjudicated bankrupt by a court in any jurisdiction? If so, give full particulars.

21. Have you failed to satisfy any debt adjudged due and payable by you as a judgement-debtor under an order of a court in any jurisdiction? If so, give full particulars.

22. Have you, in connection with the formation, control or management of a body corporate, partnership or unincorporated institution been adjudged by a court, in any jurisdiction, civilly or criminally liable for any fraud, misfeasance or other misconduct by you towards such a body or company or towards any members thereof? If so, give full particulars.

23. Has any body corporate, partnership or unincorporated institution with which you were associated as a director, shareholder, manager, officer or controller, anywhere, been compulsorily wound up or made any compromise or arrangement with its' creditors or ceased trading in circumstances where its' creditors did not receive or have not yet received full settlement of their claims, either while you were associated with it or within one year after you ceased to be associated with it ? If so, give full particulars.

24. Has any body corporate, partnership or unincorporated institution with which you were associated as a director, shareholder, manager, officer or controller, anywhere, had its authorization revoked?

25. In carrying out your duties will you be acting on the directions or instructions of any other person? If so, give full particulars

I CERTIFY that the above information is complete and correct to the best of my knowledge and belief and I undertake that, as long as I continue to be a director, shareholder, manager, officer or controller of an institution authorized under the above laws, I will notify the Reserve Bank of Vanuatu of any material changes affecting the completeness of the answers to questions 11-25 above within a period of twenty-one days.

Date Signed

____

Please refer to current and complete forms provided by each regulatory authority. The information included above is not intended to be used for an actual application for a license but merely to serve as an example of documentation required and questions asked by regulators.

Feedback

Comments?

Questions?

Please share

readers@michaelmagnusson.com

Follow Michael Magnusson on Twitter:

@magnussonwrites

NOTES

NOTES

NOTES

NOTES